Guderian's XIXth Panzer Corps

AND

The Battle of France

Guderian's
XIXth Panzer Corps
AND
The Battle of France

Breakthrough in the Ardennes, May 1940

Florian K. Rothbrust

Foreword by S. J. Lewis

PRAEGER

New York
Westport, Connecticut
London

Library of Congress Cataloging-in-Publication Data

Rothbrust, Florian K.
    Guderian's XIXth Panzer Corps and the Battle of France :
breakthrough in the Ardennes, May 1940 / Florian K. Rothbrust ;
foreword by S. J. Lewis.
        p.   cm.
    Includes bibliographical references.
    ISBN 0-275-93473-X (alk. paper)
    1. World War, 1939-1945—Campaigns—France. 2. World War,
1939-1945—Campaigns—Ardennes. 3. Germany. Heer. Panzer-Korps,
XIX—History. 4. Guderian, Heinz, 1888-1954. 5. World War,
1939-1945—Tank warfare.   I. Title.
D761.R65   1990
940.54′214—dc20   89-38182

Library of Congress Catalog Card Number: 89-38182
ISBN: 0-275-93473-X

First published in 1990

Praeger Publishers, One Madison Avenue, New York, NY 10010
An imprint of Greenwood Publishing Group, Inc.

Printed in the United States of America

∞

The paper used in this book complies with the
Permanent Paper Standard issued by the National
Information Standards Organization (Z39.48-1984).

10 9 8 7 6 5 4 3 2 1

For Gabriella, Mary-Karola, and Emma

Ich habe von Anfang meiner Karriere an nur den einzigen Leistern
gehabt—durch welche Mittel oder welche Wege kann ich
Deutschland zur Einigung bringen, und soweit dies erreicht ist, wie
kann ich diese Einigung befestigen.
(Right from the inception of my career I was guided by only one
desire—through what means or method can I unite Germany,
and, once achieved, how can this unity be maintained.)

Otto von Bismarck in an address
to the German Reichstag, July 9, 1879

Bravery and gallantry of the armored troops alone can not
make up the shortfalls of the two sister services of the
Armed Forces—the Luftwaffe and the Navy.

Colonel-General Heinz Guderian
to Adolf Hitler
August 15, 1944

Contents

Photographs follow page 96.

Tables and Figures

TABLES

FIGURES

Foreword

The German advance through the Ardennes of May 1940 has been oft recounted in English. These works usually focus their attention on the dynamic activity of well-known generals such as Heinz Guderian or Erwin Rommel. Perhaps that is only right, since the role of personality in warfare remains of great importance. Unfortunately, these works depend almost exclusively upon books published in London and New York in the decade following the war, including the altogether too self-serving memoirs of General Guderian. Strange as it may seem, English-language interpretations remain fixated upon those earlier accounts, even though more detailed studies on the French, German, Belgian, and Luxembourg armed forces in the campaign have since appeared.

What has emerged is a series of near-identical English accounts, often retelling the same stories such as Brandenburg special operations troops seizing the bridges at St. Vith for Rommel's 7th Panzer Division of Guderian in Bouillon looking upon the Meuse River crossing sites. This has made for entertaining reading and a commonality of understanding. Unfortunately, St. Vith had no bridges and Rommel's division did not pass through that town. And from Bouillon not even Guderian's eyes could see through the heights and forests to the Meuse River. Indeed, facts seem to matter little for the practitioners of this school.

Over the years a number of thinking soldiers and military historians (there are several) examining the march routes of Hoth's and Guderian's Panzer Corps have noted these discrepancies. The most common observation has been that, using English sources, one could not even follow the daily advances of the German divisions. It also became apparent that taking 100,000 motorized vehicles through the hilly and wooded Ardennes required more than a dynamic personality or two. In short, what was lacking was the actual military work of the commanders and staffs—planning, issuance of mission directives, training, and making the staff system work.

Major Rothbrust's study is therefore a most welcome corrective to the field. He has used his unique qualifications to examine the surviving German Army records along with the more reliable secondary souces to reconstruct the actual unfolding of the XIXth Panzer Corps' advance. What emerges is a new perspective of those battles and of the German Army, too. General Guderian is still present, but he is now seen within the context of the system that produced him. He did have some help in winning his victories. The German Army of 1940 emerges, not as the accustomed invincible machine, but as a traditional Western army that faced the same military problems as its opponents. Like other armies, it had training problems, traffic jams, flawed tables of organization and equipment, recalcitrant subordinates and personal rivalries. The German advance through the Ardennes in 1940 resembles the 1944 Allied invasion of Normandy in that the attacker possessed more than six months to develop the campaign plan, to elaborate the details of that plan, and to overcome deficiencies revealed in previous operations. In short, these campaigns provide an ideal opportunity to observe the military work of commanders and staffs as a campaign plan evolved.

If Major Rothbrust's study reveals the friction inherent in campaign planning, it is even stronger in demonstrating the dominance of friction and confusion on the battlefield itself. In spite of the rigorous training, revised tables of organization, meticulous planning, and detailed rehearsals, Panzer Group von Kleist faced numerous problems, as the reader shall soon see. How the German Army resolved those problems (and the earlier planning and training dilemmas) provides a unique view of the German Army performing its military work. In so doing, his narrative has placed us closer to the events as they transpired and away from the familiar mythological approach to this campaign.

S. J. Lewis

Preface

The purpose of this study is to present the operational history of Colonel-General Heinz Guderian's XIXth Panzer Corps' advance from May 10 to 15, 1940. It encompasses campaign planning at German Army High Command, the preparation for the Army's offensive against France, and the employment of a tank army as the main effort through the Ardennes, although its primary focus is directed at XIXth Panzer Corps' breakthrough at Sedan. The political and military situation influencing the decision makers of the German Army General Staff planners and the development of the campaign plan are analyzed in an attempt to provide an understanding for the rationale of the deployment, mission, and employment of XIXth Panzer Corps and its subordinate units. An appraisal of German Army reforms at the conclusion of the Polish Campaign furnishes an appreciation for the immense effort required to train and prepare the Army for the French Campaign. A discussion of Field Marshal Erich von Manstein's recommendations and operational concept clarifies his instrumental role in the development of the final campaign plan. This study also presents an in-depth explanation of the development of Panzer Group von Kleist's traffic control plan and the coordination problems involved in the movement of a tank army through the restricted terrain of the Ardennes. The operational history of the XIXth Panzer Corps includes the formation, headquarters' planning and preparation, and detailed actions throughout the initial critical days of the offensive in 1940, to demonstrate its impact on the successful conclusion of the campaign. A complete account of the daily operations furnishes an assessment of XIXth Panzer Corps' officers, men, and equipment. It provides an observation of the corps' staff in its daily evaluation of the operational and logistical situation, intelligence reports, and the endless friction with the next higher headquarters. The examination of special operations forces, air assault forces, anti-aircraft elements, and engineers during planning and execution, demonstrates their critical requirement to achieve success. Lastly, this study demonstrates the effectiveness of a well-trained, equipped armored corps, commanded by leaders who were fully cognizant of their mission, commanders' aims, and the overall operational concept.

This study encompasses much ground, although its primary focus narrows to only a five-day period during the Battle of France. I feel, however, that the stage must be set for the reader to understand the complexity of the operation and the ramifications presented to the German military leadership of the day. I have included numerous appendixes to provide pertinent information in support of this study of one of the most successful military operations in recent military history. Because of the number of German officers mentioned in this book, I have translated their military ranks into the U.S. equivalents. A table of comparative officers' ranks appears in Appendix D. Additionally, I have provided detailed biographical sketches on each officer.

German military history of World War II provides a vast number of books written by a variety of multinational authors. Literature on this critical period of the Battle of France, however, leaves much to be desired. Many of the history books written shortly after the war are biased by the authors' nationalities and wounds not yet healed. I have therefore used existing primary source documents whenever possible in order to provide the facts as they occurred during the time leading up to and the conduct of this campaign. For specific information on German documents the reader is directed to Appendix H, German Military Documents. I would like to take this opportunity to thank publicly Lieutenant-Colonel Ross Millican of the Australian Army, my Staff Group's counselor and evaluator during my year at the U.S. Army's Command and General Staff College, Fort Leavenworth, Kansas, for guiding me onto the right track for this project. His continued encouragement, invaluable assistance, advice, and kindness aided immensely in completing this work. I would also like to thank Dr. Timothy K. Nenninger and Dr. Roger Spiller for their assistance in tracking down documentation and editing this work.

Abbreviations

a. D.	ausser Dienst	retired from active service
A. H. K.	Armeehauptquartier Krieg	wartime army headquarters
A. H. Qu	Armeehauptquartier	army headquarters
A. K.	Armeekorps	army corps
Ao	Abwehr	counterintelligence section (army level)
A. O. K.	Armeeoberkommando	army high command
Abt	Abteilung	section, battalion
Abw	Abwehr	counterintelligence
Anlage		enclosure
ARKO	Artilleriekommandeur	artillery commander
Ausb.	Ausbildung	training
Befehl		order
Beilage		annex, appendix
Betr.	Betrag	reference
Chefs	Chefsache	commander, eyes only
C in C		Commander in Chief
g. or geh.	geheim	secret
Gen d. Art	General der Artillerie	Lieutenant General (basic branch, Artillery)
Gen d. Inf	General der Infanterie	Lieutenant General (basic branch, Infantry)

Gen d. Kav	General der Kavallerie	Lieutenant General (basic branch, Cavalry)
Gen d. Pz Tr	General der Panzer Truppen	Lieutenant General (basic branch, Armor)
Gen Qu	Generalquartiermeister	chief logistician and administrative officer on the Army General Staff (G4)
Gen St d H	Generalstab des Heeres	Army General Staff
gez	gezeichnet	signed
Gr	Gruppe	army group (an interim definition for army, later changed to army)
H. Qu	Hauptquartier	headquarters
Ia	Erster Generalstabsoffizier	G3 at division/corps. Since divisions had no chiefs of staff, he doubled in that capacity
Ib	Zweiter Generalstabsoffizier	G4 at division/corps
Ic	Dritter Generalstabsoffizier	G2 at division/corps
IIa	Personaloffizier	G1 at division/corps
IIb	Personaloffizier	additional G1 section/officer at corps level
K. Gef. Std.	Korpsgefechtstand	corps command post (tactical operation center)
K. H. Qu	Korpshauptquartier	corps main headquarters
Kdo	Kommando	command
Kf	Kraftfahrabteilung	motor transport battalion
Kfz	Kraftfahrzeug	motor vehicle
Kol.	Kolonne	column
KTB	Kriegstagebuch	war diary
Maint.		maintenance
MG	Machinengewehr	machine gun
Mech.		mechanized
Med.		medium
Mot Zug	motorisierter Zug	motorized platoon
Naka	Nahkampfführer	close air support coordinator
Nr	Nummer	number
O. Qu I	Oberquartiermeister I	G3. First general staff officer for operations. Army level general staff and higher

O. Qu II	Oberquartiermeister II	Second general staff officer in the G3 section responsible for training. Army level and higher
O. Qu III	Oberquartiermeister III	Third general staff officer in the G3 section responsible for organization Army level and higher
O. Qu IV	Oberquartiermeister IV	G2. Fourth general staff officer responsible for intelligence. Army level and higher
O. Qu V	Oberquartiermeister V	G5. Fifth general staff officer responsible for military history. Army level and higher
ObdH	Oberbefehlshaber des Heeres	Army commander in chief
ObdL	Oberbefehlshaber der Luftwaffe	Air Force commander in chief
ObdM	Oberbefehlshaber der Marine	Navy commander in chief
OKH	Oberkommando des Heeres	Army High Command
OKW	Oberkommando der Wehrmacht	Armed Forces High Command
Op	Operation	operation
Qu	Quartiermeister	Corps G4, logistics officer
TMR		Tactical March Route
Trans.		transportation
z. b. V.	zu bestimmter Verfügung	at the disposal for special operations

Guderian's XIXth Panzer Corps

AND

The Battle of France

1

The Cut of the Scythe

Da liegen die Würfel des ungeheuren Spiels.
Wer wagt sie zu werfen?
(Here lie the dice of this incredible game.
Who dares to toss them?)
Oswald Spengler,
in "Jahre der Entscheidung," 1932/33

Es kommt nicht auf einen schönen Befehl an, sondern auf das Niederlegen
eines Entschlusses, der mit Herz und Härte durchgeführt werden muss.
(Good looking operation orders are immaterial. What counts are clearly stated
intentions which can be executed with all of one's heart and determination.)
Generaloberst Heinz Guderian

AT WAR AGAIN

On September 3, 1939, the German Army assumed a defensive posture along the
Western Front.[1] Germany once again found itself in a two front war, worse yet,
war with Poland, France, and England. The professional military elite hoped
that Hitler would solve the situation in the West through peaceful means,
primarily, because they felt Germany was unprepared for war against the Allies,
and secondly, no plan existed for an offensive against France. Adolf Hitler, the
German dictator, however, had different ideas. His Wehrmacht Adjutant,
Colonel Rudolf Schmundt,[2] discussed the Führer's desire for a quick attack on
France with Nicolaus von Below,[3] Hitler's Luftwaffe Adjutant, as early as September 8, 1939. Throughout the following days Hitler brought up the subject of

a possible attack on France, but only within his trusted inner circle. After Germany's stunning defeat of Poland, Hitler determined that France and England would reconsider engaging the German Army on the battlefield.[4]

Hitler, with clear intentions for future operations in the West, returned from the Eastern Front with his entourage to Berlin's Stettiner railway station on the afternoon of September 26, 1939, rather unobtrusively. He returned a day early for a scheduled meeting with the three service chiefs, the Oberbefehlshaber des Heeres (ObdH)[5] Colonel-General Walter von Brauchitsch,[6] the Oberbefehlshaber der Luftwaffe (ObdL) Field Marshal Herman Göring,[7] and the Oberbefehlshaber der Marine (ObdM) Admiral Erich Raeder,[8] at the New Chancellory at 1700 hours on September 27, 1939. During this meeting, Hitler for the first time officially expressed his plans for offensive action in the West.[9]

Rumors of a pending attack against France had already filtered down to and been discussed by members of the various service staffs. Hitler, aware of Oberkommando des Heeres' (OKH)[10] opposition to any offensive action in the West, used this opportunity to reaffirm his absolute power over all matters of state, including the military. The purpose of his meeting was to present his intentions and to underscore his theory that victory in Poland resulted from superior German leadership, soldiers, tanks, and airplanes. France and England, he explained, were unable to come to Poland's aide because of military unpreparedness. Given enough time, however, they might be able to prepare themselves for a German onslaught. Worse yet, they themselves might attack Germany. Hitler declared that the minimal losses the German Army suffered in Poland would be easily replaceable.[11] He demanded the immediate activation and transfer of as many units as possible to the Western Front. Hitler thought an offensive in the West would be no more difficult than the Polish Campaign, therefore, quality soldiers were of no concern.[12] Weather, because of its effect in the first three to four days of any offensive, concerned him most. Hitler also expressed concern over Germany's industrial base, the Ruhr Valley. He feared Allied bombing raids on this highly vulnerable area.[13]

Hitler recognized his generals' sensitivity toward breaching Dutch and Belgian neutrality, and assured them that a conflict with Holland would be avoided since this problem could be solved through political means. Belgium, on the other hand, posed a direct threat to the Ruhr. The Führer expected no hesitation from France to forward deploy troops into Belgium and to use it as a staging base to threaten Germany's industrial base. He expected German forces to attack in a west-northwest direction through Belgium, with the main effort (Schwerpunkt)[14] directed towards the Channel coast. Hitler asked General von Brauchitsch for his views on this proposition. Von Brauchitsch declined to reply immediately until afforded some time to think about these new developments. Finally on the 27th, Hitler presented his military leaders with a *"fait accompli,"* demanding the initiation of an offensive not later than 20 to 25 October 1939, the war goal of which was "to force England to its knees." Hitler, usurping his advisors, declared his military aims, which were not final in the overall concept of warfare in the West, however, and left no illusions as to his motives.[15]

This amazing order marked the beginning of a great stalling maneuver by OKH, since it had no intention of fighting the West and possessed no war plan for an offensive as in 1914. This plan would truly be a challenge of enormous magnitude for the leaders of the Army General Staff. General von Brauchitsch and General of Artillery Franz Halder[16] struggled with personal conflicts as to the soldierly and moral implications of Hitler's motives in the West, even going so far as to discuss the possible elimination of the dictator. Von Brauchitsch and Halder were soldiers of the old school, however, bound by their oath of allegiance,[17] caught in a dilemma of having to plan an operation they felt was morally wrong, professionally questionable, and possibly ruinous for Germany. General von Brauchitsch attempted to stand up to Hitler; however, he found himself in a very awkward position. He had accepted 250,000 Reichsmark in the form of a loan arranged by Hitler to settle his first marriage and had recently remarried a woman with ties to the Nazi movement. General Halder's religious convictions, among other things, restrained him from committing cold-blooded murder. As Army Chief of Staff, Halder considered himself the chief representative of the German officer corps, refusing to adopt Balkan traditions into the corps to solve national problems. Murdering heads of state was not an option as long as he served as Army chief of staff.[18]

While von Brauchitsch and Halder privately discussed their concerns over Hitler's reckless intentions, the Polish Campaign presented the General Staff with issues of far-reaching consequences. It revealed significant German Army deficiencies requiring immediate attention. Among other things, military leaders at the highest levels measured the German infantry far below the standards of 1914. All offensive action depended on commanders' initiatives, since the infantry seemingly lacked élan and an aggressive spirit. The Army considered the Panzer types Mark I and II obsolete, but experienced a shortage of the modern Mark III's and IV's. Its doctrine of mobile warfare received a positive rating, although Tables of Organization and Equipment (TO&E) required numerous changes, and command and control between Panzer and Infantry formations left much to be desired. The September 27 *"fait accompli"* was a rude shock for Army leaders and in this air of misgiving OKH began to plan for an attack it did not want to conduct, against an enemy it felt it was not ready or equipped to fight, in the rain of autumn.[19]

INITIAL PLANNING

In early October 1939, General von Brauchitsch still hoped the Führer would settle for a negotiated peace, rather than forcing the Army into a winter offensive. Other senior officers at Zossen[20] expressed skepticism with Hitler's intended venture knowing full well that it would spark another world war. A comparison of the 1939 situation with that of 1914 indicates that the 1914 Great General Staff relied on a meticulously scrutinized, thoroughly war-gamed, campaign plan. In 1939 Germany had no such invasion plan against France because the General Staff did not envision offensive action against the latter. OKH therefore initially attempted to delay undertaking a campaign, but finally relented after several months when faced with repeated demands by Hitler.[21]

Hitler called in Generals von Brauchitsch and Halder again on October 7, to remind them of his intentions and to meddle in military matters. The Führer was convinced that a Belgian request for French military assistance was imminent. In his view, French troops forward deployed in Belgium along Germany's border were intolerable and answerable only by offensive action. He therefore demanded an immediate offensive. To von Brauchitsch's dismay Hitler decreed that the offensive at a minimum must gain as much ground as possible in northern Belgium and Holland to provide a protective buffer for the Ruhr and staging bases for air attacks against Britain. A seasoned military officer could not easily accept Hitler's new strategic concept. German General Staff officers had always been trained to destroy the enemy's army. Von Brauchitsch and Halder departed the chancellory for Zossen to digest their boss's new instructions, no doubt reflecting upon the previous day's Reichstag address in which Hitler offered peace to the Western Allies, concomitantly guaranteeing Belgian, Dutch, and Luxembourg neutrality. In the meantime, contrary to Hitler's public peace offer, OKH was left with no alternative but to issue new directives to commanders on the Western Front.[22]

Colonel-General Fedor von Bock,[23] Commander in Chief of Army Group B, received a mission to protect the German border from the Ems River to Mettlach where his army group linked with Army Group C, commanded by Colonel-General Wilhelm von Leeb.[24] Army Group C's front stretched from Mettlach to the Swiss border, also with a defensive mission. Von Bock's instructions not only directed him to guard the Dutch border between the Ems and the Rhine Rivers, but also to be prepared to conduct offensive operations into Holland and Belgium if required.[25]

On October 9, while von Bock visited Zossen, von Brauchitsch requested that he submit a written proposal for an offensive through Belgium and Holland. Von Brauchitsch, however, also told von Bock that he and General Halder were completely against an offensive in the West. Enroute to Bad Godesberg the following day, von Bock stopped in Frankfurt am Main to discuss the western situation with General von Leeb, who also expressed his displeasure at any attempted offensive. Not only did von Leeb disclose a lack of confidence in the planned offensive, but also expressed outrage at the Führer's motives. On the following day von Bock heard the same objections from his two army commanders, Generals Walter von Reichenau[26] and Günther von Kluge.[27]Returning to Zossen for a briefing on October 17, von Brauchitsch requested von Bock to comment on the proposed operation plan. Von Bock declined to answer "off the cuff," but the following day, after thoroughly studying the plans, sent his reply to von Brauchitsch.[28]

The Führer was aware that his generals were against an offensive in the West. His generals had always been against any type of military aggression, dating as far back as the reoccupation of the Rhineland. Hitler, therefore, occupied himself with developing a means of motivating his generals into a more offensive spirit. Sometime between October 6 and 9, he dictated a memorandum on his ideas and concepts for the continued war in the West. On the 9th, Hitler became rather nervous since the Allies had not replied to his peace offer; he ordered OKH to set the offensive for November 25, and directed von Brauchitsch and Halder to assemble in his office at 1100 hours on the 10th. Hitler personally read the entire 58-page memorandum to them. In the document the dictator underscored the reasons for his decision to initiate a quick and shattering blow to the West, should he have no other choice in wake of the political developments. Additionally, he handed them "Directive Nr. 6, for the conduct of war" which, amongst other things, specifically addressed the military situation in the West:

For the continuation of military operations the following is ordered:

a) Offensive operations are to be planned along the Western Front in the north, to attack through Belgium, Holland, and Luxembourg. This attack must be carried out with the strongest possible forces at the earliest possible opportunity.

b) The goal of this offensive operation is to defeat large elements of the French Army and her Allies, to secure as much ground as possible in Belgium, Holland, and northern France for the purpose of establishing Luftwaffe and Navy bases to conduct an air and sea war against England, and the establishment of a protective buffer for the war materiel producing Ruhr.

c) The date of the offensive depends on the availability of tanks, motorized units, and weather. All efforts must be made to harness the mobile forces as quickly as possible.[29]

This document revealed that Hitler's real strategic goal was not the defeat of France, but rather gaining the Channel coast to engage Britain in a U-Boat and air war. Her personally stated no clear political motive. However, he had probably already signified one through his attempt to win the war against the Western Allies by his northern offensive. Hitler also lacked an understanding of and a judgment for available resources to conduct war. Serious enough problems existed in the area of motorization (tanks and motorized vehicles of all types), munitions, and training to cause alarm and possibly warrant a reevaluation for an immediate offensive, especially with winter approaching.[30]

General Halder specifically worried over the establishment of additional Panzer and motorized divisions. Only by stripping several infantry divisions of motorized vehicles could he provide the necessary mobility to newly activated Panzer and motorized divisions. The shifting of vehicular assets could only be accomplished at the detriment of the entire Army. Hitler's declaration about time being in the enemy's favor was in reality false. On the contrary, Germany would benefit from delaying over the winter, raising the level of maintenance, refitting with more modern equipment, and providing the necessary training to improve the Army's combat performance.[31]

In September 1939 General Halder had five Panzer divisions at his disposal, totalling 3,195 tanks of all types. The majority of these, 2,674, were obsolete Mark I and II models. The Army lacked, in any great number, the more modern Mark III and IV models. Production capacity for the Mark III and IV still fell well below 200 a month during the 1939-40 winter and spring period. Reorganizing the existing Panzer divisions through force structure changes, OKH was able to increase the overall tank force. It reduced the number of tanks in the existing divisions from 324 to 300, lowered the number of tank battalions in newly formed Panzer divisions from four to three (in one case to two), and used the separate Panzer brigades to fill the new Panzer divisions (see Table 1.1). OKH doubled the Panzer divisions by April 1940, but severely limited the rest of the Army's mobility. Industry only increased the total production of Mark III and IV models from 525 in September 1939 to 850 in May 1940, thus confiscated Czechoslovakian 35t and 38t tanks and captured Polish equipment had to be used to bolster the German inventory to 3,381 tanks of all types by April 1, 1940. Captured Polish equipment also became a source for Germany's foreign military sales program and a way to pay for raw materials received from the USSR and Romania. Unfortunately, foreign equipment provided an additional headache for the armaments industry, because it needed to retool machinery to produce spare parts. During April and early May 1940, the Army scrapped about 807 Mark I, II, 35t, and 38t tanks. Additionally, wheeled assets required for motorized infantry brigades in new Panzer divisions were taken from existing regular infantry divisions.[32]

Transportation assets also provided a dim picture in the spring of 1940. The Army only possessed 120,000 trucks of all types to haul troops, materiel, and pull equipment and weapons. The monthly allocation of new vehicles for the Army totalled less than one percent, or 1,000 vehicles. This did not even cover normal losses, let alone losses in upcoming combat operations. In the area of specialized vehicles, an acute shortage existed. The reason for these problems were twofold: one, Germany suffered a severe shortage of steel and rubber; second, the large number of different models in production precluded sufficient quantities of one type from being produced. Vehicle shortages in regular infantry and artillery units had to be replaced by horses. This incidentally remained a problem throughout the war. Consequently, no Panzer reserves existed for the offensive in the West. Overall, the Army found itself in a situation of being less mobile in May 1940 than in September 1939 (see Table 1.2).[33]

On October 16, 1939, during a briefing by General von Brauchitsch and Admiral Raeder, Hitler stated that he gave up any hope of the Allies accepting his peace proposal. He therefore decided that the Western powers must be

Table 1.1
Panzer Division Status of May 1940

Number of Divisions	Division Number	Number of Tank Battalions	Number of Motorized Infantry Battalions
6	1st–5th, 10th	4	4
2	6th, 8th	3	4
1	7th	3	5
1	9th	2	5

Note: A four-tank battalion Panzer division fielded 300 tanks; a three-tank battalion Panzer division 210 tanks; a two-tank battalion Panzer division 150 tanks. The prime reason for the variety of organizations was because these units were not designed under a standard TO&E. New Panzer divisions were hurriedly assembled by taking equipment from the original Panzer divisions, the Light divisions, elements of motorized infantry divisions, regular infantry divisions, and existing OKH Panzer brigades.

Source: Müller-Hillebrand, *Das Heer*, p. 141

defeated militarily. The Führer separately informed the ObdH that he agreed to provide seven days' notice prior to initiating the offensive. Von Brauchitsch was told to consider November 15-20 as possible target dates. The ObdH's objections again fell on deaf ears. Hitler gave OKH no alternative but to plan for the invasion of France, Belgium, and Holland. The stalling maneuver slowly ran out of steam.[34]

The Operations Branch of OKH issued an operations plan based on Hitler's "Directive Nr. 6 for the Conduct of War" on October 19, 1939 (see Appendix A, Map 3). This plan called for the strategic concentration of the majority of the Field Army, organized in two army groups, along the Dutch, Belgian, and Luxembourg borders from north of Wesel to Trier. The point of main effort rested with General von Bock's Army Group B, headquartered in Bad Godesberg, and consisted of the 18th, 2nd, 6th, and 4th Armies. Additionally, OKH planned to employ six out of seven Panzer divisions in von Bock's sector. These Panzer divisions, concentrated in the Aachen area, formed a mighty attack wedge with the mission of rapidly driving through Belgium and northern France, opening the way to the Channel coast for the following infantry divisions. Colonel-General Gerd von Rundstedt's[35] Army Group A, headquartered in Koblenz, which consisted of the 12th and 16th Armies, received orders to advance through the Ardennes and Luxembourg in a west-northwesterly direction providing protection for Army Group B's exposed southern flank. Army Group C, considerably weaker than the other two army groups, under the command of General von Leeb, with the 1st and 7th Armies, headquartered in Frankfurt am Main, received the mission to protect the left flank of Army Group A and defend the West Wall from Trier to the Swiss border. Based on an accurate intelligence assessment by OKH's Foreign Armies West,[36] weak Belgian forces were anticipated in the Ardennes and strong forces north of Liege. OKH concentrated the armored forces in the north because planners considered the Ardennes impassable during the winter. Army group commanders and their army commanders, however, objected to this operational concept, especially with respect to employment of motorized forces in the north. Considering the multiple water obstacles in that region, they judged it ill-conceived. They questioned the entire concept of an offensive in the West. It was also an obvious duplication of the Schlieffen Plan, hence an operation the Western Allies expected. Generals Wilhelm Keitel[37] and Alfred Jodl[38] visited Zossen on October 22 to brief von Brauchitsch on Hitler's dissatisfaction with the plan, and to inform him of the Führer's intentions of using specialized troops for the securing of bridges and key installations behind the front. Jodl further informed OKH that Hitler definitely set the offensive for November 12, 1939.[39]

Table 1.2
Armored Vehicle Status from September 1939 and May 1940

Panzer Type	1. 9. 39	1. 4. 40	10. 5. 40
I	1445	1062[b]	523
II	1226	1086[b]	955
III	98	329	349
35t[a]	----	143[b]	106
38t[a]	----	238[b]	228
IV	211	280	278
Cmd[c]	215	243	135
Total	3195	3381	2574

[a] 35t and 38t model tanks were confiscated from Czechoslovakia and incorporated into the German Panzer divisions. In the 6th Panzer Division 35t's substituted for Mark III's. In the 7th and 8th Panzer Divisions, 38t's substituted for Mark III's.

[b] Indicates those models scheduled to be scrapped because of age during April and May 1940.

[c] Command tanks.

Source: Müller-Hillebrand, *Das Heer,* pp. 106, 141.

Hitler, however, dissatisfied and uneasy about the operation plan, exercised his role as Commander in Chief of the Wehrmacht by inviting General von Bock and two of his army commanders, Generals von Reichenau and von Kluge, to brief him on their plans on October 25, in Berlin. The ObdH and Army chief of staff were also asked to join the meeting. During the briefing Hitler, to the amazement of all present, asked if it were feasible to move the main effort south of the Meuse River with a direction of west-northwest towards Reims or Amiens. General von Bock immediately expressed concern over the road network, and considered the shifting of forces into this area as only compounding the problem. Von Brauchitsch and Halder were completely astonished by this new development. Hitler, as so often before, had not discussed this brainstorm with von Brauchitsch prior to the meeting. The Führer ordered OKH to investigate the possibility. Meanwhile he would defer the decision for a day or two. This constituted Hitler's first serious meddling in military operations, a development which all too soon became the norm.[40]

Hitler, in a subsequent meeting with Generals Keitel and Jodl, decided to move the main effort south of Liege with 12th Army advancing westward and isolating Belgium. This would be accomplished by attacking the Belgian forts frontally, searching for weak points, with the idea of unleashing the Panzer units held in reserve to exploit these weak points. Jodl briefed Halder about the new developments on the evening of October 26. Halder's last journal entry for that day reads: "Try everywhere."[41] Von Brauchitsch and Halder remained perplexed, unable to react in time to these changes. Hitler, obviously obsessed with this offensive, continued to suggest changes almost daily. On October 27 he recommended yet another change, this time requesting OKH to plan for two motorized groups advancing toward Ghent and southwest of Namur. His decision would follow on the 28th.[42]

At a meeting at the New Chancellory on the morning of October 28, Hitler again provided new instructions. He began by restressing his theory of defeating large formations of the French and British Armies as the first essential goal, thus securing vital territory along the French and Belgian coastline. To fulfill this plan a breakthrough should be conducted both north and south of Liege, employing one Panzer Gruppe (Group)[43] in each sector, holding 6th Army in reserve until the Meuse River crossings were secure. Based on these changes, OKH issued a new operations plan on October 29, 1939 (see Appendix A, Map 4). The struggle for the final operations plan was now well on its way.[44]

The results of the new plan were:

1. Holland would not be occupied.

2. OKH's political/strategic goal: to defeat as many French forces, and those of her allies, in northern France and Belgium thus setting the stage for further operations against Britain.

3. OKH's operational goal: to destroy the Allied forces north of the Somme River and break through to the Channel coast.

4. To meet Hitler's directive of October 25, OKH shifted units south. Fourth Army was to attack with four Panzer divisions north and south of Namur.

5. The main effort was to remain with Army Group B.

Although this new version was by no means brilliant, the obvious weaknesses of the previous one were overcome. It still did not present anything original. The three army group commanders continued to question the use of motorized units in the north, where numerous water obstacles could grind an offensive to a standstill. They foresaw a situation where, although elements in Army Group A were successful in their advance, a stall in the north would bring the entire offensive to a halt. The greatest criticism came from the Chief of Staff of Army Group A, General Erich von Manstein,[45] who became the catalyst for the development of the final operation plan.[46]

October 30, 1939, proved a significant date, since Hitler for the first time suggested a breakthrough near Sedan. The Führer discussed this possibility with General Jodl, who neglected to pass the information on to his counterpart at OKH. Dissatisfied with the latest OKH operation plan and the pace with which von Brauchitsch and Halder were implementing it, Hitler requested the ObdH for a meeting at the New Chancellory on November 5, 1939.

The November 5, 1939, meeting is recorded in history as one of the tragic moments in the continuing worsening relationship between the German Officer Corps and its head of state. (Coincidentally, November 5th was also the deadline for initiating the deployment of assault divisions into assembly areas along Germany's western borders if an offensive were to occur on the 12th.) General von Brauchitsch spent the 2nd and 3rd of November visiting the army group commanders in the West to gain a firsthand impression of their opinions of the upcoming offensive. Once again they expressed negative support for an offensive. Von Brauchitsch attempted to use the meeting on the 5th to again delay the offensive. The general prepared and read a memorandum to Hitler pointing out weaknesses within the Army. The meeting, however, turned extremely sour and ended abruptly without von Brauchitsch being able to sway the Führer. General von Brauchitsch's references, during the confrontation, to German soldiers' poor discipline and performance in Poland only served to upset further the relationship between the two men. Hitler became so furious that he immediately dictated a dismissal order for the Army commander in chief, but discarded it later. Hitler, well aware that dismissal of von Brauchitsch would only cause a further dissent among his generals, opted to cancel the order. Whatever confidence existed between these two men prior to November 5, 1939, however, was never restored. General Brauchitsch's dismissal would only be delayed by a couple of years.[47]

The Führer, enraged about his meeting with von Brauchitsch, ordered the Army's alert for the scheduled offensive on the 12th, but agreed to a postponement on the 7th. Jodl had not advised Halder of Hitler's "brainstorm" until

November 3. The Army chief of staff failed to see any point in this new development and, given the schedule for an offensive on the 12th, determined the available time to react as inadequate. On the 9th the ObdH informed Oberkommando der Wehrmacht (OKW)[48] that time still would not permit any changes in plans, even if the offensive were postponed to the 15th. Should, however, a postponement occur, the ObdH suggested organizing a motorized group, commanded by General Heinz Guderian.[49] This recommendation, though, depended on the availability of the desired units. OKW replied on November 9 that the offensive would not commence prior to the 19th and that Hitler now wanted Panzer units employed on an Arlon–Tintigny axis. Hitler also authorized the use of the 4th Light and 29th Motorized Divisions. Declining OKW's offer, the ObdH cited a lack of time to reallocate and relocate the mechanized divisions. In a discussion with General Halder, von Brauchitsch indicated that he viewed the dearth of additional Panzer divisions as unacceptable. Panzer reserves did not exist and he did not want to divert any from the planned concentration of forces in the north. Lastly, von Brauchitsch felt that Hitler did not want to scatter mechanized forces over the entire front. The ObdH would rather wait and assign the 4th Light and the 29th Motorized Divisions to the XIXth Corps once fully combat-ready. However, later on the same day von Brauchitsch changed his mind and ordered an additional Panzer division added to Guderian's XIXth Corps. On the 10th, OKH informed OKW that it wanted the 10th Panzer Division, 2nd Panzer or 29th Motorized Division, and Leibstandarte-SS ''Adolf Hitler'' (LAH) for the purpose of advancing to Sedan. The 4th Light Division would remain in OKH reserve. Von Brauchitsch requested permission to issue orders to this effect. Hitler considered these forces inadequate and ordered the 2nd Panzer Division added along with the 29th Motorized Division to ensure success. Hitler was correct in not piecemealing Panzer divisions over the entire front; however, he failed to provide his Army commander in chief any clear statement of intent. Instead the Führer suggested a new whim each day, causing OKH to remain in a constant state of reaction, rather than being able to plan and test the feasibility of some of these theories in war games.[50]

The lack of Panzer reserves resulted in a shifting of all motorized forces along the Western Front to organize the necessary Panzer group. Panzer divisions could only be obtained at the expense of already existing forces. On November 11th OKH issued orders to Army Groups A and B, instructing them to release the 2nd and 10th Panzer Divisions, one motorized division, LAH and Infanterie Regiment ''Grossdeutschland'' (GD) for assignment to the XIXth Corps. The mission of XIXth Corps was to advance, as lead echelon, in front of 12th and 16th Armies to the Meuse River near Sedan, and force a crossing, thereby establishing favorable conditions for a continuation of the offensive. Thus was born XIXth Panzer Corps. Upon receipt of this message General von Bock informed OKH that, unless provided with additional forces, he could no longer accomplish his assigned mission.[51]

Postponements of the offensive continued throughout the winter, primarily because of poor weather. The real struggle for the operation plan and employment of armored forces, however, had not yet been fought. With Guderian in command of XIXth Panzer Corps and von Manstein as chief of staff of Army Group A, a new chapter in the planning process commenced.[52]

THE QUESTION OF MAIN EFFORT AND THE CUT
OF THE SCYTHE

Both operations plans, issued by OKH in October 1939, failed to establish a military goal that would satisfy the political aims of Adolf Hitler for Western Europe. Hitler, untrained in the art of warfare, was incapable of presenting recommendations to his military advisors that he derived through a sequence of logical military deductions, but rather based his suggestions on intuitions and voiced thoughts. The Army's leaders, von Brauchitsch and Halder, failed to understand Hitler's military goals because they did not support his political aims. Von Brauchitsch and Halder also concluded that the military offensive in the West was wrong and, judging the Army unprepared, could only view it as an imminent failure. Thus, the Army's leaders never supported their political leader, and the two October plans amounted to nothing more than reluctant obedience or improvisation upon Hitler's orders. The main effort remained ill-conceived, army group commanders had no confidence in the OKH plans, and several senior Army officers began to question OKH's ability to plan an offensive.

The question of main effort and the employment of Panzer assets was a burning issue right from the beginning of the planning process. However, with General Guderian earmarked as a possible contender to lead this effort and General von Manstein as chief of staff of Army Group A, OKH began to feel increasing pressure from the field. Guderian, commanding XIXth Corps, became intimately involved in the planning process after November 11, when he received information that his XIXth Corps might lead the armored thrust. He agreed that a thrust through the Ardennes was feasible, but felt the allotted forces were insufficient.[53]

General von Manstein's involvement began on October 21, 1939, when en route to Army Group A's headquarters in Koblenz, he visited Zossen and received his first briefing on the operation. As early as October 31, von Manstein, with von Rundstedt's endorsement, wrote the first of many memoranda to OKH advocating a main effort further to the south, in Army Group A's sector. After General von Bock was required to transfer both of his reserve Panzer divisions to Army Group A, he expressed dissatisfaction with von Manstein's plan because it not only threatened to wrestle the main effort from Army Group B, but also meant a reduction of the size of his army group. Von Bock talked to Halder and von Brauchitsch several times over the next few weeks, expressing his concerns over the constant fluctuations in mission requirements. He considered continuous changes, both in mission and offense dates, a hindrance to preparation, and warned OKH about the long-term negative impact the perpetual alert status would have on his soldiers.[54]

The question of main effort became critical since reserves were usually positioned to support the main effort. This caused a triple rivalry between the commanders of Army Groups A, B, and General Halder. Halder, caught in the middle, received pressure not only from field commanders, but also from Hitler, who demanded immediate action.[55]

Von Manstein's theory envisioned an offensive resulting in a decisive victory through means of a two-phase battle. Phase one was conceptualized as the main effort south of Namur, breaking through to the Somme and destroying or cutting off all Allied forces moving into Belgium. Phase two was visualized as the forces turning south to envelop and defeat the Allies. Von Manstein based his plan on the Allies expecting a repeat of the 1914 Schlieffen Plan. He figured that Allied countermeasures would call for stopping the Germans as far northeast as possible, attacking the German southern flank, and rolling up the entire front. He planned the main effort in Army Group A's sector, with one army attacking in a westerly direction between Dinant and Fumay in conjunction with Army Group B (to the north) trapping and destroying enemy forces in Belgium. An additional army would also advance and cross the Meuse River on both sides of Sedan in a southwesterly direction opposing enemy forces expected to counterattack north. Having eliminated the enemy's counterattack forces, the northern armies could drive westward unimpeded, resulting in a decisive victory (see Appendix A, Map 7).[56]

In several memoranda General von Manstein provided planning figures to OKH delineating the minimum forces required to achieve victory. He requested two mobile corps, at a minimum one Panzer corps, to defeat enemy forces in southern Belgium. Following von Moltke's view that no operation plan should be planned beyond its first engagement, von Manstein's further employment of mobile forces depended on the enemy's reaction. Eliminating the dangers of an exposed flank, mobile forces from Army Group A could strike north, assisting in the destruction of encircled enemy forces. Von Manstein, however, recommended the mass of the armored forces in Army Group B's sector. A third army would have the responsibility of establishing a defensive front between the Meuse River at Carignan and the Moselle River at Metlach. Von Manstein also envisioned the simultaneous destruction of Allied reserve forces moving north toward Fumay and Laon (see Appendix A, Map 7).[57]

General Halder, in the meantime, also investigated the operational possibilities, and as an able General Staff planner did not dismiss von Manstein's ideas. Von Manstein's plan called for offensive flank protection using motorized units (2nd Army). Halder stated as early as November 1939 that a possible attack against the left flank of Army Group A was consistent with German doctrine, but not contemporary French doctrine. In his own scheme, Halder relied on infantry divisions for defensive flank protection while rapidly advancing motorized units toward the Somme River. He disliked von Manstein's plan, partly because it lacked unity of effort. Halder wanted to avoid "private campaigns" with Army Group B advancing northeast and Army Group A southeast. He envisioned 4th Army advancing (south of Namur) rapidly to the Somme River on the northern flank of Army Group A, thus trapping and destroying the Allied armies north of the Somme River. Halder planned for five Panzer and three motorized divisions to lead the attack. Von Manstein, on the other hand, envisioned a strong Army Group B pushing Allied forces toward the Somme, while engaging Army Group A both in destroying Allied reserves and attempting to drive to the Channel coast. Halder's plan hinged on Army Group B feinting in the north, thereby deceiving the Allies into committing their mechanized reserves to the north. He likened this to a hammer and anvil approach where Army Group B, the anvil, would fix the Allies in the north while Army Group A, the hammer, would provide the decisive blow with the Panzer and motorized divisions. General von Manstein's theory consisted more of a double hammer approach where 2nd Army in the center could act as an anvil.[58]

General Halder found it difficult to change his October 29 plan because of Hitler's sole control of all armored and motorized assets and the continuous rescheduling of the Western offensive. It was postponed 14 times between November 12, 1939, and January 16, 1940. The Army chief of staff did, however, incorporate significant changes directed in OKW's Directive Nr. 6 issued on November 20, 1939, for the January 17, 1940, target date. These changes did not incorporate his own concepts on how the offensive should be conducted (see Appendix A, Map 5). Hitler, however, cancelled the offensive for an indefinite period on January 16, 1940, since the long-range weather forecast remained poor, but more important, an incident on January 10 may have revealed his intentions to the Allies.[59]

The incident on January 10, 1940, known as the "Mechelen Affair" changed the entire situation. A Luftwaffe paratroop officer carried the top secret operation plan, against orders, while on a flight from Münster to Köln. During the trip the pilot became lost and strayed into Belgian territory. After a forced landing, caused by aircraft engine trouble, the Belgians captured parts of the German war plan. Although only fragments of the plan fell into Belgian hands, Hitler did not believe the testimony of the officers and postponed the offensive until some time in the spring. This, for the first time since September 27, 1939, provided OKH with an opportunity to fundamentally change the October plans. More important, the Army General Staff was now afforded time to test changes through its traditional methods and could properly plan a logical deployment.[60]

General Halder and the army groups conducted a series of war games to test several scenarios, ultimately convincing the Army chief of staff that von Manstein's overall concept was correct. These wargames led OKH to shift the main effort south of Liege in an advance through the Ardennes to Sedan. Halder, in an effort to assert his control over the army group commanders, also shifted army group boundaries, placing 4th Army under Army Group A. In mid-February he also placed all armored and motorized forces under a separate army headquarters. His plan was not without risk. Halder himself, after analyzing his decision, determined that OKH had to take the risk. He summarized it by saying: "It would be impossible to justify to military historians not to have taken a risk so promising and filled with the possibility of decisive victory."[61]

In mid-January 1940, the Army Personnel Office informed General von Manstein that he would be replaced as Army Group A's chief of staff to assume command of the XXXVIIIth Corps, a third echelon infantry corps in the upcoming offensive. Coincidentally, von Manstein, while en route to his new corps command, briefed Hitler on February 17, 1940, in Berlin. Hitler was impressed by von Manstein's ideas and immediately summoned von Brauchitsch and Halder for a meeting the following day. Halder and von Manstein had only two or three occasions where they personally interacted. Even though the two Army leaders had no idea what von Manstein's briefing contained, it was very similar to their own and Hitler accepted OKH's concept. This plan is recorded in history as the "Sichelschnitt Plan" (Cut of the Scythe) (see Appendix A, Map 6). General Halder based his plan on several war games. Although the plan contained many of von Manstein's ideas, Halder actually developed the plan through meticulous General Staff work. Hitler, finally satisfied, accepted the plan and OKH issued it to the army groups on February 24, 1940. General Halder vehemently defended his plan against any major changes by either Army Group A or B after this point, making it clear that his Sichelschnitt Plan was final.[62]

The plan, published on February 24, 1940, provided a sound foundation, although many of the details that would ultimately make it so successful still required meticulous staff work. In retrospect the operation plan was not conceived by any one individual, but rather through a combination of General Staff planners employing all the specialized knowledge, weighing risks in order to arrive at the best possible solution. The Sichelschnitt Plan evolved over time, probably through a match of von Manstein's strategic concepts and Hitler's ideas. Halder, the technocrat, absorbed and analyzed all the varied ideas and developed it into the actual campaign plan. Finally the General Staff tested it for feasibility. The Sichelschnitt Plan, however, like its October 1939 predecessors, did not reach beyond the fall of France. The General Staff still lacked an overall political and military strategy for war with all belligerents because of OKH's reluctance to undertake any offensives. This shortsighted outlook became the seed for future disasters.[63]

The road was now open to began preparations and to dedicate training for an offensive in the spring. Despite the difficulties of continuous alert conditions, the German Army did conduct training over the winter months to rectify tactical, disciplinary, and equipment problems identified in after-action reports from the Polish Campaign. General Halder and the army group commanders had their hands full over the next 12 weeks preparing the German Army for the execution of this offensive, while at the same time fixing major problems in the areas of organization and training.[64]

2

The Army Prepares

Es kommt darauf an, ohne Rücksicht auf Rechts und Links schnell
in die Tiefe durchzustossen und den Verteidiger immer zu überraschen.
Sperrungen und Geländehindernisse sind mit allen Mitteln schnell zu
überwinden oder zu umgehen.
(It is imperative to break through rapidly to the enemy's rear. To accomplish this,
we must disregard left and right flank security and employ every available means to
cross quickly or to bypass his barriers and obstacles. Surprise him continuously.)
General der Kavallerie Ewald von Kleist

TRAINING

Most armies experience difficulties in their first combat actions. These are
usually as a result of the process of changing from peacetime training conditions
to the realities of war. Previous deployments of the German Army occurred
during the Austrian Anschluss and the Czechoslovakian invasion and, although
these actions provided interesting lessons for logisticians and organizational
planners, they did not test the young army in combat. The Polish Campaign
served as the actual proving ground for the German Army, and as such identified
some unique problems for the German Army's General Staff. The General Staff
and field commanders analyzed the Army's performance and utilized the lessons
learned for improvements. It therefore becomes rather obvious why the German
General Staff was so opposed to an immediate winter offensive in the West.
General von Brauchitsch wanted his regular units to digest the lessons from the
recent campaign, but more important, hastily organized divisions called up for

the Polish Campaign flagrantly lacked training and toughness. Reorganization and training thus became the Field Army's top priority. Continuous alerts and the coldest winter in recent history, however, prevented an orderly reorganization of forces and affected all aspects of training in a negative manner.

Before the guns of the Polish Campaign fell silent, the German General Staff began to evaluate the Army's performance. It quickly became apparent that a number of problems required solutions, most important of which were training and unit cohesion. Lack of training and impetus within the Army had caused the German officer corps a proportionately high number of losses in Poland. The credit for the campaign went to the senior army leadership, superior weapons, and materiel. German employment of Luftwaffe and Panzer formations presented the Polish General Staff with a hopeless situation.[1]

The German Army chief of staff began to evaluate the Army's performance toward the end of the Polish Campaign, and thus was able to plan for and initiate changes immediately. He rejected any large-scale activation of new units with the exception of five previously planned infantry divisions. These divisions received confiscated Czechoslovakian equipment since no German equipment was available. OKH originally planned for a defensive posture in the West and started reorganizing, training, and equipping forces on the Western Front. Not discarding a war of movement in the West, however, the Army General Staff planned for and expected two-thirds of the field army to quickly undertake offensive operations in the West. Thus, OKH ordered the filling of the first through fourth draft infantry divisions to full strength.[2]

The accelerated build up of forces from 1934 to 1939 produced divisions with varied grades of combat efficiency. This became primarily noticeable in the motorized infantry divisions when they proved too cumbersome in Poland under the 1939 organization. As a result of these deficiencies, OKH initiated organizational changes, adjusted its TO&E's, and reorganized motorized infantry divisions from three to two regiments (see Appendix E, Tables of Organization and Equipment). Reducing the three regiment (motorized) infantry divisions by one regiment served to streamline that organization. Extracted regiments were used to increase the number of infantry battalions in Panzer and light divisions from three to four. Under a long-term project, light divisions converted to Panzer divisions as new tanks became available. Most of these long-term changes were already in progress when Hitler presented his generals with the *"fait accompli"* on September 27, 1939. Acting immediately to meet the Führer's goals, OKH dropped a meticulous organized transition in favor of a high speed reorganization, resulting in a non-uniformly equipped army with questionable combat efficiency.[3]

On September 1, 1939, the majority of active duty divisions deployed to the Eastern Front, while several active but mostly reserve divisions deployed to the West. Typically, reserve divisions had few regular Army officers. Normally one would only find them in command and operations officer/chief of staff positions. The 58th Infantry Division, for example, had 300 out of 490 officers with no combat experience or training since 1918. About 90 percent of the troops were either World War I veterans or had only received short-term military training. The operations officer/chief of staff of this division reported his unit as not combat-ready in November 1939 and, unless given a rigorous training program behind the front at an army training center, predicted no change in readiness status. The 58th Infantry Division was not an isolated case, since only 11 of 35 divisions in the West were active duty divisions.[4]

General Halder directed his efforts at improvements not only toward the organization of the force, but also at the weapons systems and training. Initial impressions indicated problems with the MG 34.[5] It became easily dirtied by dust and mud because of delicate workmanship. Although the Army adopted the weapon as the standard machine gun shortly before the war, Poland served as its proving ground. Halder immediately ordered the Army Weapons Office to take corrective action. The 81 mm mortar, on the other hand, proved its worth in the short conflict.[6]

At the tactical level, the General Staff identified serious problems that would have to be addressed prior to the campaign in the West. Camouflage against air attack, although deemed very bad, could probably be attributed to a nonexistent Polish air force shortly after the conflict started. Consequently, units relaxed antiaircraft defense. Infantry tended to bunch up. Also deficient were combat reconnaissance and defensive postures by units during rest periods, especially after long marches. Halder requested his staff to look into establishing reconnaissance units at corps level. In the area of traffic control, vital to moving large motorized formations, the Army also rated itself below standard. Police employed for the purpose of traffic control proved ineffective, prompting Halder to direct the immediate formation of a military staff solely for the purpose of traffic control. Marksmanship received excellent ratings.[7]

Upon completion of the Polish Campaign OKH began collecting official after-action reports to formalize its conclusions. Although a successful campaign, German commanders and staffs spared no criticism in their reports. Indications from all levels suggested that problems existed in the Army's performance during the Polish Campaign, although, by and large, the Army and the individual soldier fought well. The Army's fundamental doctrine and structure were sound, but changes proved necessary.[8]

Light divisions fared well in Poland against a disorganized enemy; however, OKH acknowledged the Western Allies as a more potent challenge, forcing an accelerated reorganization of all light divisions into armored divisions. Panzer and motorized formations lived up to their pre-war expectations, although a lack of initiative plagued the ranks of mid- and junior-grade officers. Panzer and infantry cooperation still left much to be desired. In one case General Guderian personally intervened at company level to maintain the momentum of an attack.[9]

Infantry did not show the same resilience as in 1914, and reservist units especially suffered high rates of exhaustion during long approach marches. Infantry night fighting and combat in rough terrain acquired inadequate ratings. Transition from offense to defense presented German units with difficulties, occupying linear defenses rather than the doctrinally correct defense in depth. General Halder noted in his journal, on September 14, 1939, "delaying defense" must go. German soldiers of 1939 seemed pampered compared to those of 1914. Hitler spent enormous sums of money to build model barracks for his new army, and treatment of soldiers became less severe and frugal compared to the pre-1914 Army. Previously members of the Hitler Youth and having served six months in the Reichsarbeitsdienst (Reich Labor Service), these young soldiers were full of faith and ideals. However, their spiritualized principles failed to match the hardness required for battle.[10] The tremendous expansion of the German Army from 1935 to 1939 actually led to a decline in the overall performance of its soldiers. The relatively small Reichsheer cadre found itself incapable of singlehandedly supporting such a dramatic expansion. Too many inexperienced junior officers and NCOs conducting training resulted in an overall decrease in basic soldier skills. Trench warfare mentality still plagued some of the World War I officer veterans, stifling their reaction to mobile warfare.[11]

The accelerated growth of the German officer corps from 1933 to 1939 diluted the junior ranks of the professional officer corps of the Reichsheer, resulting in leadership problems during the Polish Campaign that required immediate attention. The poor leadership of junior officers therefore became a major concern of the Army's commander in chief after the Polish Campaign. Well-trained soldiers, poorly led, are an ineffective force. The German Army officer corps grew at a tremendous rate from its 4,000 professional Reichsheer officers in 1933 to 25,000 active Army officers in 1939. One must consider that about 500 officers of the original Reichsheer cadre transferred to the newly formed Luftwaffe in 1935. An additional 450 were medical and veterinary officers. Officers of the State Police transferred into the Army when Hitler ordered their incorporation as part of the expansion program. After the Anschluss, Austrian officers and Czechoslovakian officers of German origin filled available officer billets. Officer candidates, however, provided the vast majority of junior officers.[12]

Soldiers and NCOs who met the necessary qualifications attended officer candidate schools. After completing the course, they returned to their units and, having demonstrated the ability to lead, received commissions. By spring of 1940, 1,500 to 2,000 officer candidates a month returned to units. In contrast, Reichsheer officers required the Abitur[13] and received military education in the tradition of the old Imperial Army. This new officer corps, fragmented by old traditions and a new way of life, did not have time to solidify with a cohesive esprit de corps by 1939. During and after the Polish Campaign discipline, behavior, and dress code violations outside military installations became so rampant that von Brauchitsch ordered the formation of the Heeresstreifendienst, Army Military Police Patrols, with the sole mission of enforcing discipline and order. These units, assigned to army level headquarters, were directly responsible to the Army's chief of staff and had complete authority to punish soldiers in the absence of their commanders. In February 1941, the Heeresstreifendienst became part of the Wehrmacht-Streifendienst, Armed Forces Military Police Patrol, because each service had established its own version and a consolidation seemed more appropriate. The Army's Streifendienst, however, already enjoyed full power of authority over all three branches' soldiers.[14]

General von Brauchitsch set the training wheels in motion by issuing the first of a series of directives to correct training deficiencies. In the directive, titled "The Training of the Field Army," the ObdH insisted commanders utilize the lull before the campaign in the West to perfect the Field Army's performance, discipline, and cohesion. He expected realistic training for his soldiers, emphasizing soldier education and a toughening of character to ready them for the challenge of fighting a well-equipped and trained enemy. General von Brauchitsch expected marked improvements in reconnaissance and security, march discipline, infantry fire discipline, preparing units for long marches, improved stamina, better cooperation between arms, offensive and defensive tactics during limited visibility, and a clear understanding of defensive doctrine.[15]

In the second half of his directive, the Army commander in chief stressed combat leadership in the officer corps. General von Brauchitsch expected units to train their reserve officers to the same standards as regular Army officers. The general also wanted an intensified noncommissioned officer (NCO) training program, with special emphasis in the reserve NCO ranks. He demanded high standards to avoid their position as leaders, trainers, and educators from sinking as it had in the last years of World War I.[16] Lastly, General von Brauchitsch, emphasizing a traditional Prussian notion, expressed in his military philosophy that "discipline is the foundation of victory in both military form and courtesy." He expected this subject to receive particular attention at every school or command.[17]

OKH issued a second key document on October 13, aimed at reorganization at the tactical level from company down to squad. This change resulted in a significant retraining program for the Army. Based on conclusive evidence that the infantry company's organization resulted in a lack of maneuverability and too little capability in the way of rapid fire weapons, General von Brauchitsch directed a reorganization of the infantry squad. Under the new organization the squad consisted of ten men (see Appendix E, Infantry Company (motorized)). Arming the squad leader with a submachine gun rather than a K98 rifle and issuing each squad an MG 34 significantly improved the unit's firepower. Changing the composition of the infantry squad also caused a reorganization of the infantry platoon. Previously operating on the half-platoon principle, one half of the platoon consisted of machine guns and mortars, the other half of maneuver troops. Under its reorganization the infantry platoon consisted of four rifle squads, one three-man 50 mm mortar section, and a headquarters section. This new organization forced lieutenants and NCOs to lead troops rather than position machine guns and mortars.[18]

In October 1939, von Brauchitsch reinstituted a World War I monthly status report on combat readiness at division and corps levels. The significance of this report was that commanders did not have to fear retaliation for submitting unfavorable comments and evaluations. Von Brauchitsch wanted to avoid the mistakes of 1914-18, when the German High Command overestimated the fighting capability of frontline units.[19] These evaluation reports formed the basis of training programs for the 1939-40 winter period, and clearly implicated the Army as ill-prepared for a campaign in the West. Von Brauchitsch expected to utilize the status reports to convince Hitler of the Army's unpreparedness, hoping the Führer would concede to a lengthy postponement of the offensive, and thereby provide the necessary time to correct shortcomings.[20]

OKH established and supervised training programs for commanders. Von Brauchitsch entrusted company and battery commanders' training to field army headquarters; however, OKH maintained control of courses for battalion and regimental commanders. Only combat experienced officers and NCOs would fill the school staffs. OKH instituted and monitored the objective standards set for these schools. Case studies of officers failing to show initiative during the Polish Campaign became the basis for leadership instruction. As a result, OKH encouraged senior commanders to inspire junior officers and NCOs to take initiative, while at the same time not ignoring their stated orders; thus failure to display initiative became equated to disobeying an order. Compelling officers and NCOs to perform under conditions of constant physical and mental duress served to identify weak leaders.[21]

There were, however, problems in the implementation of unit training since most of the German Army was on the Western Front and remained on constant alert. There also existed a lack of training areas along the Western Front that were capable of accommodating large-scale maneuvers. Units began to experience deteriorations in troop morale because of the long period of position warfare and on account of working on construction projects along the West Wall. OKH's training concept also included divisions scheduled to deploy from the East. In early November, Halder determined that these divisions required two full weeks of intensive training to prepare for combat in the West.[22]

Army commanders at all levels concerned themselves with the offensive spirit of soldiers and leaders. The Army Group B commander, General von Bock, as late as April 28, 1940, gave critiques of units after training exercises. During these critiques he emphasized his displeasure with "over cautious" leadership. Von Bock wanted to instill "attack, attack, attack"; however, he cautioned against irresponsible incitement. Most importantly, he realized the mission of his army group in the overall scheme. The deception plan depended on Army Group B gaining and maintaining pressure on the Allied armies. Success rested on aggressive leadership at all levels, but especially at company and platoon levels. Disengaging would provide the Allies an opportunity to shift forces and possibly jeopardize the armored breakthrough in the Ardennes and the subsequent thrust to the Channel.[23]

In early December the Army commander in chief realized that an opportunity for more structured training existed, so he had OKH issue another directive to

Army Groups A and B. Halder ordered accelerated training for both army groups and reserves through Christmas. Training focus shifted to battalion through division level exercises. Corps were to establish 10-12 day training courses for officers, NCOs, and prospective NCOs. Only officers having previous command experience could serve as instructors. Infantry units were instructed to train in offensive tactics under their new TO&E. Unfortunately not all units in the field had switched to the new TO&E's. XXIInd Corps, later Panzer Group von Kleist, complied and conducted reorganization at double time even though the required new weapons and equipment had not arrived. Artillery units underwent extensive live fires and engineers began practicing laying and clearing minefields and river crossing operations. Since mobile warfare relied on good communications, signal units were directed to develop training programs to increase their levels of proficiency.[24]

OKH restricted training exercises to units' present field locations or the nearest military installation. Some commanders obtained authority to remove units from front lines for training, provided that designated reserves were available to fill the gaps. OKH, however, denied commanders the use of rail transport for these training activities because the Reichsbahn (German Railroad) could not support the Army. An unprecedented harsh winter and fuel shortages coupled with high usage and poor maintenance of locomotives, railroad yards, and rail lines during recent years caused a deterioration of the entire rail network. This reached alarming proportions during the winter 1939-40 when elements of the war industry came to a standstill because the Reichsbahn could not deliver coal. Only upon Hitler's orders and the introduction of Four Year Plan initiatives in early January 1940 did things finally begin to roll again. Consequently, OKH imposed limits on distances of troop movements to preclude over-ambitious leaders from going to extremes. Marching units could not move farther than two night marches and motorized units no more than one night march. General von Brauchitsch privately discussed his concerns over training with his chief of staff. He feared commanders would place their sole focus on training behind the front. Von Brauchitsch, well aware of problems associated with training in the vicinity of the frontier, informed Halder that some units would just have to accept the circumstances and train there.[25]

Engineers, destined to carry a heavy burden in the coming offensive, received special instructions to conduct waterborne assaults and bridging operations at predetermined locations along the Rhine and Moselle rivers. However, much of the engineer bridging equipment consisted of captured stocks, resulting in many engineer units having to dedicate valuable training time just familiarizing themselves with this equipment. Regimental engineer commanders of army level headquarters supervised these training and exercise activities.[26]

The German General Staff was well aware of the numerous water obstacles in the path of the advancing armies. The Army, however, experienced an acute shortage of both engineer personnel and equipment that could not be remedied until February or March 1940. As a result OKH issued orders in the spring of

1940 to train infantry units in engineer assault tasks. This freed sufficient engineers for the technical requirements of bridging, but placed a tremendous burden on the infantry to conduct its own sapper missions. Motorized machine gun battalions, often operating independently without help from engineers, became the first units to undergo special engineer assault training. These units trained in the removal of explosives from barriers and clearing mine fields. Each infantry platoon trained one machine gun crew as assault engineers. Thus, when needed, one NCO and five enlisted men per platoon or nine NCOs and 45 enlisted men per battalion were capable of filling the assault engineers; role. Each motorized infantry company, in addition to its normal equipment, carried 20 shaped charges, 10 satchel charges, 540 handgrenades, 18 mine detectors, 36 rolls of white engineer tape, an assortment of blasting caps, and a variety of materials to rig explosives and clear and mark paths through mine fields.[27]

Reviewing the enormous training requirements, OKH became increasingly concerned with the unauthorized use of military vehicles. A number of factors contributed to this concern: a shortage of petroleum, poor road conditions, a shortage of vehicles, low maintenance standards, and poor driving standards of soldiers. General von Brauchitsch concluded that officers and soldiers were using military vehicles to visit wives and girlfriends, while training in rear areas. General Halder discussed possible solutions with army group commanders.[28]

The 1939-40 winter, the worst in several years, caused an inordinate amount of frost damage to roads on the Western Front. As late as April 15, 1940, frost levels extended 60 cm below the surface. In the 12th and 16th Armies' sectors road conditions became catastrophic causing numerous accidents. Drivers, poorly trained and unaccustomed to winter road conditions, were incapable of coping with the situation. As a consequence, OKH required commanders to solve traffic problems and deployed road construction battalions to repair damaged roads. In 12th Army's sector these units replaced 330 km of road on the Main Supply Route (MSR) alone.[29]

In response to traffic accidents caused by poor road conditions, maintenance, and driver discipline, Army Group A issued supplemental traffic regulations and a strict policy on vehicle usage. It ordered units to consolidate and coordinate all truck movements to eliminate one stop, one mission type hauls. Dispatch authority became an officer function and roadside spot checks enforced the new rules. Poor driving habits and road conditions, however, were not the only contributors to decreased unit readiness.[30]

Decreased readiness caused by bad maintenance, a result of repair part shortages, and low training standards of maintenance crews also contributed to this dilemma. In a report submitted to Army Group A in January 1940, 12th Army's commander clearly stated his maintenance problems and questioned his army's ability to perform offensive missions.[31] The immediate impact of these maintenance problems resulted in 12th Army's inability to transport properly and resupply itself for an offensive. One of 12th Army's infantry divisions, during a no notice night march on January 14, had several trucks break down because of maintenance failures, and accidents caused by icy roads could have been avoided through proper reconnaissance. In a letter to his corps' commanders, Colonel-General Wilhelm List[32] placed the blame on poor leadership by junior officers. Had officers taken the initiative to reconnoiter routes, he summarized, then ice covered sections would have been identified and covered with sand prior to movement. General von Bock on several occasions echoed similar impressions to von Brauchitsch and Halder regarding his army group.[33]

A combination of bad road conditions, negligent management, and stupidity resulted in units not receiving desperately needed repair parts. In one instance a depot returned to units parts requests submitted during the Polish Campaign for not using proper request forms. Fortunately the affected division commander mentioned this to General von Bock during one of his visits, who immediately brought the problem to the attention of General Halder.[34]

Measures initiated to educate officers, NCOs, and soldiers on maintenance aided in alleviating the problem, but vehicle shortages remained. The German Army as a whole only received 1,000 replacement vehicles per month. As a result, infantry divisions resorted more and more to horse drawn transport, since motorized divisions had priority for motor vehicles.[35]

During the winter General Halder developed a plan for extended training periods in the event of a six to eight week postponement of the offensive. This in fact occurred after the Mechelen Affair. Thus the new directive issued by OKH on January 19, 1940 established the tone for training well into spring. Prior to the Mechelen Affair, the Army remained on virtually continuous alert because Hitler postponed the offensive every seven to ten days. Assault divisions, stationed at their home bases in many cases required a seven day (six night marches) deployment into their assault positions along the border. One can only imagine the turmoil these alerts caused on a routine basis. Eventually, the army group commanders convinced OKH to deploy assault divisions closer to the frontier, resulting in significantly reduced transit times. Deployment was thus reduced to five days, and later to 24 hours once assault divisions moved into permanent deployment areas along the Western Frontier. Even after February 1940, however, entire divisions including motorized and Panzer divisions, and a number of their commanders, remained east of the Rhine River training.[36]

OKH in the January 19 memorandum stressed training as the prime objective for the immediate future of the Army on the Western Front. Halder ordered the movement of several motorized infantry divisions and infantry brigades of Panzer divisions of Army Groups A and B to training centers at Ohrdruf, Gross Born, Grafenwöhr, Senne and Altengrabow respectively for three-week rotations. The infantry units during these rotations practiced assaulting fortified positions. Rail transport, now a necessity, became immediately available.[37]

In an effort to use properly limited time and to provide realistic training, General Halder ordered selected units to provide aggressor forces[38] and school detachments for unit rotations. One battalion of "GD" provided aggressor forces for Army Groups A, B, and C from February 5 to 12. After February 12, field units provided their own aggressors. Company and battery commanders continued attending their respective schools, and battalion commanders of motorized units attended a special course from February 5 to 24 under the direction of the Armor School Commander. First Panzer Division had to provide one Panzer battalion, one battery of artillery, and one engineer company as a school detachment. Tenth Panzer Division, likewise, provided a battalion staff, signal platoon and an antitank battalion for the same purpose. The Army chief of staff maintained great emphasis on training until the campaign against France opened on May 10, 1940. Training, however, was not the only issue that preoccupied German staffs.[39]

THE MAIN EFFORT AND PANZER GROUP VON KLEIST

The main effort, Schwerpunkt, a hotly contested issue in the planning process throughout the 1939-40 winter, was finally resolved by General Halder in his February 24, 1940 operation plan. He placed the main effort in Army Group A's sector, employing armored and mechanized forces in a magnitude heretofore unimagined. Convinced that this armored force required a separate headquarters, OKH activated Panzer Group von Kleist, commanded by Colonel-General Ewald von Kleist,[40] on March 7, 1940 and placed it under Army Group A. The Panzer Group consisted of five Panzer divisions, three motorized divisions, and numerous General Headquarters Troops,[41] organized into three mobile corps (see Appendix G, Order of Battle).[42]

General Halder relied on his intelligence section, Foreign Armies West, to provide accurate information on Allied forces and intentions in order to formulate his decision. As previously mentioned, the Army chief of staff, as early as November/December 1939 viewed the Ardennes as the weakest point along the Allied front.[43] The war games of December 27, 1939 and January 12, 1940 led OKH to believe that the Allies would most probably deploy their main forces toward the Dyle River in northern Belgium, in anticipation of the German main effort in that region.[44]

German intelligence located and identified the Allied reserves spread thinly across the enemy's entire rear area. Based on this information, OKH's Foreign Armies West made several important assumptions. It meant the Allies were incapable of quickly reacting to the German main effort, and second, once identified it could not employ a *masse de maneuvre* against Army Group A's left flank. German intelligence drew a fairly accurate picture of the enemy's situation, which totally supported OKH's operation plan of February 24, 1940.[45]

By late April 1940, however, German intelligence gathered enough information to positively identify 82 of 96 suspected French and British divisions along the northeastern front, providing a nearly complete image of Allied intentions. Earlier assumptions about Allied reserves proved correct. The weakest point along the Western Front remained with the French 9th Army's third rate divisions defending the sector between Sedan and Dinant. Facing von Bock's army group, the French employed their 1st Army Group consisting of a majority of active duty divisions, prepared to advance north to meet the expected German main effort. These divisions were deployed for movement, not for defense.

Along the Maginot Line the French employed the 2nd Army Group, estimated to be greatly overstrength.[46]

Foreign Armies West not only provided the necessary information on France, but also on Belgium. It identified the 1st Chasseurs Ardennais[47] as defending the entire frontage of the Ardennes, and the 1st Cavalry Division was being observed in St. Hubert. German intelligence experts reckoned that, based on the disposition of Belgian forces, they would fight no more than a delaying action, hoping for a quick intervention by the allies. This was confirmed shortly before the invasion, when a signal unit intercepted Belgian radio traffic discussing a planned Belgian delaying action from the frontier to their second defensive belt, along the line St. Hubert–Neufchâteau–Mellier, as soon as the German offensive started. In essence, Foreign Armies West provided the Army chief of staff with the information to make the necessary decisions, almost guaranteeing little or no French interference on the first and possibly even the second day of Panzer Group von Kleist's advance through the Ardennes. The success of the operation inherently depended on the surprise advance through the Ardennes and it seems that the prerequisite had been met.[48]

The February 24 OKH plan called for Army Group A's employment of deeply echeloned mobile forces to advance toward the Meuse River sector between Dinant and Sedan. Employing the element of surprise, these forces were to gain quickly a bridgehead west of the Meuse River, thereby establishing preconditions for the continuation of an advance to the English Channel. Having designated Panzer Group von Kleist as the main effort, Army Group A issued the following mission to General von Kleist: "Panzer Group von Kleist, as lead echelon of Army Group A, advancing in front of 12th and 16th Armies (Vianden–Echternach), attacks in deep echelonment through Luxembourg–southern Belgium. Employing surprise and rapid movement, the Panzer Group, with the main effort on both sides of Charleville-Mézières, secures the west bank of the Meuse River between the Semois River (where it feeds into the Meuse) and Sedan. Subsequently, Panzer Group von Kleist continues its attack to Abbeville and the Channel coast." The key to Panzer Group von Kleist achieving operational surprise rested in its unexpected arrival, in great numbers, along the Meuse River.[49]

Upon assuming command of the Panzer Group, General von Kleist first addressed the problems of command relationships, equipment readiness, echelonment of the Panzer Group, and traffic control. Von Kleist's immediate goal was to solve his command relationship. His Panzer Group's deployment area was amidst 12th and 16th Armies. He would also have to pass through these infantry armies to assault positions and subsequently advance directly in front of them. General List commanded 12th Army to the north of Panzer Group von Kleist, and General of Infantry Ernst Busch[50] commanded 16th Army to the south. Each army commander demanded the Panzer Group be under his own operational control. General von Kleist, however, viewed a subordination to an infantry army as a restraint on his operational mission and his freedom to maneuver. He concluded that the Panzer Group should remain directly responsible to

Army Group A. After several briefings and discussions between the infantry army commanders, von Kleist and Army Group A's commander, General von Rundstedt, the latter decided that as long as the Panzer Group maintained operational freedom it would remain directly under Army Group A. Should, however, the Panzer Group lose the initiative and find itself bogged down and entangled with stiff infantry resistance in front of one of the infantry armies, it would become subordinate to that infantry army.[51]

Army Group A confined Panzer Group von Kleist's advance to a narrow front, with one corps leading, thus forcing the group into a deep echelonment of the entire Panzer force. Dissatisfied with this arrangement, von Kleist discussed the echelonment with von Rundstedt. Von Kleist recommended an advance of two corps abreast (XIXth Panzer Corps and XLIst Panzer Corps, commanded by General Georg-Hans Reinhardt[52]) followed by the XIVth Motorized Corps, commanded by General Gustav von Wietersheim.[53] General von Rundstedt disagreed and directed echelonment in depth, XIXth Panzer Corps leading, followed by XLIst Panzer Corps and XIVth Motorized Corps. Although tactically more feasible, von Rundstedt rejected von Kleist's approach because of traffic control problems. Thus XLIst Panzer Corps would have to follow XIXth Panzer Corps through Luxembourg before shifting to Guderian's right flank for the breakthrough at the Meuse (see Figure 2.1).[54]

Traffic control, previously identified as a problem during the Polish Campaign, presented a monumental challenge once OKH published the operation plan in late February 1940. Panzer Group von Kleist, spearheading the offensive in front of 12th and 16th Army, would have to negotiate a very difficult piece of terrain known as the Ardennes Forest. The Ardennes Forest covers vast areas of eastern Belgium, the Grand Duchy of Luxembourg, and the French Department of Ardennes. It forms an area of about 2,600 sq. km (1,000 sq. miles) and is dissected by deep narrow valleys and gorges. Several rivers create formidable obstacles. Its dense forests offered only narrow roads and trails interlaced with streams, deep valleys, and gorges creating a planner's nightmare. The most difficult terrain of the Ardennes lay in the path of Panzer Group von Kleist.[55]

The German General Staff planned to employ Panzer Group von Kleist as lead echelon through the Ardennes with 134,000 soldiers, 41,000 motor vehicles, 1,250 tanks, and 362 reconnaissance vehicles. Massing and employing these forces, without alarming the Allies and tipping the German hand, introduced special traffic problems. Commanders agreed that the slightest slowing of these forces, once the advance began, presented a potential disaster. To ensure success, Army Group A and Panzer Group von Kleist's staffs conducted a thorough road analysis, developed special traffic control plans, published detailed traffic control orders, and disseminated information down to the last soldier.[56]

TRAFFIC CONTROL

The deployment of 42,000 vehicles and tanks into forward assembly areas and then rapidly moving them through the confines of the Ardennes presented the

Figure 2.1
Panzer Group von Kleist Echelonment

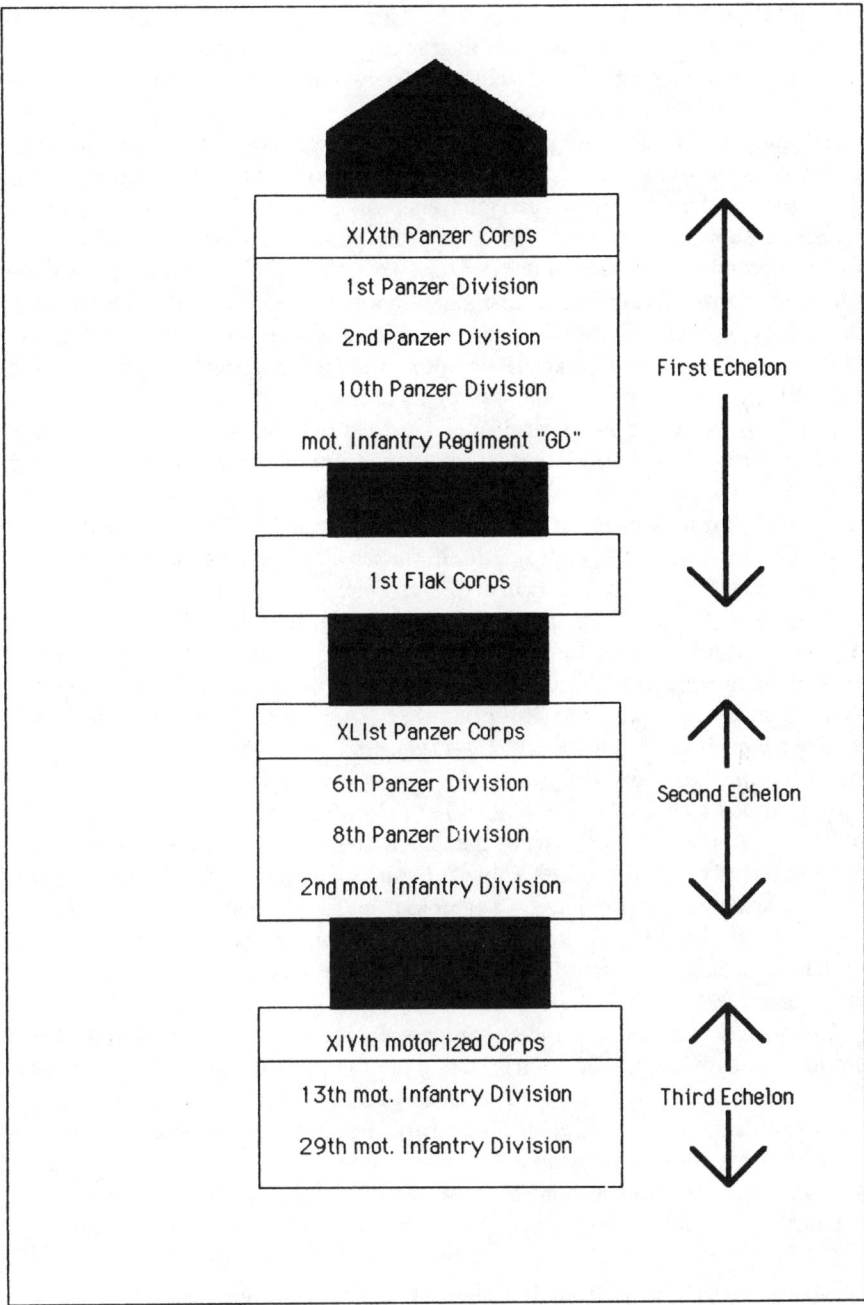

XIXth Panzer Corps	
1st Panzer Division	
2nd Panzer Division	First Echelon
10th Panzer Division	
mot. Infantry Regiment "GD"	
1st Flak Corps	
XLIst Panzer Corps	
6th Panzer Division	
8th Panzer Division	Second Echelon
2nd mot. Infantry Division	
XIVth motorized Corps	
13th mot. Infantry Division	Third Echelon
29th mot. Infantry Division	

General Staff with serious concerns. Since this was the first time a mobile force of this type had ever been assembled, no institutional knowledge existed. The Polish Campaign, on a much smaller scale, demonstrated a need for tight traffic control. However, until OKH issued the operation plan on February 24, 1940, no one imagined the magnitude of this traffic problem. General Halder provided General von Rundstedt, as well as the other two army group commanders, full authority to deal with traffic control.

Positioning of forces along the Western Frontier presented unique challenges to Army Group A's planners. Infantry armies, occupying the defensive line along the border, required garrisons and towns stretching 40 km east. The Panzer Group therefore deployed east of the infantry armies, creating the first major dilemma: movement of the Panzer Group through the infantry prior to the offensive. Panzer Group von Kleist's deployment area (Daun, Bernkastel, Idar-Oberstein, Giessen, Marburg), amidst and immediately to the rear of 12th and 16th Armies, was about 75 km in breadth and 250 km in depth. The immediate implication of this arrangement was that Panzer Group von Kleist, designated main effort, exercised no control over the road network it required for movement to forward assembly areas. The Army General Staff wanted the Panzer divisions deployed without alarming the Allies, and also in a way to aid rapid integration and movement to the border assembly areas. To facilitate this plan Army Group A agreed to deploy XIXth Panzer Corps west of the Rhine River, leaving the remainder of the Panzer Group east of the Rhine.[57]

Army Group A provided the Panzer Group with four Tactical March Routes (TMR) as thoroughfares for combat formations and one Main Supply Route (MSR) for movement from deployment areas to the frontier, through Luxembourg, and Belgium. Panzer Group von Kleist assumed control of these TMRs the afternoon prior to attack day (D–Day), and would be the only authorized formation on these roads. On a single TMR, Panzer Group von Kleist would have occupied a road distance of 1,540 km. Von Kleist's staff, assigning TMRs to the Group's corps in support of the echelonment, reduced the column length to 300-500 km on each TMR.[58] Table 2.1 shows a disposition of forces along the TMRs and Table 2.2 provides an example of a TMR's depth. Although Panzer Group von Kleist enjoyed exclusive use of the four TMRs, many infantry units ultimately needed to cross them, thus creating the possibility of confusion and traffic snarls.[59]

Through a series of war games testing possible traffic control measures, Army Group A categorized traffic control in two major areas: traffic control in deployment areas in Germany and traffic control in enemy territory. In Germany traffic control remained under the control of Army Group A, but became the responsibility of corps and divisions upon entering enemy territory. The Panzer Group, however, received sole responsibility for traffic control of its four TMRs from D-1 until the entire Group passed through, at which time control reverted to Army Group A.[60]

General von Kleist personally conducted a reconnaissance of the four roads and, noting a poorly marked road network, directed his chief of staff, Colonel

Table 2.1
Disposition of Forces

TMR A	TMR B	TMR C	TMR D
2nd Pz Div	1st Pz Div	(1/2) 10th Pz Div	(1/2) 10th Inf Div
6th Pz Div	2nd mot. Inf Div	Inf Reg "GD"	29th mot. Inf Div
(1/2)	(1/2)	(1/2)	
8th Pz Div	8th Pz Div	13th mot. Inf Div	
	(1/2)		
	13th mot. Inf Div		

Kurt Zeitzler,[61] to design a thorough traffic control plan incorporating strict
instructions and rigid time tables (see Appendix B, Movement Orders). Von
Kleist's staff, with some previous traffic control experience in Poland, devised
ingenious methods for controlling the flow of the Panzer Group's 42,000
vehicles. All four TMRs became one way traffic routes to the west. Only special
designated messengers, medical, and firefighting vehicles received authorization
to drive in an easterly direction. The Group ordered all assigned and attached
vehicles marked with a white "K" on the right front and left rear fender to
facilitate identification. The Group issued code words for quick identification to
all units designated to use a TMR. Code words also served to reroute lost drivers
to the correct TMRs. Fixed wing Fieseler Storch aircraft, employed as airborne

Table 2.2
Tactical March Route B

1st Pz Div		1st echelon, 12 hours
Corps Troops		180 km depth
2nd mot. Inf Div		2nd echelon
8th Pz Div (1/2)		150 km depth
13th mot. Inf Div (1/2)		3rd echelon
Service Support		165 km depth

Note: Wheeled vehicles 25km/hour/day, 15km/hour/night; tracked vehicles 20km/hour/day, 15km/
hour/night

traffic patrols, provided immediate reports and updates to von Kleist's headquarters.[62]

Not all units of the Panzer Group deployed along the four TMRs, creating a traffic control problem for feeder roads. The Panzer Group with only enough assets to control the four TMRs, requested assistance from Army Group A and the latter agreed to the Panzer Group's divisions controlling traffic from deployment areas, on designated feeder roads, to their main TMR. The Panzer Group also requested assistance for control of the Rhine River bridges, since two-thirds of its units deployed east of the river. The military commander of Koblenz, ordered to support the Panzer Group, provided the necessary assistance. Once the Panzer Group passed all its vehicles through, traffic control on the four TMRs reverted to the 12th and 16th Armies. The Panzer Group maintained control of its MSR. Von Kleist left the administration of traffic control west of the border to his corps commanders who delegated the responsibility to division commanders. Traffic restrictions remained until contact with the enemy, when tactical requirements would supersede all restrictions.[63]

Army Group A provided Panzer Group von Kleist with two military police (MP) battalions to control the four TMRs and MSR. The Group placed one MP company commander, reinforced in some cases to battalion strength, in charge of each TMR. The TMR MP commanders' mission was to keep the roads open and traffic moving, while preventing unauthorized units from using the TMR. TMR commanders, aided by local police authorities, could draw on additional male personnel living in villages along the routes to assist in their mission. Traffic checkpoints, established as reporting stations, served as a means of controlling units, rerouting traffic if necessary. TMR commanders, after conducting thorough reconnaissances of their routes and using a color code system, identified and marked all danger areas along the roads. Maintenance units positioned at danger areas assisted in accidents and other mishaps. Regular infantry divisions, expressly forbidden to use the Panzer TMRs, however, had to cross them on a northeast to southwest direction. This presented a problem of some magnitude even though infantry commanders received specific orders to cross the roads only in "very small elements" through gaps between tanks.[64]

In an effort to facilitate movement and traffic control beyond the designated end of the TMRs, von Kleist's staff, with Army Group A's approval, extended the Tactical March Routes. TMR A continued to Harlingen, Longlier, and Membre, TMR B extended to Martelange and Neufchâteau, TMR C went on to Attert and Florenville, and TMR D to Arlon and Bellefontaine. Following established rules, the roads remained one way traffic west. The two center TMRs, designated MSRs once XIXth Panzer Corps passed through, became the responsibility of the two MP battalions.[65]

The traffic control plan ensured Panzer Group von Kleist's orderly movement to the border, through Luxembourg, and into the immediate frontier area of Belgium. Intelligence sources, however, identified the construction of obstacles along the narrow restricted roads through Luxembourg. Foreign Armies West also identified the bridges along the four march routes between the Belgian border and the Meuse River as possible bottlenecks. Based on the intelligence reports, the war games that incorporated representative obstacles, and realistic assessments made by commanders within Army Group A and OKH, all agreed that the vital bridges and obstacles needed to be secured forward of the advancing Panzer forces.[66]

ENGINEER OPERATIONS

Panzer Group von Kleist negotiated some of Europe's most restrictive terrain, and conducted six major river crossings in the initial five days of the Battle of France. Engineers played a key role in the successful effort of these operations, and their employment, especially with limited bridging assets, required detailed planning and close husbanding of resources. Von Kleist's staff and XIXth Panzer Corps conducted several war games incorporating engineer operations to determine the number required, and their most effective use. As a result of these war games the Panzer Group established the following priorities for engineer tasks:

1. Breach or cross the undefended obstacles along the German-Luxembourg border, and the Our and Sauer border streams.
2. Clear obstacles in Luxembourg, and support the assault and breaching of the first Belgian defensive line.
3. Clear roads, minefields, and support the assault and breaching of the second Belgian defensive line. Construct assault bridges as required.
4. Support the crossing of the Semois River. Construct assault bridges as required.
5. Support the crossing of the Meuse River. Construct assault bridges as required.

To complete the multitude of engineer missions, Panzer Group von Kleist procured additional engineer units to reinforce the normal divisional and corps assets. One regimental engineer headquarters for planning and coordination, three engineer battalions, one assault engineer battalion, and three type B bridge columns were placed under operational control of Panzer Group von Kleist for the breakthrough operation and the crossing of the Meuse River.

Each engineer battalion had one type B bridge column and one type K[67] column organic to its TO&E. The 12th and 16th Armies' engineers were responsible for clearing obstacles at the Our and Sauer Rivers, relieving the Panzer Group's engineers for bridging missions in Belgium and France.[68]

Motorized engineers of 1939 were capable of performing a variety of missions, and enjoyed use of fairly advanced equipment for their time. Being fully motorized, they were integrated well forward in the armor columns, and were thus able to respond quickly. Additionally, engineers were always included in the formation of forward detachments and advance guards. The advance through the Ardennes depended on mobility; engineers were trained and equipped accordingly. The three regular engineer companies' equipment included 9 large (trailer mounted) air compressors, 20 power saws, 6 welding sets, 9 flame throwers, 10 searchlights for night operations, and a variety of axes, picks, hand saws, shovels, etc. As barrier materials the engineers carried 379 rolls of barbed wire, 121 rolls of regular wire, and 1,550 sandbags. The engineer battalion also carried 1,140 antitank mines, 1,934 antipersonnel mines, and an assortment of explosive materials. The most important pieces of equipment, however, were the B and K type bridges.[69] This equipment could be constructed to span short gaps (3.9 meters) or long gaps (32 meters). Under normal conditions, a 32-meter 16-ton pontoon bridge required about eight hours to construct. The equipment was extremely versatile and could be used to not only construct bridges but also ferries. German doctrine called for moving essential combat power across a water obstacle first. Bridge construction then followed. Thus the use of ferries was an essential part of any bridging operation.[70]

The type K bridge, available only in small numbers in the spring of 1940, was a small box girder bridge with a maximum carrying capacity of 16 tons. Unlike the type B bridge, the type K was less versatile, but could cover spans twice the length (76 meters). The desired bridging mix in the engineer battalion was one of each type bridge, but because of the limited number of type K bridges available in the spring of 1940, Panzer Group von Kleist was one of the only units with type K bridging columns.[71]

Detailed reconnaissance provided the Panzer Group with the necessary information to plan its engineer assets accordingly. Close liaison with VIth and VIIth Corps, through which Panzer Group von Kleist passed on D-Day, ensured the speedy removal or bridging of obstacles at the German–Luxembourg border. Seven bridges were required for the Panzer Group's sector on the morning of May 10, and all were completed within two hours. Once across the initial obstacles, XIXth Panzer Corps became responsible for all other bridging within the group's sector to the Meuse River. The Panzer Group provided Guderian with an additional engineer battalion and three type B bridging companies to carry out its main missions. The assault engineer battalion, specially equipped to neutralize bunkers, was not employed until the Meuse River crossings. The Panzer Group, properly reinforced with engineer assets, was thus able to conduct its speedy advance in a minimum amount of time.

OPERATION NIWI

War games in early January 1940 clearly linked success of an armored breakthrough in the Ardennes to surprise and speed. Planners determined that Luxembourg would fall rather quickly. Belgium, with enough warning however, would occupy prepared defensive positions along Belgium's first defensive belt on the Belgian–Luxembourg border. German intelligence sources identified numerous bunkers and fortifications along the four designated TMRs which could possibly slow the Panzer divisions. The fortification at Bodange caused planners the greatest concern.

In January, XIXth Panzer Corps coordinated with the Luftwaffe on the availability of airborne forces to aid the corps in its speedy drive through the Belgian defensive belt. After consultation with Field Marshal Göring, a Luftwaffe staff officer briefed the XIXth Panzer Corps chief of staff, Colonel Walther Nehring[72] on the Luftwaffe's response. The officer proposed the use of 100 Fieseler Storch aircraft[73] to transport about 180 men behind the Belgian defensive line. Once on the ground soldiers could attack and secure specified targets from the west, in the enemy's rear, assisting the Panzer divisions with their advance from the east. Fieseler Storch aircraft, the staff officer reasoned, could transport initial assault elements to seize landing zones, followed by gliderborne troops. With Luftwaffe airborne and airlanding units already scheduled for commitment in northern Belgium and Holland, he recommended that XIXth Panzer Corps use elements of the elite motorized Infantry Regiment "Gross deutschland" or Leibstandarte-SS "Adolf Hitler."[74]

Continued emphasis on a mission of this type and further staff studies resulted in the corps adopting the Luftwaffe's "poor man" solution and selecting one battalion of "GD" to carry out the operation. Guderian appointed Lieutenant-Colonel Eugen Garski and his 3rd Battalion for the mission. In late February Garski moved his 400-man battalion to Crailsheim to begin familiarization training with the single-engined aircraft.[75]

Planners initially developed two options for the employment of the Garski battalion. Option one, code named "Operation NIWI," entailed air assaults near the towns of Nives and Witri (see Appendix A, Map 1), about 15 km inside Belgium to disrupt communications and traffic between Neufchâteau and Bastogne, and Neufchâteau and Martelange and to prevent Belgian units in Neufchâteau from reaching their first defensive line. Additionally, they were to attack the Belgian bunkerline at Bodange from the west to assist 1st Panzer Division in its breakthrough of the fortifications from the east. German planners conceived the second option, code named "Operation Rosa," as a raid to secure the Sauer and Alzette River bridges along the four TMRs. The execution of option one depended on the situation at the Sauer and Alzette River bridges. If intelligence determined that the bridges were rigged with explosives for destruction, Operation Rosa would take priority over Operation NIWI. Without control of these bridges, XIXth Panzer Corps did not want to risk Garski's men on such a deep operation. Although well aware of the consequences of a hold up at the bridges, Colonel Nehring favored Operation NIWI from the start. In mid-April intelligence sources provided the necessary information to go ahead with Operation NIWI.[76]

Lieutenant-Colonel Garski's men spent early March training in air transport and air assault techniques. The Fieseler Storch, not designed for nor previously used in this manner, offered everyone a chance to learn, develop, and employ a new technique. General of Fliers Hugo Sperrle,[77] Commander of IIIrd Air Corps (Luftflotte III), whose organization supported Operation NIWI, visited Garski at Crailsheim in mid-March to observe training. Sperrle considered the support of Panzer Group von Kleist, specifically XIXth Panzer Corps, one of his primary missions in the initial phase of the offensive. To ensure proper support the Luftwaffe assigned a special liaison officer, Major Förster, to Garski's battalion. Förster had a two-fold mission: "coordinate and/or request all Luftwaffe assets during training and, as air mission commander, command and control the actual air operation." Garski would assume control once the aircraft landed at the Landing Zones (LZ). In his capacity as air mission commander, Förster, in conjunction with Garski, made all air-related decisions and selected the LZs (see Appendix A, Map 1).[78]

Förster and Garski decided to divide the battalion into two assault groups, NORTH and SOUTH, designating "Group SOUTH" the main effort (Table 2.3), as a result of aircraft availability and a mutual study of the overall operation. Garski assigned Captain W. Krüger to command "Group NORTH." Because of the limited capability of Fieseler Storchs, Garski planned to transport his forces in three lifts. Since Garski's people would operate well outside of friendly artillery range, Förster secured two groups, Staffeln, of Stukas as airborne artillery and some transport aircraft for resupply (see Table 2.4).[79]

Garski's men completed familiarization training with the aircraft at Crailsheim in early April. Their next step in preparation for their mission would take them to Baumholder Training Center, an Army maneuver area, for intensified ground combat training. At Baumholder the battalion trained rigorously, assaulting mock fortifications and neutralizing bunkers. Baumholder, an excellent training facility, also simplified the battalion's drive to the airfields at Bitburg and Deckendorf on D-1. Garski's battalion required 110 trucks to transport men and equipment.[80]

While Garski's battalion trained at Crailsheim and Baumholder, the staffs of the Panzer Group and XIXth Panzer Corps developed detailed plans for the secret movement of the unit from Baumholder to the airfields. The aircraft were not scheduled to arrive at Bitburg and Deckendorf until late afternoon on D-1. In order to maintain the secrecy of the operation, the Luftwaffe did not alter the configuration of the aircraft prior to arrival at the airfields. Loading and rigging[81] of the aircraft would have to be accomplished by Garski's men, once transported to the airfields. During training it routinely took four to five hours to rig and load the small aircraft. Garski therefore urged XIXth Panzer Corps to devise a plan to move his troops to their respective airfields no later than 1415 hours on D-1. This would allow time for the necessary rigging and for leaders to attend a final briefing. The German Army in the West began its movement from deployment areas to assault positions at H-18,[82] causing Garski to compete for the same road space (see Appendix B, Movement Orders). Attempting to avoid a TMR conflict and to maintain a veil of secrecy around Operation NIWI, XIXth Panzer Corps agreed to notify and transport the 400 men well ahead of the rest of the Army. This also meant that XIXth Panzer Corps required earlier notification. Garski's vehicles, after dropping the troops at the airfields, would filter in behind 1st Panzer Division for link-up with the battalion on the objectives.[83]

The last update briefing at 1900 hours on D-1 revealed only two significant changes. XIXth Panzer Corps, worried about compromising the main effort of the entire operation, decided to hold Stuka support back until the air assault land-

Table 2.3
Operation "NIWI" Task Organization

OIC: Captain W. Krüger	OIC: LTC Garski
1 Infantry company	Battalion staff
1 Machine gun squad	1 Infantry company
1 Engineer squad	1 Machine gun squad
1 Signal squad with	1 Mortar platoon (3 x 8 cm mortars)
a 5 Watt wireless radio	2 Engineer squads
for communication with	1 Signal squad with a 5 Watt
Group SOUTH.	wireless radio for communication
42 Fieseler Storch aircraft	with Group NORTH and one 15 Watt
Departure airfield: Bittburg	wireless for communication with XIXth
Landing Zone: vicinity Nives	Panzer Corps.
	56 Fieseler Storch aircraft
	Departure airfield: Deckendorf
	Landing Zone: vicinity Witry

Source: Hans von Dach, "Panzer durchbrechen eine Armeestellung," *Schweizer Soldat* (47) 1972, no. 2, p. 58.

ings were complete. Fearing that confused German soldiers could mistakenly fire on the Fieseler Storch planes both going and coming, Förster and Garski requested that ground units along the flight paths be briefed. The corps agreed to release a message through Panzer Group von Kleist requesting all units to brief their soldiers about the low level flights of the Fieseler Storch formations. Returning to their assault groups, Garski and Krüger briefed their soldiers one last time. The two leaders would not communicate again for the next 21 hours until their link-up inside Belgium.[84]

XIXTH PANZER CORPS

When OKH published the final version of the operation plan, it became apparent to XIXth Panzer Corps' staff that it would form the point of the spear-

Table 2.4
Air Assault Organization

Close Air Support	Logistics/Communication/ Reserve Forces	Assault Element
No fighter cover	3 x Junkers 52 for ammo	Elements of
2 x Squadrons of	resupply (parachute drop)	3rd Battalion,
Stukas	2 x Fieseler Storch as	Infantry Regiment
Junkers 87 as	back up aircraft,	"Großdeutschland"
airborne artillery	reconnaissance, and	98 Fieseler Storch
(~ 24 aircraft)	airborne communication	aircraft

Source: Dach, "Panzer durchbrechen eine Armeestellung," *Schweizer Soldat* (47) no. 2, p. 61.

head in the Western offensive. The Corps controlled 1st, 2nd, and 10th Panzer Divisions, Infantry Regiment "Grossdeutschland," and a variety of corps support units. Guderian immediately had his staff establish an intensive training program for his divisions, since the offensive would surely commence in early spring.[85]

Guderian and his chief of staff understood the requirement of impressing upon their junior commanders the necessary initiative to conduct mobile warfare. A clear understanding of the commander's concept and aims were a prerequisite for every leader. A rigorous training program encouraged leaders to exercise initiative and to become experts in their fields. The intensified training period from February to May 1940 saw General Guderian continuously visiting units at various training centers throughout the Reich.[86]

The Polish Campaign successfully demonstrated the multiple capabilities of the Luftwaffe's Flak (antiaircraft) artillery. Army commanders realized the potential of the 88 mm Flak guns as back up artillery. More important, however, the Army viewed the 88 mm Flak gun, with its pinpoint accuracy, as a decisive weapon to combat tanks and ground targets. Thus, antiaircraft gun crews trained not only in their traditional role, but also practiced firing at ground targets. The Luftwaffe's 88 mm gun crews of the 1st Flak Corps,[87] placed under operational control of Panzer Group von Kleist for the offensive, followed this training pattern at the Ahrbrück Luftwaffe Training Center. The Panzer Group relied upon the Flak Corps to provide effective antiaircraft cover, engage enemy tanks, and neutralize enemy bunkers. The troops of 1st Flak Corps, in their support of

Panzer Group von Kleist, experienced tremendous physical demands during the advance to the Meuse River. Ground and antiaircraft roles alternated altogether too rapidly. In many cases units had to occupy positions three and four times a day. Because of the rapid advance of the armored forces, Flak units proved unable to rest. Day and night, Flak units moved forward on the TMRs to provide the air umbrella for the Panzer Group, or to occupy assembly areas for the following day's operations. On numerous occasions single gun crews were called upon to engage enemy tanks or points of resistance along the TMRs.[88]

XIXth Panzer Corps, through several map exercises, realized that in addition to Operation NIWI, only well-trained and properly equipped engineers would be able to maintain the momentum of the advance. Infantry and assault engineers practiced many river crossings in rubber boats. Construction engineers exercised bridging operations and ferried tanks and mechanized vehicles across the Moselle River in an effort to perfect their skills. The crossing sites served as dress rehearsals, since they resembled actual sites on the Meuse River. XIXth Panzer Corps alone possessed five engineer battalions and nine bridging companies for the advance through the Ardennes. As Guderian gathered new ideas at each exercise, he passed the information to his planners at corps headquarters for dissemination and implementation throughout the Corps.[89]

Guderian was familiar with the terrain in the Ardennes from his World War I experiences and he realized the potential for disaster in this constricted area. Directing purposeful questions at junior leaders and providing them with candid assessments of their performances, Guderian trained leaders to make quick estimates of the situation and draw proper conclusions. He became affectionately known to his troops as "Der Schnelle Heinz" (fast Heinz) because he appeared, disappeared, and reappeared at the same training exercises, travelling tirelessly from one training center to another. In his education of junior leaders he stressed what later became known as a joke, "Klotzen, nicht Kleckern," don't feel around with your fingers at several different places, but hit hard with a determined fist.[90]

In spite of the well-prepared training of the divisions, major hurdles still lay in the way. Guderian's Panzer Corps, although ranking number one on the priority list for the modern Panzer types Mark III and IV, did not receive the tanks on time. Finally, when the tanks were delivered on March 12, they came directly from the factories without the necessary breaking in. Worse yet, with so few Mark III's and IV's in the divisions, commanders tended not to use them in training exercises, only operating with the old Mark I's and II's. When General von Kleist, visiting Guderian's headquarters on March 14, was briefed on this subject the old gentleman's temper flared. Guderian briefly outlined a training program designed to remedy the situation. He estimated that drivers would complete training by March 24, followed by crew level training, a live fire, and company and battalion maneuvers. General Guderian assured his boss that everything would be accomplished by mid-April. Von Kleist remained extremely upset, unable to determine whether to admonish Guderian for failing to initiate a proper training plan earlier, or the Army General Staff for not

Figure 2.2
Close Air Support Map

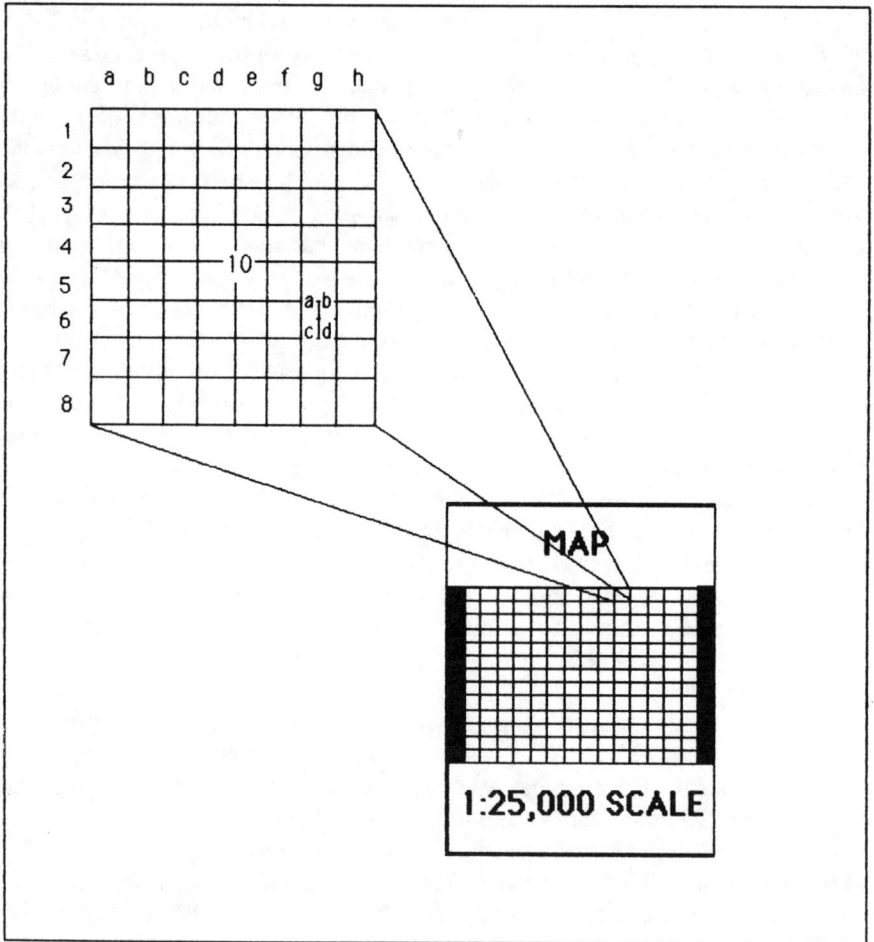

ensuring timely deliveries. Nevertheless, he ordered company and battalion level training at Wahn and Baumholder.[91]

War games, previously discussed as a means to identify and solve problems, greatly aided the various staffs in their preparation for the upcoming offensive. During one of the war games organized by XIXth Panzer Corps in early March, Colonel Nehring observed a problem that could have far-reaching consequences: the Army and the Luftwaffe used different types of maps. Army locations for close air support (CAS) did not match Luftwaffe locations and lengthy CAS requests failed to provide sufficient information. Additionally, Foreign Armies West determined that Germany only possessed 7,378 artillery pieces against the Allies' 13,974. That corresponded to about a 50 percent gap. OKH relied on the more modern German artillery, and more important, on its Luftwaffe to close and overcome this deficiency.[92] Thus, Army and Luftwaffe coordination with respect to CAS was essential. Colonel Nehring had his operations officer, Major Fritz Bayerlein,[93] design a special map and support request for common use.

Major Bayerlein overprinted a 1:25,000 scale map with 1 cm squares (see Figure 2.2). Simplifying the CAS request, he further overprinted a larger square over the 8×8 1 cm squares, creating 196 large squares per map sheet. The large squares were numbered from 1 to 196. The new call for close air support consisted of five items:

1. Large target square (1-196).
2. Small target square a-h, then 1-8.
3. When requesting CAS on small target area, provide location, identifying the quarter of the small square.
4. Type and activity in target area.
5. Time of observation and time CAS requested.

An example of a CAS request: "Target area 10 g 6 a, artillery battery moving into position, 16:20, 17:30." This system ensured a common, quick solution to calling for close air support. A normal request went through division to the corps Close Air Support officer (Nahkampfführer (Naka)), a close resemblance to the U.S. Air Forces Tactical Air Control Party. The Naka sent the report to the Luftwaffe Close Air Support Element (Nahkampfführer II) of IInd Air Corps (Fliegerkorps II). IInd Air Corps was the Luftwaffe unit that provided direct support to XIXth Panzer Corps.[94]

Shortly after issuing this CAS directive, 1st Panzer Division decided to become innovative. The division operations officer requested permission for his Panzer crews to talk directly to Stuka pilots, to guide them to their targets, and second, to identify the friendly line of troops. Interestingly, the Naka II rejected the first proposal on grounds that the still technically inferior equipment would not allow this, and that he did not want ambitious young tank commanders to divert Stukas destined elsewhere. On the second issue, purple or red smoke grenades or swastika flags became markers for identifying friendly troop locations.[95]

One other major problem that Guderian's staff, as well as von Kleist's, pondered was how to handle resupply. The Panzer Group brought this problem to the attention of Army Group A in early March. The latter managed to secure an additional three motor transport battalions for the Panzer Group. Both Panzer corps received one battalion, while the third remained under Group control. This provided XIXth Panzer Corps with an additional 1,600 tons of hauling capability. A Panzer or motorized division required 49,735 gallons of fuel for every 100 km. Planners also determined that during the breakthrough operation units would need to be refueled and rearmed several times. As a result, OKH established fuel storage areas close to the border, so that units could fill up and cross the border with full tanks of gasoline. Several trains consisting solely of Class I, III, and V[96] were held ready for immediate movement into Luxembourg to provide a forward resupply base. Each tank carried extra 20 liter fuel canisters (Jerry cans) that crews discarded when empty. Following combat service support units eventually recovered the canisters.[97]

In early March, the Quartermaster (General quartiermeister (Gen Qu)) of the Army General Staff, Colonel Eduard Wagner,[98] reported to General Halder that the possibility of resupply by air, in addition to the ground motor transport battalions, was feasible. Wagner estimated that by D+4 a group of 50 Junkers (Ju) 52 transport planes could transport 100 tons of fuel to forward Panzer elements. One such lift provided sufficient fuel for one Panzer division to travel 75 km. In the absence of airfields the Ju 52's would drop supplies by parachute. To minimize damage to parachutes and containers during recovery operations, XIXth Panzer Corps requested parachute rigger personnel to conduct classes on the subject.[99]

Army Group A's quartermaster studied the proposal by OKH's Quartermaster-General and found it to be inadequate. Army Group A experienced some difficulty in attempting to coordinate the air resupply with the Luftwaffe. Third Air Corps, which would be providing the transport planes, felt their assets could not support both Army and Luftwaffe needs. Army Group A, furthermore, requested that the Army Supply Depot at Hanau be made available for storing prepackaged loads of ammunition for specific combat formations that could be delivered by air on a moment's notice. The Army Group's Quartermaster requested and stored additional fuel cannisters for the same purpose.[100]

The Army's Quartermaster-General settled the dispute between Army Group A and the Luftwaffe and organized a training exercise from April 8 to 10, 1940, to practice resupply by air. To prevent unnecessary use of aircraft, Army Group A agreed to Luftwaffe demands that aerial resupply missions be flown in emergency situations only. Parachute rigger crews travelled to the respective airfields to practice their skills in preparing parachute loads. Army personnel received training on prepackaging ammunition and fuel containers. The exercise culminated with several resupply missions being carried out.[101]

As the attack day drew nearer the generals assessed the Army's readiness. They viewed junior officers and NCOs with renewed confidence, and more important, young leaders developed confidence in themselves. Indeed, the majority of the problems identified as a result of the Polish Campaign had been rectified, however, at tremendous cost. German industry remained unable to support the dramatic expansion from 105 divisions in November 1939 to 156 divisions on May 10, 1940. The Army transferred vast numbers of wheeled vehicles from regular infantry divisions to newly formed Panzer and motorized divisions. The poor state of German industry caused infantry divisions once again to become solely dependent on the horse as prime mover for artillery and services. In Army Group A, the 12th and 16th Armies relied on 22,000 and 33,000 horses respectively for transportation in May 1940. A number of Panzer divisions equipped with captured vehicles and tanks experienced maintenance problems for lack of spare parts. A general shortage in steel production caused concern amongst the military leadership, especially with the impending violations of Belgian, Dutch, and Luxembourg neutrality. Germany relied on neutral Sweden's iron ore. Nevertheless, on May 9, 1940, XIXth Panzer Corps stood ready, poised for action, its soldiers and leaders completely confident of victory. One must keep in mind, however, that a vast majority of Germans, soldiers included, were incapable of focusing beyond the facade.[102]

3

Advance to the Meuse

Nach dem Durchbruch ist von entscheidender Bedeutung, ohne Rücksicht auf Flankenbedrohung, unter voller Ausnutzung der Motoren, ohne Ruhe und Rast, Tag und Nacht marschierend so weit vorzustossen, als es der Brennstoff gestattet. Ausschaltung von Flankenangriffen des Feindes ist Aufgabe aller nachfolgenden Korps.
(After the breakthrough is achieved, it is of decisive importance that we advance as quickly and as far as fuel will allow. The advance must continue relentlessly, day and night, without possibility of rest. Flank threats must be disregarded and engines utilized to their maximum capability. The elimination of flank attacks is the responsibility of all follow-on corps.)
General Heinz Guderian, May 1940

THURSDAY, MAY 9, 1940

At 1648 hours Hitler and his personal staff departed Berlin–Finkenkrug train station. For security reasons only a select few knew the destination. The train initially headed toward Hamburg but changed course at Hagenau–Land toward Hannover. This alteration in course, noticed by members of the staff, resolved any questions regarding the trip's purpose. The train made one last stop at Burgdorf, where Major Nicolaus von Below called Luftwaffe headquarters for the latest weather report. The voice of the Luftwaffe meteorologist on the other end assured von Below that Western Europe would be dominated by a high pressure system for the next few days, and that the outlook for May 10, 1940 would be clear and cool with a light wind. Based on this weather report Hitler issued code word "Danzig" at 2100 hours, authorizing the crossing of the international border and the initiation of the Battle of France.[1]

XIXth Panzer Corps received its official notification at 1300 hours from Panzer Group von Kleist ("Gelb 10.5.40, 5.35 Uhr"), and notified its subordinate units. Since there were no last minute changes in the mission the Corps executed the March 28, 1940 operation order, and began deploying the Panzer Corps forward according to schedule. Final authorization to cross the international border came later in the evening. The opening day of this offensive was surely one of the closest held secrets within the German Army. The XIXth Panzer Corps' chief of staff and the intelligence officer were on leave when the Corps received its notification. Both, recalled, joined the Corps on the morning of the 10th. The tactical command post (TCP) under the direction of the corps operations officer arrived at Sonnenhof at 1900 hours. General Guderian joined the TCP at 1925 hours.[2]

At 2000 hours, the Panzer Group notified XIXth Panzer Corps that it had allocated an additional engineer battalion and four bridging companies to the Corps. The Corps held the 70th Engineer Battalion with one bridging company in reserve while attaching the 1st Company/406th Engineer Battalion to the 2nd Panzer Division, 2nd Company/406th Engineer Battalion to the 1st Panzer Division, and 1st Company/430th Engineer Battalion to the 10th Panzer Division. At 2015 hours the XIXth Panzer Corps, notified by its divisions that the assault elements had reached their start points short of the border, was prepared to commence the offensive on schedule. Garski's air-land groups, having loaded and rigged their aircraft and completed last minute checks, stood ready, awaiting the final go ahead.[3]

Panzer Group von Kleist issued codeword "Danzig" to the XIXth Panzer Corps at 2230 hours. Based on the final go ahead the Corps completed the deployment phase by advancing the assault echelons of the divisions into assault positions at Sinspelt, Mettendorf, Irrel, and Eisenach along the Luxembourg border. The remainder of the Corps stretched as far east as Monreal–Cochem. This was accomplished at 0130 hours. In the assault positions units refueled and soldiers welcomed a final hot meal, resting as much as possible.[4]

While the troopers of XIXth Panzer Corps were preparing themselves for the next day, specially selected soldiers stole across the order to seize key defiles and obstacles to help speed the morrow's advance. These soldiers, from the 12th Army and the Lehr and Bau Bataillon z. b. V. 800[5] (Brandenburg), dressed in civilian clothes, carried no identification cards or tags but only submachine guns, flashlights, and specially selected equipment and demolitions. Their instructions included the securing of bridges before they could be destroyed, preventing road blocks from being emplaced, and occupying government buildings, such as police stations, city halls, railway stations, and telephone exchanges. These troops captured Luxembourg's police and soldiers, and held them until the German Army arrived on the morning of the 10th. Previously recruited Luxembourgers, trained in espionage and sabotage, provided the necessary information on locations of radios within the small villages along the border with Germany.[6]

German intelligence sources inside Luxembourg and Belgium fed the Army's General Staff with precise information, providing a clear picture of what to expect. More important, it disseminated the information to units in the field so they could properly prepare. The Army had evaluated the information on enemy activity and obstacle construction projects, and as a result, positioned engineers well forward in the movement order. When XIXth Panzer Corps invaded Luxembourg on May 10, it knew where to expect obstacles, often with detailed technical information.[7]

The steel gate at Fouhren and the Diekirch railroad bridge were two of the Special Operations Forces objectives in XIXth Panzer Corps' sector. Securing the Fouhren gate was essential since it could potentially halt the 2nd Panzer Division for an extended period of time, and the destruction of the bridge would interrupt resupply operations. The position of the Fouhren steel gate was such that on one side of the barrier a steep grade led into a deep gorge, while the other side bordered a solid wall of bedrock. The two Luxembourg guards assigned to it received orders to close and lock the barrier at 0315 hours. After carrying out their orders, the two returned to Fouhren to meet with the rest of their Gendarmerie detachment. Standing outside the local cafe, at 0400 hours, the group noticed four men in civilian clothes approaching them. It seemed strange to the Gendarmes that anyone would be out walking at this late hour. The four had yellow scarfs protruding from pockets or tied around their necks. When the strangers were within five meters, they threw open their overcoats and confronted the Gendarmes with submachine guns. Simultaneously, they ordered them to raise up their hands and turn over the keys to the Fouhren steel gate. It quickly became evident to the Luxembourgers that these strangers were in fact no civilians, rather German soldiers dressed in civilian clothes. What the Gendarmes, however, did not know was that these men were specially trained soldiers of the elite Brandenburg Battalion z. b. V. 800. The leader of the Gendarmes attempted to explain to the Germans that once the steel gate was shut, it could not be opened. The Brandenburgers would not hear of such nonsense, lined up the Gendarmes, and marched them to the obstacle. At the site of the steel gate the Germans quickly assessed the situation and, with several failed attempts to open the gate using handgrenades, decided to employ demolitions on the barrier. The team leader placed the explosives and the other three took the Luxembourgers into the nearby woods. Within minutes the Fouhren gate disintegrated, clearing the path for 2nd Panzer Division. While waiting in the forest for the advancing German units, another Brandenburg group joined them. This team had just secured the open Logsdorfer steel gate without incident (see Figure 3.1).[8]

Further west at Diekirch, Luxembourg Gendarmes received a call from their headquarters shortly after midnight, alerting them to be on the lookout for strangers, and to patrol the railroad bridge. The detachment commander directed

Figure 3.1
Obstacle Sketch

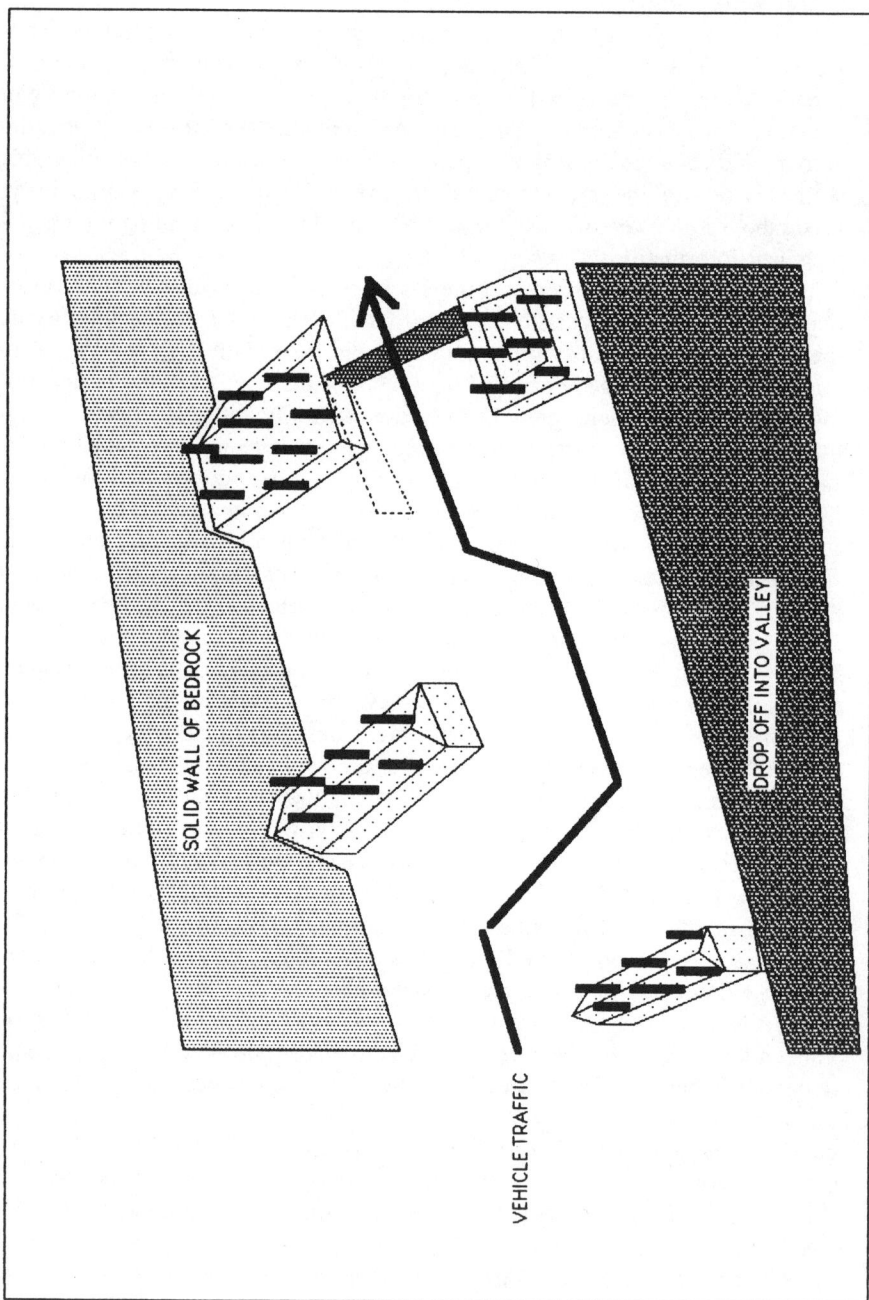

two Gendarmes to the bridge for what he thought would be another routine patrol. The German Army knew that Luxembourg bridges were not prechambered and therefore could not be destroyed by their defense forces. However, OKH worried about vital bridges falling into French or Belgian hands. After completing their patrol to the railroad bridge, and finding everything in order, the two Gendarmes posted themselves at the main road intersection about 200 meters east of the bridge. Shortly after 0100 hours the two noticed two bicycles, without lights, approaching from the east. Immediately suspicious they stepped out onto the road to stop them. However, before realizing what happened, they found themselves on the pavement with several submachine gun barrels staring them in the face. The Germans, dressed in civilian clothes, took the Gendarmes to the bridge, and established defensive positions while waiting for the advancing 1st Panzer Division. When the regular German forces arrived, the civilian-dressed soldiers turned over the Gendarmes to the Army and departed. The Army released the Gendarmes at 1100 hours.[9]

Not all special operation missions fared as smoothly as the two just described. The prime targets throughout Luxembourg were communication facilities, telephone exchanges, and Gendarmerie headquarters. These facilities could be used by the Luxembourg government to alert the French or Belgians of the imminent invasion. The mission to destroy the most important telephone exchange located in the main Post Office in Luxembourg failed. The Brandenburg team, led by a young German lieutenant, ran into an alert three-man Luxembourg patrol at the Fehls Mill near Mandernach. Following a brief firefight, the Germans suffered several casualties and three missing in action. The Luxembourgers had one killed and two wounded. However, one of the wounded soldiers crawled to the main road and stopped a civilian car, whose driver took him to the Gendarmerie Station at Grevenmacher. The station chief alerted his higher headquarters and sent two men to the mill to recover the presumably dead Luxembourg soldiers. At the mill, they instead found three wounded civilians informing them to stay away from the old mill. The Luxembourg soldiers suspected the three were Germans, arrested them, and drove the invaders to the Luxembourg hospital.

Back at the mill, the German lieutenant decided that, because of his compromised team, the best alternative would be to stay there and await the advancing German Army. This critical decision precluded the destruction of the vital telephone cables at the Luxembourg Post Office, which no doubt transmitted important messages to France and Belgium during the night. The three wounded Germans at the hospital identified themselves as Sergeant Herbert Swirzy from Kattowitz, Alfred Wolny from Ridneten/Silesia, and Heinrich Kalsmarzk from Oberradosche. The origin of the names and the location of their hometowns clearly connected them to Upper Silesia, the roots of the Brandenburg Battalion. Brandenburgers and specifically selected units conducted special operations throughout Luxembourg on the night of May 9 to 10, 1940, and no doubt as a result of some badly mishandled operations authorities became suspicious and alerted Gendarmerie Stations to close all the steel gates. This prevented a number of these barriers from falling into German hands open. However, the Special Operation Forces were well-prepared for their missions and carried the necessary tools and equipment to ensure a smooth passage for the advancing Panzer divisions. Suffice it to say, these actions left the Luxembourg government under no illusions about the imminent German offensive.[10]

FRIDAY, MAY 10, 1940

Precisely at 0535 hours, XIXth Panzer Corps commenced the offensive. The weather report issued late on the 9th predicted clear, cool conditions, and a light wind. Guderian, like many of his contemporaries, intended to lead his corps from the front and thus departed his headquarters about 0400 hours to join the 1st Panzer Division at Wallendorf.

XIXth Panzer Corps crossed into Luxembourg in three main spearheads (see Appendix B, Movement Orders): 2nd Pz Div: (north) Vianden, Tintange, Libramont to the Meuse at Flize and Sedan; 1st Pz Div: (center) Wallendorf, Martelange, Neufchâteau, Bouillon to Sedan; 10th Pz Div: (south) Echternach, Arlon, Rosignol, Florenville to the Meuse south of Sedan.

First Panzer Division, the main effort of the Corps, had the corps artillery, the TCP, and the mass of the antiaircraft units following in its path. Each Panzer division and the Corps headquarters had a reconnaissance squadron of 12 Heinkel (HE) 126 aircraft at their disposal to provide combat intelligence throughout the breakthrough. The invasion of Luxembourg proceeded as scheduled. It took the engineers about two hours to remove the barriers and reconnaissance units took the lead. Guderian's ultimate goal for the Corps simply called for reaching the Channel. The entire Corps advanced west in a tight formation, presenting an excellent target for enemy air forces while in the restricted terrain of the Ardennes. Since, however, the Luftwaffe succeeded in completely surprising the Allies and delivering a decisive blow against the French and English air forces on May 10, no Allied air attacks hindered the Corps' movement. The Luftwaffe targeted 72 French, Belgian, and Dutch airfields up to 300 km behind friendly lines. Its pilots, practicing for weeks in advance, led the German Army with 3,200 aircraft, 1,500 of which were bombers. Besides the unconventional warfare tactics used in Luxembourg, the airborne and glider landings in Holland and northern Belgium, and the Luftwaffe's deep strikes into the Allied rear, the German Army held one more surprise in store. The world would witness the first air assault operation in history. The Luftwaffe transported specially trained soldiers behind the Belgian lines with orders to disrupt communications and to assault the enemy's defensive line from the west to aid the 1st Panzer Division's breakthrough.[11]

Operation NIWI

The 3rd Battalion, Infantry Regiment "Grossdeutschland" led XIXth Panzer Corps, in the same fashion as the 82nd and 101st Airborne Divisions would lead the Allied assaults on the Normandy beaches only four years and 26 days later. Garski's men rested little before the air assault, spending a night of anticipation, contemplating their mission and wondering when they would meet their families again. As scheduled the first lift departed at 0530 hours, but soon after take-off many pilots lost contact with the formation and became disoriented. This resulted in the formation's breakup into several small groups searching for the LZ. Captain Krüger landed near the village of L'Eglise at 0600 hours, about 10 km from the planned LZ (see Appendix A, Map 2). Other airplanes in Krüger's group spotted his aircraft and landed alongside. Several aircraft were damaged during the landing at L'Eglise with two catching on fire. A third group seeing the burning aircraft guided in on them. Krüger's men, thoroughly dissatisfied with the Luftwaffe's delivery, expressed some choice phrases in its honor as they carried ammunition boxes and equipment to the nearest woodline. Nevertheless, the first order of business was to get somewhat organized, set up a small perimeter, and determine their location. Stopping some Belgian civilians, Krüger learned they landed along the road to Ebly. In the confusion several more aircraft landed near the village of Rancimon at about 0600 hours, 5 km south-west of L'Eglise. The battalion staff from Garski's lift, carrying a 15 watt radio, also mistakenly landed at Krüger's location. Thus Krüger established the first radio contact with XIXth Panzer Corps. The second and third lifts arrived at 0800 and 0830 hours respectively to join Krüger.[12]

Group South, led by Lieutenant-Colonel Garski, did not fare much better. The pilots experienced the same problems as Group North. Garski landed with five aircraft near the village of Traimont at 0600 hours, while his staff and the rest of Group South landed near L'Eglise. Garski and nine men spent the next three hours alone, until the second lift's two platoons joined them. The pilots of this lift reported to Garski that they spotted Fieseler Storch aircraft 5 km south of Traimont. Garski's third lift arrived at 1000 hours, completing the air assault operation. Both groups failed to land at their intended landing zones.[13]

The air landings went completely unopposed, and in both cases found Belgian civilians on their way to work or farmers tending fields. Krüger's men had their first contact with Belgian soldiers, retreating west according to the Belgian defensive plan, at 0830 hours and managed to take several prisoners. Captain Krüger authorized his men to requisition bicycles, horses, and motorcycles to form a mobile column to march northeast and link up with Garski. While his soldiers conducted the necessary requisitioning, a Luftwaffe Ju 52 transport dropped ammunition. The element from Rancimon linked up at L'Eglise at 1000 hours, and a bicycle patrol from Garski's group made contact with Krüger. Having organized enough transportation assets, Krüger began his advance to Garski's location, leaving the prisoners behind locked in a cellar. Belgian troops supported by a tank, probably the 10th Company, Chasseurs Ardennais stationed at L'Eglise, appeared north of the town at 1100 hours just as Krüger's group began to depart and a firefight ensued. Krüger's men warded off the enemy with machine guns and antitank rifles (Panzerbüchsen), but the Belgians did not withdraw. At 1300 hours, Krüger gave up his planned motorized push to Traimont, disengaged from the enemy and started a cross-country march. Time did not allow for locking up the latest batch of Belgian prisoners, hence they were taken along. The Belgian attackers did not pursue, enabling Krüger to link up finally with Garski west of Fauvillers at about 1600 hours.[14]

Garski's group also spent an interesting day. His third lift brought along three mortars and several antitank rifles. Having finally gathered most of his people at about 1000 hours, Garski decided to push toward the objective, Bodange. Initially the group met weak resistance and continued to press on. However, they ran up against stiff resistance in an attempt to capture some bunkers protecting the approaches west of Fauvillers. The Belgian defenders held firm, stopping Garski in his tracks. He decided to wait for the arrival of Krüger's group; before trying again. The Belgian 2nd Battalion headquarters and the 4th Company, Chasseurs Ardennais, defended Fauvillers. Linking up with Krüger at 1600 hours, Garski finally assembled about 80 percent of his original force. Wasting no time, he attacked with the entire force, capturing the bunkers shortly after 1700 hours. Garski's soldiers occupied Fauvillers sometime between 1700 and 1800 hours. The Belgians were able to disengage and retreated westward. Garski planned to continue the advance toward Bodange immediately.[15]

The airlandings apparently did not alter the plan of the Chasseurs Ardennais to continue their withdrawal westward. Although the German landings were reported to the regimental headquarters at Neufchâteau, no major counterattack was planned or attempted. The Belgian Chasseurs Ardennais that Garski's air assault forces encountered were simply retreating according to plan. However, at Bodange, one of the prime objectives of Operation NIWI, a Chasseurs Ardennais company, under the command of Captain Bricart, succeeded in halting the advance of the German Army through the afternoon of May 10. This company continued to resist although the entire Belgian Army had withdrawn. As ordered, Bricart destroyed the telephone exchange in Bodange, eliminating one of three means of communication with his higher headquarters. The air assault forces interrupted Bricart's second means of communication: messengers. Garski's men also cut telephone lines, causing considerable confusion in the Belgian headquarters' decision cycle. Thus communication between the regimental headquarters at Neufchâteau, the battalion headquarters at Fauvillers, and the company at Bodange depended on very unreliable radio equipment. The radios failed and messengers were unable to get through to Bodange because of Garski's control of the roads. An order to retreat, sent at 1300 hours, reached neither the 2nd Battalion at Fauvillers nor Bricart's company at Bodange. Bricart's last message at 1230 hours ordered him to stand his ground. Following those orders, Bricart dutifully defended Bodange.[16]

Second Panzer Division

On the right flank of XIXth Panzer Corps, 2nd Panzer Division, commanded by Major-General Rudolf Veiel,[17] conducted its movement on the worst of the available road networks within the Corps' sector. Narrow roads winding through deep valleys and gorges with numerous hairpin turns hindered the division's movement the entire first day. Second Panzer Division encountered all bridges along the Belgian frontier destroyed. In addition, troops found it very difficult to maneuver around the 6-meter deep and 15-meter wide craters the Belgians left behind. Even though enemy resistance remained fairly weak throughout the day, obstacles and chaotic traffic conditions in the rear limited the division from advancing any further than Menufontaine–Hotte by 1900 hours. The division advanced roughly 65 km on its first day, and was about 15 km short of its objective (see Appendix A, Map 3).[18]

First Panzer Division

The 1st Panzer Division, commanded by Brigadier-General Friedrich Kirchner,[19] as the main effort of the Corps, had the best of the four TMRs at its disposal. Guderian directed it to dash through Luxembourg and breach the Belgian fortifications between Warnach and Martelange. No resistance was expected in Luxembourg. OKH intelligence expected the Belgian Army to defend the Ardennes Forest, with the Chasseurs Ardennais conducting a delaying action back to the Our River. They anticipated the Our River to be defended by the Chasseurs Ardennais and the 1st Belgian Cavalry Division, later reinforced by French forces. The Luxembourgers constructed a series of obstacles with steel gates, with a particularly important one on the mountain road near Mössbach. Right at the beginning, 1st Panzer Division ran into difficulty caused by enemy obstacles. The first barrier blocked the Our River bridge at the German–Luxembourg border. The Luxembourg defense forces constructed a two-meter thick by two-meter high concrete barrier with railroad rails imbedded in the top on the west side of the bridge at Wallendorf. The 1st Infantry Brigade commander, Colonel Walter Krüger,[20] observing the construction of this obstacle earlier, organized a forward detachment from within the division advance guard, consisting of an ad hoc bicycle company and a motorized detachment to ford the river quickly, conduct route reconnaissance, and locate obstacles along the division's TMR (see Table 3.1). Once locating a barrier the forward detachment would either seize and remove it, or locate a detour around it. The advance guard and the remainder of the division would wait for the engineers to position a prefabricated wooden ramp over the concrete bridge barrier. Twelve HE 126 reconnaissance aircraft also assisted the forward detachment.[21]

Heavy fog severely hindered visibility along the Our River at 0530 hours as a small German assault group crossed the bridge at Wallendorf to disarm the Luxembourg customs agents. Simultaneously, the forward detachment forded the river and began its advance west. Engineers completed the ramp across the barrier at 0730 hours and Lieutenant-Colonel Hermann Balck[22] led the advance guard into Luxembourg. Balck, the commander of the 1st Infantry Regiment, commanded the advance guard because Colonel Krüger was still on leave. The forward detachment, unopposed, made excellent time and seized the road barrier at Mössbach at 0800 hours before the defenders could close the steel gate across the narrow road.[23]

The Belgian government, informed of the attack by German anti-Nazis within the military and diplomatic community, ordered the blowing up of bridges and deployment into forward defensive positions at 0100 hours on May 10. By 1000 hours the Belgians had destroyed most of the bridges, including the ones over 1st Panzer Division's TMR at Bodange and Martelange.[24]

At 1000 hours the forward detachment reached the Belgian border just east of Martelange. According to plan, the detachment commander began to deploy his unit into designated assault positions to observe the Belgians until the advance guard and the rest of the division arrived. Lieutenant-Colonel Balck, however, deciding to drive ahead of the advance guard, arrived at the forward detachment's location just as they began to dismount and settle down. Balck identified two bunkers on the Belgian side, made a quick assessment of the situation, and decided to attack without waiting for the advance guard, artillery, or air support. His scout cars fired on the bunkers, while the riflemen crossed the river to the Belgian side. Within 30 minutes the troopers maneuvered to the rear of the bunkers, neutralized them, and captured five Belgians and two machine guns. A hole had been breached in the Belgian border defenses and Balck, realizing the opportunity at hand, radioed division for permission to advance to Fauvillers. The division commander agreed. In the meantime the advance guard arrived and at 1030 hours Colonel Krüger pulled up in a commandeered motorcycle to take command of his brigade. Balck returned to his regiment, with Krüger now leading the advance guard. One engineer company remained at Martelange and began constructing a bridge at 1130 hours. By 1200 hours the advance guard reached Bodange, where it was halted by a well-constructed Belgian strongpoint and found itself in an intense firefight.[25]

The Belgian commander at Bodange, Captain Bricart, constructed a formidable obstacle network along TMR B just south of the village. Antitank ditches, minefields, and wire obstacles, covered by fire from well-camouflaged fighting positions, prevented the two battalions of the Grman advance guard from unseating the Belgian defenders. The Germans tried to use the high ground to the south and east of Bodange to maneuver around the defenders but failed because of a lack of fire support. The 2nd Battalion/73rd Artillery Regiment moved forward and occupied firing positions at 1650 hours near Warnach to support the assault. Bricart's men, out of ammunition, and unable to disengage, surrendered at 1730 hours after resisting five and one-half hours. Bricart was killed during a last attempt to disengage his company at Bodange. The dust had not settled and 2nd Company/37th Engineer Battalion began constructing a bridge. The advance guard continued west.[26]

Garski, in Fauvillers, prepared to advance east toward Bodange at about the same time. The 1st Motorcycle Battalion, however, arrived in the village at 1900 hours to link up with Garski, sparing the exhausted group another march. The advance guard remained at Fauvillers, while the forward detachment drove to

Witri to link up with the rest of Garski's men. By and large the division proceeded no further on the 10th.

At Martelange, the newly constructed bridge had been opened for traffic at 1600 hours. Vehicles crossed for an hour and a half when a German officer approached a group of captured Belgian Chasseurs. One of the Belgian officers stood shaking his head while watching the German vehicles cross the bridge, and the German officer asked him what was bothering him. The Belgian answered that he simply could not understand the rapidity of the river crossing, since he and his men had mined the obvious crossing site on the west bank of the Sauer. The Germans stopped the crossing immediately and began clearing the minefield. The Belgians had placed the minefield some time ago and, planting the mines too deep in the ground, soil compacted around them enabling motorcycles and small vehicles to pass unhindered. The crossing site opened again at 2115 hours; the minefield, however, had served its purpose. General Kirchner called off the advance for the day. Nightfall, chaos on the road behind, and the need to bring supplies forward undoubtedly influenced his decision (see Appendix A, Map 3).[27]

Table 3.1
First Panzer Division Advanced Guard Organization

```
┌─────────────────────────────────────────────────────────┐
│                                                           │
│           1st Panzer Division Advanced Guard              │
│                                                           │
│       Commander: Lieutenant-Colonel Hermann Balck         │
│                                                           │
│                    Advanced Guard                         │
│                                                           │
│                 1st Motorcycle Battalion                  │
│              3rd Battalion/1st Infantry Regiment          │
│                37th Engineer Battalion (-)                │
│           1st Company/Panzer Jäger Abteilung 37           │
│                 one battery 88mm Flak (mot)               │
│       three platoons heavy Panzer Jäger (88mm) (mot)      │
│                                                           │
│                   Forward Detachment                      │
│                                                           │
│                     Detachment A                          │
│                                                           │
│           Bicycle Company (Abteilung Fischer)             │
│                                                           │
│                     Detachment B                          │
│                                                           │
│         1st Company/4th Reconnaisance Battalion           │
│           1st Company/37th Engineer Battalion             │
│                    three scout cars                       │
│                                                           │
└─────────────────────────────────────────────────────────┘
```

Note: All assets for the advance guard came from the 1st Infantry Brigade.

10th Panzer Division

The 10th Panzer Division, commanded by Major-General Ferdinand Schaal,[28] like the other two divisions, began its advance through Luxembourg at 0530 hours. The two TMRs allotted to the division led over fairly open country, scattered with rolling wooded hills. The 10th reached the Belgian border near Redingen at 0630 hours. Breaching the border defenses by 1000 hours, it proceeded westward, rapidly penetrating 10 km into Belgian territory. At noon, however, the division met the first enemy resistance at Hachy, Vanen, and Étalle and quickly came to a halt. The enemy turned out to be reconnaissance elements of the 2nd French Cavalry Division advancing northwest into Belgium to meet the invaders. General Schaal, sensing a threat to his left flank, immediately deployed "GD" forward to cover the exposed left flank. The 2nd Battalion/IR "GD" attacked in the early afternoon and pushed the French forces back to Ste. Marie. In the course of this action the commanders of 2nd Battalion/IR "GD" and 69th Infantry Regiment were killed. By 2000 hours the division advanced to the line Rulles-Ste. Marie, where it stopped for the day. The 10th also suffered from chaotic traffic conditions with units strung as far back as Echternach. The Division advanced roughly 75 km on the first day, but failed to reach its objectives of Rosignol-Bellefontaine. Those last five km would have to be accomplished on the 11th.[29]

Corps Headquarters

General Guderian spent most of the day with forward elements of his divisions. At 1900 hours he had visited every division headquarters to get a first-hand impression. The corps' main tactical operation center (TOC) displaced twice during the day, settling at Ettelbrück for the night. The tactical command post (TCP) set up at Rambruch at 2200 hours. Von Kleist issued the Panzer Group's operation order for May 11 to XIXth Panzer Corps at 200 hours. It was in essence a fragmentary order, simply reiterating the Group commander's intention of clearing and securing the near bank of the Meuse River on May 11. The Panzer Group allocated additional artillery and engineer assets from the General Headquarters troop reserve to XIXth Panzer Corps.[30]

German intelligence reports had proven correct. The enemy provided only limited resistance in the Ardennes and German armor had made fairly decent progress, although not reaching its objectives. Guderian, concerned about not reaching the day's objectives, would not allow his divisions a very long rest on the night of May 10. Belgian troops had removed road signs and village name signs, interdicted the entire road network, and successfully placed numerous road craters slowing the advance. The Belgians, however, committed a fatal error by failing to effectively cover the obstacles with direct or indirect fire (Bodange was the exception to the rule). Consequently, German engineers and assault troops rapidly cleared the obstacles. The majority of obstacles not protected by minefields were simply bypassed. The greatest problem the XIXth Panzer Corps faced on the first day of the offensive was not created by the enemy, but by units failing to obey traffic regulations.[31]

XIXth Panzer Corps as well as other elements of the Panzer Group experienced numerous traffic jams and delays. German infantry divisions, relegated to inferior sideroads and tracks, crossed the TMRs at unscheduled times. The infantry armies, pumped full of élan and offensive spirit, found openings between Panzer march groups and some stubborn infantry commanders used TMRs, causing enormous traffic jams. This massive concentration of vehicles created a rather sizeable target, extremely vulnerable to enemy air attacks. Elements of the XIXth Panzer Corps, having priority on the TMRs, at times forcefully attempted to pass interlopers, causing accidents. Tempers flared along the congested march routes. Everyone seemed to concern themselves with their own unit's interests, resulting in a complete breakdown in traffic discipline. All three divisions had units bogged down and stretched back into Germany as late as 2300 hours on the 10th. German supply columns were particularly hampered, integrated further to the rear, and could not move forward. Furthermore, the entire traffic management plan was at risk, since XIVth Panzer Corps and XLIst Motorized Corps, as second and third echelon, relied on the same roads (see Appendix B, Movement Orders). The XIVth Panzer Corps reached none of its march goals on the night of the 10th. It continuously ran up against tail elements of the XIXth Panzer Corps. The use of the Fieseler Storch aircraft for observation aided the Panzer Group, which dispatched staff officers to sort out the worst of the traffic jams. On the evening of May 10, General von Kleist issued an order that, "any unauthorized persons using Tactical March Routes and, using rank to usurp Military Police authorities risked immediate field court martial proceedings resulting in the severest possible punishment." The term "severest punishment" did not exclude the death penalty.[32]

The chaos in march discipline resulted from several factors. The Military Police company commanders, too young and low in rank, proved unable to enforce traffic rules against higher ranking commanders. Military Police units, not sufficiently trained in their traffic control duties, failed to understand the importance of traffic regulations. Because of negligence and an apparent lack of authority, Military Police commanders failed to enforce the rights of Panzer formations on TMRs. The Military Police, however, were not the sole offenders. Troops were not properly educated or trained, nor were they disciplined enough to follow orders or to subordinate themselves to the overall concept of the operation. The infantry wanted to advance quickly to share in a victory obviously destined for the Panzer arm. In many circumstances infantry commanders purposely prevented Panzer formations from advancing by wrongfully obtaining permission to utilize the Panzer division's TMRs.[33]

Operation NIWI, although not executed according to plan, was a complete success because the Germans managed to disrupt the enemy's lines of communication. Garski's battalion captured 82 Belgians, but also paid a heavy toll: nine men killed, seven wounded, and three missing. The Corps failed to achieve its objectives on the first day even though enemy resistance was lighter than expected. Guderian temporarily halted movements around 2000 hours, probably in an effort to clear up the traffic problems and to allow the divisions to bring supplies forward. In the early evening the XIXth Panzer Corps headquarters received intelligence reports indicating enemy tank formations assembling and preparing to advance on Guderian's left flank. Based on this information Guderian ordered the 10th Panzer Division, at 2250 hours, to proceed northwest along the Rulles-Habich road on the 11th, to secure the southern flank, and to cross the Semois between Cugnon and Mortehan. The missions for the other two divisions remained unchanged.[34]

Luftwaffe reconnaissance provided excellent information throughout the day, enabling Guderian to extend his view of the battlefield well beyond his lead elements. The Corps advanced the safety line for bombing to the railroad line "Liege-Marche-Libramont-Neufchâteau-Virton," effective until 1200 hours on May 11. The 102nd Flak Regiment (minus the 2nd Battalion) occupied positions in the vicinity of Bourscheid-Ettelbrück-Berg-Merch to provide the necessary air defense umbrella for the Corps. The 2nd Battalion/102nd Flak Regiment remained attached to the divisions. The 91st Battalion/1st Flak Corps deployed between Echternach and Attert for air defense protection along the Corps' Main Supply Route.[35]

The Corps staff's estimate for May 11 predicted heavier enemy resistance along the second Belgian line of defense. Based on the reorientation of the 10th Panzer Division, and OKH intelligence reports, the XIXth Panzer Corps' intelligence officer evaluated the flank threat as minimal. Thus ended XIXth Panzer Corps' first day of combat in the Battle of France. Casualties had proven light and divisions remained fully combat-capable, with the exception of the traffic dispersion to the rear. Corps' air defense units shot down three enemy aircraft and over 160 enemy were captured including one French scout car. While the XIXth Panzer Corps' staff prepared orders for the next day's anticipated breakthrough of the Belgian second defensive line at Libramont and Neufchâteau, supply officers aged prematurely attempting to move supply columns forward. Guderian, however, did not allow his divisions to rest for very long; instead he ordered them to continue the advance throughout the night. Lead elements reached the line Nives-Witri at 0430 hours on May 11. The Corps' objective for May 11 was to secure the near side of the Meuse River and, if possible, send forward detachments across the river to establish small bridgeheads.[36]

OKH's Foreign Armies West correctly predicted the enemy's intentions for May 10. The French Army, as expected, reacted very slowly, resulting in only minor engagements with the 10th Panzer Division along the left flank. By 2100 hours OKH intelligence evaluated reports from signal units monitoring French radio traffic, indicating that the French 2nd Infantry Division (motorized) had advanced elements to just south of Namur. Further south, the French 2nd and 3rd light Cavalry Divisions advanced forward to Arlon and Esch. A captured enemy operation order, however, revealed they were only to remain there long enough to ensure destruction of the vital industrial complexes at Esch. The most critical information that OKH Foreign Armies West needed next, to develop a clear picture of the enemy's operational intentions based on the German attack, was to determine the fate of the French divisions along the Maginot Line and the forward defenses facing the southern elements of 16th Army and Army Group C.[37]

SATURDAY, MAY 11, 1940

The eve of Whitsunday promised to be another beautiful day. The weather report predicted more of the previous day's sun and cirrus clouds. At 0745 hours, Panzer Group von Kleist reported the latest positions of XIXth Panzer Corps to Army Group A as being along the line Vaux les Rosiers–Witri–Rosignol–Bellefontaine. The night was rather uneventful, with the exception of a disagreement between Generals Guderian and von Kleist, on the employment of 10th Panzer Division.[38]

XIXth Panzer Corps received a message at 0030 hours on May 11, ordering the immediate halt of 10th Panzer Division. The Panzer Group, anticipating a French motorized threat on the left flank, wanted the 10th to establish a hasty defense between Étalle and Arlon to secure the Group's exposed flank. Guderian vehemently disagreed with this concept, but did not request to have the order rescinded nor did he alter his orders to 10th Panzer Division. The XIXth Panzer Corps' commander waited until 0430 hours to call the Panzer Group chief of staff, Zeitzler, demanding adherence to the original plan. The Corps commander further explained to Zeitzler that he did not view the potential flank threat significant, and that turning 10th Panzer Division northwest already negated any possible threat. Guderian insisted that the Meuse river operation remain the main effort and that any diversion of forces would endanger its outcome. Flank protection in his opinion was the responsibility of follow on divisions. Shortly after their lengthy telephone conversation, Zeitzler called back and informed XIXth Panzer Corps' chief of staff that after having discussed the issue with General von Kleist, the Panzer Group agreed with Guderian's concept and rescinded the order. Having weathered this storm, Guderian departed the corps' tactical operation center for the divisions' headquarters to discuss the day's operations with his subordinate commanders.[39]

The three Panzer divisions continued to press the attack throughout the night until about 0430 hours, when units occupied defensive positions for a rest. The Corps reached the line of Nives–Witri in the north. However, 10th Panzer Division became bogged down in the forested area around Anlier and Rulles, making progress during the hours of darkness virtually impossible. Guderian's orders for the 11th called for reaching the Meuse River, but like May 10, enemy road destruction and obstacles prevented XIXth Panzer Corps from reaching its objectives.

2nd Panzer Division

The 2nd Panzer Division faced stiff resistance at Libramont, but secured the town at 1500 hours. It was the first division to break through the second Belgian defensive line, but again was slowed by numerous road obstacles. At 2100 hours the 2nd Panzer Division's main combat elements reached Ochamps, about five km west of Libramont. The advance guard pushed as far west as Paliseul, which is about 15 km from Libramont. The division operations officer established the command post at Ste. Marie (see Appendix A, Map 4).[40]

1st Panzer Division

General Guderian's intention for the 1st Panzer Division on May 11 was to break through the second Belgian defensive position at Neufchâteau and, if possible, reach Sedan. The Division, however, did not begin its advance until noon. Obstacles and minefields forced its halt. In all probability, needed supplies and fuel contributed as much to the halt as the required engineer work. In the division's rear, traffic conditions remained confused. The Belgian Chasseurs Ardennais continued their withdrawal, offering little resistance, but added to the confusion by removing road signs and village name markers. Chasseurs Ardennais' engineers conducted numerous road demolitions, leaving holes six to eight meters in depth, ranging in diameters from 15 to 20 meters. Like the day before, the Belgians left the obstacles undefended. Therefore, they again had little effect other than delaying the Germans' advance and forcing the engineers to expend an inordinate amount of time, energy, and technical equipment.[41]

Shortly after 1500 hours, the 3rd Battalion of Balck's infantry regiment, supported by the 2nd Battalion/56th Artillery Regiment, secured Neufchâteau. Earlier in the day, much of the 73rd Artillery Regiment and the 1st Panzer Brigade, commanded by Colonel Karl Keltsch,[42] remained mired in traffic east of Bodange. After noon, however, with the fall of Neufchâteau elements of the 1st Panzer Regiment advanced to Grapfontaine, while available units of the 2nd Panzer Regiment captured Petivoir.[43]

First Panzer Brigade, now reinforced with the division's reconnaissance battalion and supported by the 1st Battalion/73rd Artillery Regiment, exploited the breach in the Belgian defensive line and continued the advance west. At 1700 hours this reorganized advance guard of 1st Panzer Division, for the first time, encountered troops of the French 5th Division Legere Mecanique at Bertrix. OKH intelligence had done its work, and French intervention forces appeared as predicted on the afternoon of May 11.[44]

After a short engagement, the French retreated westward, and the Panzer Brigade continued its advance to Bouillon. Captain Wedige Graf von der Schulenburg's 3rd Company/1st Battalion/1st Panzer Regiment led the advance through the Foret de Bouillon, arriving at the outskirts of the town at 1800 hours. Bouillon is a key defile on the Semois River leading to the Meuse River at Sedan.

Von der Schulenburg's company immediately received fire from the French and Belgian antitank guns positioned on the west bank. Air reconnaissance, however, reported a stone bridge just upstream of the city still intact. Colonel Keltsch promptly ordered 4th Company/1st Battalion/1st Panzer Regiment, commanded by First Lieutenant Ernst Phillip, to seize the bridge by a *coup de main*. During the attempt Phillip's tank was taken out of action, forcing him to mount one of his platoon leader's tanks to continue the assault. The French managed to blow up the bridge just as Phillip was ready to cross it. The 1st Battalion's commander, in the meantime, sent the 2nd Company to assist von der Schulenburg in Bouillon. Since, however, the 1st Panzer Regiment's reconnaissance platoon located a ford, the 2nd Company's commander decided to use it instead and crossed the river to the west bank. Simultaneously, 25 Stukas mistakenly attacked Bouillon and the west bank, adding confusion to the already ongoing battle, forcing Keltsch to withdraw 1st Battalion from the city and the west bank.[45]

French resistance began to dwindle soon thereafter. Under the cover of darkness the 1st Motorcycle Battalion located another ford near Mouzaive, just north of the 1st Panzer Division's main spearhead, crossed the river and established a small bridgehead. Third Company/1st Battalion/1st Panzer Regiment immediately followed the motorcyclists to reinforce them. Later in the night the 2nd Battalion/2nd Panzer Regiment crossed the river to help expand the bridgehead. By 2100 hours the 1st Panzer Division had advanced 100 km in two days and made up its shortcomings of the previous day. The division staff set up at Bertrix. The Division stood at the outskirts of Bouillon, managed to seize a bridgehead, and was just five km from the French border, and 20 km from Sedan, but that battle would have to be fought another day.[46]

10th Panzer Division

The 10th Panzer Division spent another interesting day, since both the order to turn northwest and numerous obstacles and road demolitions in the Foret d'Anlier and Foret de Rulles caused it to be considerably behind the other two Panzer divisions. By 2330 hours, its lead elements reached Straimont and Suxy. The division's staff set up at Mellier. Although forced to change its direction on this second day of the offensive, the division's staff and units performed well. The dispute over its objective bewildered both XIXth Panzer Corps and General Schaal.[47]

XIXth Panzer Corps

The controversy of 10th Panzer Division's objective continued to plague the corps staff throughout May 11. While Guderian was at the front, General von Kleist visited the corps tactical command post. After an operations update by

Colonel Nehring, von Kleist recommended that the 10th Panzer Division be directed toward Florenville to roll up the Semois defenses from the south. The Corps chief of staff, however, pointed out that the Division was previously redirected to the northwest and had probably already reached the area south of Neufchâteau. Nehring went on to emphasize that massing the Corps' forces for the Sedan operation was a precondition. Diverting 10th Panzer Division again would further slow the Division's advance. After listening to Nehring, von Kleist departed without providing an answer, and 10th Panzer Division's orientation remained unchanged. At 1600 hours an orderly officer from the Panzer Group delivered a message from the operations officer of Army Group A, directing 10th Panzer Division's advance along the southern bank of the Semois River. Shortly thereafter the Panzer Group operations officer came to the XIXth Panzer Corps' command post and, after being briefed by the chief of staff, recommended that at least the Division's Panzer brigade ought to advance toward Florenville. He also stressed that OKH supported the concentration of strong forces toward Florenville.[48]

By late afternoon 10th Panzer Division advanced far enough northwest to preclude any change in orders for the infantry brigade, IR "GD," or the Panzer brigade, toward Florenville. To satisfy the wishes of OKH, however, XIXth Panzer Corps ordered 10th Panzer Division at 1700 hours to organize and dispatch a battalion task force to Florenville.[49]

It is interesting to point out that, less than 24 hours before, the Panzer Group was ordered to halt the 10th Panzer Division to secure the left flank, because the Group feared a counterattack. General von Kleist's staff required thorough convincing by both Nehring and Guderian to change their attitude about that alleged threat. On the afternoon of May 11, however, the Panzer Group advocated the complete opposite and supported a quick advance to Florenville, disregarding flank protection altogether. Florenville was well within range of French artillery units along the Maginot Line. The Corps' command group, however, not overly concerned with its latest order to 10th Panzer Division, displaced the Corps' tactical command post to Neufchâteau. Nehring probably figured that 10th Panzer Division would resist the order anyway and develop a reasonable excuse to be freed from the mission; however, in the meantime he satisfied higher headquarters' requirements. After numerous detours, the small staff reached its destination at 2100 hours and found the city deserted. Guderian returned from the front a short time thereafter. He was in an ebullient mood and spent several minutes describing heroic deeds of soldiers to his staff.[50]

In the meantime, General Schaal pondered over the Corps' order he received at 1700 hours, but took no serious action to execute the directive. At 2330 hours, Schaal personally contacted the Corps' tactical command post by radio and reported that the formation of a battalion task force was impossible. He explained that the 10th Panzer Division's three columns would be required to secure Straimont and Suxy. Like any good officer, however, Schaal recommended an alternate solution to his corps commander. He suggested that the advance guard of VIIth Corps provide flank security with the 29th Infantry Division (motorized) advancing to Florenville. Guderian immediately agreed with this idea, since it would keep his corps intact while still conforming to OKH's intent of securing the southern flank. XIXth Panzer Corps notified Panzer Group von Kleist of this suggestion, and von Kleist also agreed. The Panzer Group issued orders to the 29th to dispatch its advance guard to Florenville. Guderian, although narrowminded in his concept of the overall mission, maintained his freedom of action and probably prevented a stalling of the main effort through a diversion of the 10th Panzer Division.[51]

On May 11, XIXth Panzer Corps made significant progress. Air and ground intelligence deserved substantial credit because they kept the Corps' staff informed. Air reconnaissance throughout the day confirmed that there were no major enemy movements into the Ardennes. There were, however, reports of French columns advancing toward the area of Sedan–Carignan–Montmedy–Virton. Single French motorized columns, bicycle units, and horsedrawn units crossed into Belgium at Bouillon, Florenville, Geronville, and Virton. There were no reports of significant movements west of the Meuse River. Enemy bombers and fighters began to appear in the sky, but their intervention remained insignificant.[52]

OKH intelligence estimates again proved correct on May 11. French and British forces moved to the Dyle River, taking the bait of the feint in the north. The Belgian cavalry division and the Chasseurs Ardennais continued to delay to the Semois River. The most important information, however, was that the French did not extract forces from their Army Group 2 to reinforce the Sedan–Dinant sector, verifying they had not yet identified this sector as the German main effort. Heavy rail traffic between Hagenau, Saaralben, and Berndorf led OKH to conclude that the French also expected a German attack against the Maginot Line. All retreating Belgian forces were moving toward the Dyle River. By evening of May 11, OKH Foreign Armies West positively identified the Allied main effort along the Dyle River.[53]

The XIXth Panzer Corps' intelligence officer analyzed the available information from OKH, Army Group A, Panzer Group von Kleist, air reconnaissance elements, and prisoners of war and, combined with stiffer resistance on May 11, determined that the enemy had recovered from the initial shock and would provide a more organized defense in the future. The northwest troop movements in the Sedan–Carignan–Longuyon sector indicated the enemy's intention of strengthening the Semois sector, suggesting a fierce fight between the Semois and the Meuse on May 12.[54]

The second Belgian defensive line did not present as tough an obstacle as anticipated, probably because the Belgians never had an opportunity to occupy their intended positions. During May 11, the XIXth Panzer Corps' situation developed according to plan, but again still did not achieve its objectives. The traffic situation remained chaotic, but less of a hindrance than the previous day. It rapidly became clear that the centralized traffic control suffered from faulty organization and a lack of signal assets, which precluded a timely response to higher headquarters' needs. Logistics ran smoothly, primarily because the system had not yet been sufficiently taxed. The rapid advance combined with minimal resistance contributed to low consumption of fuel and ammunition, and most important, it kept operational losses in terms of men, equipment, and supplies at a minimum.[55]

Guderian's concept or intent for the operation remained the same and his staff issued the corps' order shortly before midnight. For May 12, orders reiterated the crossing of the Semois River, the clearing of the enemy from the northern bank of the Meuse River, and, if possible, the establishment of small bridgeheads across the Meuse. Guderian directed the 1st and 2nd Panzer Divisions to debouch from their Tactical March Routes to facilitate XIVth Panzer and XLIst Motorized Corps' deployment on the right and left of XIXth Panzer Corps. Second Panzer Division would cross the Semois at Membre and Alle, and head toward Sugny. First and 10th Panzer Division's routes remained the same. Infantry Regiment "GD" became the corps reserve. The Panzer Group's operation order, although issued at 2100 hours on May 11, did not arrive at the XIXth Panzer Corps headquarters until 0545 on May 12. Fortunately it mirrored Guderian's intentions, since it would have been too late to effect any changes. A comment berating XIXth Panzer Corps' failure to achieve the objectives set by the Panzer Group on May 11 caused the tempers of both Guderian and Nehring to flare up. The subject of this statement continued to strain the relationship between the staffs of XIXth Panzer Corps and Panzer Group von Kleist, and became the topic of several heated discussions on May 12. The 12th of May, Whitsunday in Germany, when all young Catholics receive their first holy communion, would start with another confrontation between von Kleist and Guderian.[56]

SUNDAY, MAY 12, 1940

May 12, 1940, was a clear and warm day and proved to be one of the most successful days of XIXth Panzer Corps. By the end of Whitsunday, the Corps was in position to strike across the Meuse River, and commence one of the more successful exploitation operations in modern military history. Even though the advance on May 10 and 11 had not achieved the daily objectives, the Corps made up all its shortfalls on the 12th. XIXth Panzer Corps' advance between the Semois and the Meuse rivers proved so successful that Guderian's tankers reached the Sedan sector in two and one-half days instead of the planned three.

First, however, the business of XIXth Panzer Corps' pride needed to be settled. Colonel Nehring telephoned his counterpart at Panzer Group at 0630 hours and vehemently protested the context of the intent paragraph of the Panzer Group's Fragmentary Order Nr. 2 from the previous night. Nehring reminded Zeitzler of the difficult road conditions and the élan with which XIXth Panzer Corps tackled its missions over the past two days. The Corps chief of staff further insisted that the soldiers were doing their best and that the divisions not reaching their designated goals was not the fault of XIXth Panzer Corps, but rather that of the Panzer Group in assigning objectives too distant. Colonel Zeitzler finally agreed with Nehring and recognized the divisions' achievements. This newly established truce, however, only lasted a short time.[57]

2nd Panzer Division

Second Panzer Division spent a frustrating day and was unable to reach the Meuse River by nightfall. Prior to crossing the Semois River, the Division resorted to several detours because the enemy destroyed virtually all main roads. In spite of these difficulties, the Division crossed the Semois at 0900 hours at Vresse, but a lack of roads between the Semois and Meuse Rives, and constant enemy artillery interdiction, resulted in a significant slowdown. By nightfall the 2nd Panzer Division reached Bosseval, seven km from the Meuse River. General Veiel hoped to gain the Meuse at Donchery sometime during the night of May 12 to 13 (see Appendix A, Map 5).[58]

1st Panzer Division

The 1st Battalion/1st Infantry Regiment supported by two platoons of tanks from the 1st Panzer Regiment and the 2nd Battalion/73rd Field Artillery Regiment began its attack on Bouillon at 0500 hours and secured the town by 0745 hours, at which time the engineers began construction of a bridge over the Semois. The enemy resisted with artillery and bombing attacks. German tanks, crossing a ford, pursued their next objective, the heights just north of Sedan. At 0930 hours lead elements of the 1st Panzer Division crossed the French border, and with German forces prepared to approach the Meuse, the Luftwaffe directed its aircraft to switch to targets on the south bank of the river.[59]

Elements of the French 5th Division Legere Mechanique remained on the north bank of the Meuse, but with only twelve tanks could put up little resistance. Lead elements of the 1st Panzer Regiment entered the forest east of Sedan near 1030 hours. About the same time French artillery began to interdict the defiles and roads leading into Sedan. Its aim was so accurate that at times single soldiers and vehicles were taken under fire. The interdiction fire, however, did not stop the German tanks. At 1100 hours the 2nd Battalion/2nd Panzer Regiment exited the Foret de Ardennes north of St. Menges, while the 3rd Battalion/1st Infantry Regiment debouched from the Ardennes north of Sedan. The German soldiers observed smoke rising from Sedan, where the Luftwaffe just finished a bombing raid. In the meantime 2nd Battalion/2nd Panzer Regiment continued its advance to St. Menges. Above them across the Meuse River the Bois de la Marfee looked down upon them, the site where Emperor Napoleon III surrendered to King Wilhelm I of Prussia in 1870.[60]

The 1st Panzer Division covered the last 20 km from the Semois River to the Meuse River in four hours, covering the entire distance from its original assault positions at the Luxembourg border in just 60 hours. The rest of the division spent the afternoon hours clearing the north bank of the Meuse. Most of the Corps' artillery, Flak, and Infantry Regiment "GD" remained stuck in traffic east of Bouillon. Balck's infantry regiment occupied Fleigneux and St. Menges at 1800 hours and the Division Command Post set up in a small forest house two km from Fleigneux. First Panzer Division certainly achieved its main objective on May 12, but a crossing of the Meuse River could not be accomplished. Retreating across the Meuse, the French destroyed all bridges with the exception of the ones in Sedan, which they blew at 2045 hours, thus curtailing any attempt to capture them by a *coup de main*. In any event, the division staff was busily preparing for the river crossings the following day.[61]

10th Panzer Division

The 10th Panzer Division did not rest during the night of May 11 to 12, but continued its advance, crossing the Semois between Cugnon and Mortehan before daybreak. At 1000 hours lead elements reached the Bouillon–Florenville road, but like the 2nd Panzer Division, made only slow progress from that point on. Road conditions and traffic problems continued unabated, particularly since all vehicles had to pass through the few defiles debouching into the Meuse River valley. Finally, near 2400 hours the 10th Panzer Division began to deploy about Sedan.[62]

Enemy artillery, as previously mentioned, interdicted the XIXth Panzer Corps' march routes with deadly accuracy. Only the 1st Battalion/73rd Field Artillery Regiment deployed forward, in support of 1st Panzer Division. It occupied firing positions along clearings of the Foret de Sedan, north of Fleigneux. Later in the day, the 2nd Battalion/73rd Field Artillery Regiment also managed to get forward and occupied firing positions near Corbion. From observation points north of Fleigneux, the two artillery battalions supported the infantry attacks at St. Menges and Fleigneux. Although the enemy was driven from St. Menges and Fleigneux, French artillery continued to engage German units along the Meuse River approaches. The remarkable effect of French artillery resulted from the enemy's thorough knowledge of the terrain. The rest of the 73rd Artillery Regiment did not partake in any of the day's action, since it remained behind stuck in traffic.[63]

XIXth Panzer Corps

There was no doubt in anyone's mind that the XIXth Panzer Corps had to reach the Meuse River on May 12 to maintain the element of surprise. General Guderian departed at 0630 hours to personally influence his divisions' actions. He returned at 1545 hours to the new Corps command post, located at Bouillon. Shortly after his arrival the command post was relocated to Noirefontaine, because the enemy continued to bomb Bouillon. At 1715 hours the command post moved a third time, when the enemy shifted the bombings to Noirefontaine. Nehring opted for a forest not far from Noirefontaine.[64]

The Luftwaffe would play a significant role in the Meuse River crossings at Sedan. General von Stutterheim, commander of the 2nd Close Air Support Group assigned to Guderian for May 13, visited the Corps at 1700 hours to confirm the prearranged Luftwaffe support. Guderian and von Stutterheim agreed in early May that the Luftwaffe (Stukas and fighters) should systematically engage designated target areas and individual targets, and be incorporated as part of the artillery Fire Support Plan (see Appendix F, The Meuse River Crossing). The aim of this coordinated air and artillery assault was the programmed destruction of the enemy's artillery batteries prior to the river crossings. XIXth Panzer Corps' chief of staff, at 1750 hours, published a warning order for May 13, since Panzer Group von Kleist issued neither an operation order nor a directive by late afternoon. The order went out immediately and directed the divisions to prepare for the river crossing on May 13. As a precondition, the divisions were required to advance to the east bank of the Meuse River on the 12th, and draw all artillery and engineer assets forward. Specific instructions, they were told, would follow later in the night. At 1800 hours a Fieseler Storch landed near the Corps command post to pick up General Guderian for a meeting at the Panzer Group's headquarters at Ebly.[65]

General von Kleist conducted the meeting and stated that time was of the essence. Von Kleist did not want to lose the element of surprise, so he directed Guderian to cross the Meuse at 1600 hours on the following day. Von Kleist and Guderian, however, did not share the same concept of the operation. The Panzer Group commander met with General Sperrle, 3rd Air Corps commander, earlier in the day and they agreed on a massive bombing attack on large zones rather than on specific targets to isolate the battlefield. This did not fit into Guderian's scheme of systematic destruction of the enemy's artillery. Von Kleist refused to change his mind, while Guderian kept insisting that the Group's artillery assets were not strong enough, and that they could not be brought forward in time. Under these circumstances, Guderian recommended a postponement of the crossings until the morning of May 14, so that a more thorough preparation could be made. The Group commander rejected that proposal too. General von Kleist was one of the more soft-spoken gentlemen of the senior German commanders. He was chosen to lead the Panzer Group because General Halder wanted someone with strong leadership capabilities, yet clever enough to not be too bold or foolish. General Guderian required strong control at times, and General von Kleist was familiar with his subordinate's penchant for excitability and enthusiasm. Von Kleist knew he had to strike while the iron was hot, therefore he cut short any further discussion and told Guderian to obey his orders.[66]

Guderian, earlier disregarding his commander's intent, maneuvered the XIXth Panzer Corps to a different location for the crossings than von Kleist had anticipated. General von Kleist wanted to cross the Meuse between Sedan and Flize with the main effort west of the Ardennes Canal. The advantage of this maneuver kept the Panzer Group in the proper operational heading (west) and would avoid having to make two additional river crossings over the Baar Stream and the Ardennes Canal. This also supported Army Group A's and OKH's operational concepts. Crossing east of the Ardennes Canal restricted initial movements to the south, an unnecessary waste of time, people, and material. Von Kleist personally discussed this concept with Guderian on May 9, and also incorporated it as part of the intent statement in Panzer Group Order Nr. 2, issued on May 11, 1940.[67]

Unfortunately, Guderian's divisions were positioning themselves east of the Ardennes Canal. At the meeting, Guderian explained that he could not carry out von Kleist's concept without a delay of the attack until May 14. Von Kleist reluctantly agreed with the stubborn tanker's positioning of forces, since he did not want to sacrifice an extra day. The remainder of the meeting consisted of coordinating the next day's attack. While en route back to his command post, Guderian's pilot became disoriented and mistakenly strayed over French lines. Fortunately for Guderian, they were undetected and managed to return and land safely near Noirefontaine.[68]

In the German rear traffic problems continued unabated. Elements of the 16th Infantry Division decided to use one of the Tactical March Routes, and as a result blocked the XLIst Panzer Corps' advance guard, precluding it from reaching the Meuse River on schedule. Army Group A intervened and ordered the infantry unit off the road in the vicinity of Witri. Farther south, the 29th Infantry Division (motorized) was also hampered in its advance. A later investigation revealed that the traffic problems on May 12 occurred because of irresponsible leaders and drivers, mostly with only single vehicles. Even though the roads were taxed beyond limits, supplies still moved forward. There were no complaints from units of shortages of ammunition or fuel. The Panzer Group, however, did request the delivery of 13,000 gallons of fuel by air at 1400 hours to XIXth Panzer Corps. The Luftwaffe responded by delivering 5,200 gallons of fuel west of Fay les Veneurs.[69]

On May 12, OKH's Foreign Armies West section placed the Allied intelligence picture into clearer focus. OKH intelligence determined with certainty that the enemy would defend along the line: western Holland, Antwerp, the Dyle River line, and the Meuse River, from Namur, to its connection with the French Maginot Line. Foreign Armies West dismissed any danger of a flank attack from the north through the Ardennes, but did begin to focus on the more vulnerable southern flank. Aircraft spotted two columns of vehicles early in the day, one heading from Rocroix to Fumay and another from Vouziers to Mouzon. The Luftwaffe struck both columns; however, precise damage reports were not available. On May 12, the French again did not remove any units from the Maginot Line. In addition to OKH intelligence reports, XIXth Panzer Corps' air reconnaissance elements provided continuous information throughout the day. The Corps' intelligence officer rated the enemy in front of the Panzer divisions as weak, but expected a strong defense of the Meuse River by the French 55th Infantry Division on May 13.[70]

XIXth Panzer Corps used all of the remaining 20 hours to prepare for the Meuse River crossings. Nehring and his staff worked the entire night to finalize the Corps operation order. Since the intended plan almost mirrored one of the war games conducted along the Moselle River, Nehring simply changed dates, times, and incorporated specific information and changes coordinated at the Panzer Group's commanders' meeting. The order, finally published at 0815 hours on May 13, left little time for the divisions to react (see Appendix F, The Meuse River Crossing).[71]

4

The Breakthrough

Joyriding canoes on the Meuse is forbidden.
General Heinz Guderian, April 1940

XIXth Panzer Corps' advance to the Meuse River was a remarkable achieve-ment. Halder's calculated risk paid off and the enemy's defense consisted of a mere delaying action, resulting in minimal losses in both personnel and equip-ment. However, the most difficult task—that of conducting a river crossing into the enemy's jaws—still lay ahead. The Army General Staff spent many hours during the previous winter and spring determining the best course of action. Guderian convinced his superiors and the Army General Staff that crossing the Meuse at Sedan would open the door to the Atlantic coast in the shortest time and most effective manner. General von Kleist agreed with the concept; however he injected an even riskier proposition than the Ardennes breakthrough. Von Kleist, not willing to forfeit the initiative by waiting for the 12th and 16th Armies' infantry, decided instead to conduct the river crossing with dismounted infantry from the march. The river crossings had been rehearsed in detail on the Moselle River only eight weeks earlier, and Guderian's chief of staff, Colonel Nehring, spent most of the night of May 12 to 13 updating the war game's operation order, which he issued at 0815 hours on the 13th. The actions of XIXth Panzer Corps over the next two days would be remarkable achievements in modern military history and ultimately decide the outcome of the Battle of France.[1]

MONDAY, MAY 13, 1940

Throughout the night of May 12 to 13 Guderian coordinated with his chief of staff, artillery commander, and Luftwaffe liaison officer to incorporate the

Panzer Group's changes. Because of the traffic snarls Guderian worried about all the artillery getting forward on time. A second issue that Guderian discussed with Nehring was the Panzer Group's concept of the bridgehead's size. Panzer Group von Kleist ordered XIXth Panzer Corps to cross the Meuse River between Flize and Sedan, and to establish a bridgehead along the line Boutancourt–Sapogne–Chehery–Noyers–Pont-Maugis.[2] Since under the German system the maximum amount of freedom was provided to subordinates to execute their mission, Guderian maneuvered his corps a few kilometers south of Flize and planned to push further south to the heights of Stonne before turning it westward. Although Guderian failed to execute his commander's intent, the resulting changes were minimal and did not effect the Meuse River crossing operation.[3]

The French continued to impede German movements north of the Meuse River. As on the previous day, French artillery forward observers engaged anything that moved. This proved extremely costly, at dawn, for reconnaissance elements of the 37th Engineer Battalion. As a result many young engineers were killed along the river banks attempting to confirm previously selected crossing sites. First and 10th Panzer Divisions worked throughout the night, clearing the remainder of the French forces from the north bank, and by 0800 hours had all elements in assault positions in the woodlines contouring the river from St. Menges to Balan. Every division faced several hundred meters of open flat grass, leaving every movement outside the cover of the woodline to enemy observation and fire. Second Panzer Division advanced much slower and was still located in the forest of Sugny at 0815 hours, about five km from its crossing site at Donchery.[4]

The Luftwaffe initiated its attack at 1000 hours instead of the previously coordinated 0800 hours, bombing prepared enemy positions, artillery batteries, and unit assembly areas. During the course of the morning a Stuka squadron mistakenly attacked the assault positions of the 1st Motorcycle Battalion, but only caused minimal injuries and damage. The battalion commander, Major Wend von Wietersheim,[5] promptly contacted the 1st Panzer Division's headquarters and told the operation office, Lieutenant-Colonel Walther Wenck,[6] that he could do without this type of support from the Luftwaffe. Wenck immediately contacted XIXth Panzer Corps to ensure that there would not be a repeat.[7]

General Guderian spent the entire morning visiting the three division commanders, conducting face-to-face coordination and explaining his aims for the upcoming operation. At Sugny, he informed Major-General Veiel that the attack would commence as scheduled, and that he was to have all available combat elements at the river on time. Traffic conditions were especially bad on the morning of May 13 since all artillery assets, engineers, and Flak units congested the limited road space between the Semois and Meuse Rivers. The situation deteriorated when the Corps' Military Police company commander was killed during one of the bombing raids on Sedan. At 1030 hours, the Nebelwerfer regiment's commander reported that he would be unable to bring his units forward in time to support the river crossing. As the Corps attempted to position its combat support elements, the Luftwaffe continued the air raids. The French, however, began firing some long-range artillery in the rear of Guderian's assault positions, which rather surprised the Germans.[8]

General Wilhelm Berlin, the Corps' artillery commander (ARKO 101), spent a hair-raising morning concentrating the artillery units around Sedan. The 73rd Artillery Regiment finally occupied its firing positions about noon, and the rest of the artillery units managed to somehow occupy theirs by 1530 hours. This accomplishment reflected the tremendous leadership capabilities of General Berlin. The Luftwaffe's effort began to increase after 1400 hours, culminating at 1500 hours with a massed raid of 900 to 1,000 Stuka/fighter aircraft for the next hour. At 1530 hours, the artillery joined the Luftwaffe, commencing the combined one-half hour concentrated fire support preparation prior to the assault (see Appendix F, the Meuse River Crossing). Infantry and engineers used this "Götterdämmerung" as cover while moving boats and equipment to the river's edge. As the last bombs and artillery shells struck the enemy's side of the river, elements of XIXth Panzer Corps started their historic assault.[9]

The Luftwaffe demonstrated the effectiveness of a coordinated air bombardment, virtually driving the French 55th Infantry Division into panic. Intelligence officers within the French division received instructions on how to use machine guns in the antiaircraft role only on the morning of May 13. At 0730 hours, the French 10th Corps commander telephoned the 55th Infantry Division commander and assured him that a German attack was unlikely over the next four to six days, since their artillery and ammunition had not yet been brought forward.[10]

1st Panzer Division

The soldiers of the 1st Panzer Division, main effort of Panzer Group von Kleist, observed the devastating Luftwaffe attack the entire day. Nevertheless the situation was chaotic when they began their river crossing, with French bunkers spitting intense fire at them from the far side of the river. The soldiers had actually spent a fairly calm day, resting as much as possible. The signal battalion finished laying all telephone lines by 0400 hours, placing division headquarters in contact with the infantry brigade, Panzer brigade, and ARKO 101.[11] The engineers produced only scant information on the crossing sites as a result of their costly reconnaissance efforts early in the morning. Although the crossing sites had previously been selected from aerial photography, commanders wanted to confirm the actual locations. Any attempt at further reconnaissance during daylight became impossible. Thus, at 1500 hours, under the protection of the massive air attack and the subsequent artillery preparation, infantry and engineers carried their boats to the water's edge. The Division planned its assault as follows: 1st Motorcycle Battalion assaulted the Iges loop, the 1st Infantry Regiment assaulted north of Gaullier towards Frenois, and Infantry Regiment "Grossdeutschland" south of Gaullier (inclusive) on Torcy. Earlier in the morning company 1st Sergeants instructed the mechanized infantry soldiers to prepare and carry assault packs, since they would be without their vehicles for the next day (see Appendix A, Map 6).[12]

The 1st Motorcycle Battalion began its river crossing, at 1600 hours, southwest of St. Menges. The Meuse was shallow at this location and presented the motorcyclists with little difficulty. Clearing of the Iges loop proceeded rapidly and by 1800 hours the battalion secured the French positions on Mont D'Iges. The battalion continued its advance reaching and securing Glaire de Villette at 1900 hours. The 1st Company's commander was killed and Major von Wietersheim was wounded during the attack on Glaire de Villette. Bunkers south of the Canal de l'Est were cleared by elements of 1st Infantry Regiment, so the motorcyclists could cross the canal.[13]

Lieutenant-Colonel Balck, commander of the 1st Infantry Regiment, accompanied his soldiers to the river at 1500 hours, and became the focus of a classical breakdown in communications. The regiment's transportation column delivered the pneumatic boats for the river crossing, but no operators, since someone forgot to inform the engineers where to go. In the meantime "Grossdeutschland's" engineer battalion commander arrived at the scene and Balck directed him to operate the boats. The engineer commander reminded Balck that his soldiers were assault engineers and not boat operators. Balck had trained his soldiers in the use of pneumatic boats, thus he decided to conduct the assault crossing without the help of the engineers. He crossed the river with the first wave and within minutes reached the initial bunker line along the far bank. The advance slowly began to increase momentum, since the French in Balck's sector only rendered isolated resistance. At 1730 hours lead elements of the 2nd and 3rd Battalions reached the Donchery–Sedan rail line, about one and one-half km southwest of the crossing site. General Guderian, whose command post moved to La Chapelle at noon, drove to elevation 266, southwest of Givonne at 1600 hours to observe the river crossings. From this location he could see the entire battlefield and observe the progress of his corps. His patience, however, was short-lived and by 1800 hours, Guderian proceeded to the river, crossed, and joined the 1st Infantry Regiment in the forward lines.[14]

Balck knew the next defensive line had to be breached before his soldiers could receive a well-deserved rest. The French main defense lay south of the Sedan-Bellevue road. The 2nd and 3rd Battalions assaulted at 1830 hours and breached it by 2030 hours, opening a gap in the French defensive system between Frenois and Wadelincourt. Balck kept pressing the attack, although his battalion commanders recommended against it. He realized the surprise the regiment achieved, and wanted to carry the bridgehead as far forward as possible. Since French resistance at this point was almost nonexistent, Balck did not want to pay a high price on the 14th for something available so cheap on the 13th. By midnight, Balck had led elements of his regiment to just south of Cheveuges and the southern edge of the Bois de la Marfée. He sent two companies of 2nd Battalion on ahead to Chehery to secure the high ground west of the village, in essence cutting off the French artillery positions in the southern confines of the Bois de la Marfée.[15]

Infantry Regiment "Grossdeutschland" was attached to 1st Panzer Division on May 13 for the river crossing. It arrived late in the division's sector, not reaching Gaullier until 1430 hours. The main effort of the regiment rested with the 2nd Battalion. The battalion commander decided to use a factory adjacent to the river as his command post, and established machine gun positions on the upper floors of the building to engage three French bunkers on the opposite river bank. As scheduled, the first assault squad carried its boat to the water's edge at 1600 hours, but was immediately engaged by the French from the bunker positions. The entire squad was mowed down and killed, and the boat destroyed. The second squad met the same fate. When a 3.7 cm half-track mounted Flak gun arrived at the scene, the battalion commander ordered its crew to engage the bunkers. The gun crew expended all its ammunition, engaging the bunkers, but the third squad met the same fate as the first two. Only the direct fire support of two 7.5 cm armored assault guns, Sturmgeschütz, and a Stuka attack finally subdued the French in the bunkers. At 1650 hours, the 2nd Battalion made its first successful crossing managing to establish a small bridgehead by 1730 hours. The commander immediately sent the rest of the battalion across the river and began the advance on Torcy. At 2000 hours, the regiment progressed to the northeastern edge of the Bois de la Marfée. Engineers ferried the entire infantry brigade and Infantry Regiment "Grossdeutschland" across the Meuse by midnight. The 1st Panzer Division's execution of the river crossing proved successful, reflecting the hard training practiced weeks before along the Moselle.[16]

10th Panzer Division

The other two Panzer divisions did not have the same good fortune. Tenth Panzer Division, faced with incredible odds, finally managed to get some weak elements across the river by 1800 hours. Flat, open terrain leading to the water's edge, sighted by enemy forward observers and machine gunners nestled in bunkers under the railroad embankment 300 meters from the river, enabled the French to saturate the assault forces with devastatingly accurate fires. German bombers and artillery missed those fortifications throughout the day's bombardment. The Division also received artillery fire from heavy guns positioned near Remilly. The lack of the Division's heavy artillery battalion subordinated to the 1st Panzer Division severely hampered its ability to support properly the river crossing. Crossing attempts at Bazeilles ended in complete disasters, resulting in heavy casualties, and the loss of much of the bridging equipment.[17]

A company size force, at about 1930 hours, finally crossed at the Division's second crossing point at Wadelincourt. One squad spent several hours clearing bunkers along the water line, taking pressure off the crossing sites. As soon as the French defensive fire began to slacken, the Division sent two battalions of infantry across. Like the earlier assaults at Bazeilles casualties were extremely high, but the assault succeeded. The Division continued to receive heavy flanking artillery fire from French batteries located at Noyers–Pont-Maugis and

Remilly. The division commander refused the aid of a Stuka attack against the batteries, in light of his destroyed bridging assets, rendering him incapable of constructing a bridge until new equipment could be brought forward. Later, during the night, the Division began constructing a bridge just south of Sedan, while the two infantry battalions advanced to Noyers and Pont-Maugis. Thus by midnight the Division established a bridgehead running from Wadelincourt to 500 meters east of the Bois de la Marfée–Noyers–Pont-Maugis. The 10th Panzer Division paid a heavy price for such a modest bridgehead (see Appendix A, Map 7).[18]

2nd Panzer Division

The 2nd Panzer Division suffered a much worse fate than the 10th. Similar problems with open terrain along the approaches to the river plagued General Veiel's infantrymen. Only a few small elements managed to get to the south bank of the Meuse, west of Donchery. Because of extremely heavy losses, and the unlikelihood of constructing a bridge near Donchery under the present conditions, Guderian redirected elements of the 2nd Panzer Division, at 2100 hours, to the Iges loop hoping a strike in the enemy's flank would be more successful.[19]

The ability to bridge the Meuse rapidly would prove as important as securing a bridgehead. Engineers began constructing an assault bridge at Gaullier at 1800 hours. Initially, however, the 37th Engineer Battalion, reinforced by the 505th Engineer Battalion, constructed ferries, beginning operations with the first one at 1815 hours. These ferries transported the initial armored cars and antitank guns to the other side, while pneumatic boats carried five battalions of infantry across the river. Actual construction of the bridge, once proper reconnaissance of the sites were completed, began at 2015 hours. The engineers opened the bridge for traffic at 0200 hours.

The engineers had only 70 meters of bridging equipment, since a previously constructed bridge over the Semois, the day prior, could not be taken down. The location selected by the engineers was just under 70 meters. If the French airforce or artillery had taken out only one section, bridge traffic would have been halted for an extended period of time. The 37th Engineer Battalion would have had to borrow equipment from another unit.[20]

While General Guderian accompanied the 1st Infantry Regiment, Nehring began planning operations for May 14. Throughout the day visitors arrived at the Corps' headquarters for update briefings. Two of those distinguished guests were Generals von Kleist and von Stutterheim. Nehring impressed upon von Kleist the importance of expanding the bridgehead to Stonne, and with von Stutterheim he coordinated the air effort. Nehring and the Luftwaffe commander agreed on the area south of Attigny–Steny as a free-fire zone. Among other things, the chief of staff assessed the day's operations. He attributed the failures of 2nd and 10th Panzer Divisions to a lack of fire support. At 2130 hours Nehring directed 1st Panzer Division to detach the two heavy artillery battalions to 2nd and 10th Panzer Divisions. The artillery's massing in 1st Panzer Division's sector had paid off, but the two flanking divisions now required heavier fire support to catch up with 1st Panzer Division. Nehring also recognized the vulnerability of the two bridges at Gaullier and south of Sedan. Since the French had attempted several times already to destroy the bridges with their air force, the Corps' chief of staff ordered all available Flak guns concentrated around the crossing sites. German Flak crews managed to drive off the attacking Allied aircraft on May 13. However, the intelligence officer expected heavier air activity on the 14th. The significance of those bridges can not be over-emphasized, for without them the Panzer brigades would not have reached the infantry on the following morning. As the Corps' center of gravity, the bridges had to be protected at all costs since they not only carried the tanks, but also the vitally important supplies required to sustain the forces.[21]

The initial advance across the river produced little usable intelligence. As predicted, the French fought hard, but the Luftwaffe generated such a fear that many soldiers were found hiding in corners of bunkers. Intelligence officers, after interrogating French soldiers and officers, concluded that the enemy caught in 1st Panzer Division's sector was completely demoralized and no longer willing to fight. Air reconnaissance, at 1615 hours, reported enemy tank formations moving north toward Bulson, possibly indicating a French armored or motorized counterattack. No such large formations, however, had yet been reported within the vicinity of the bridgehead. The enemy was expected to continue his stubborn resistance, although a major counteroffensive by the French was not anticipated since a sizeable movement of reserves had not been initiated.[22]

At 2230 hours Nehring issued the operation order for May 14, reflecting the estimate of the intelligence officer that French armored forces would reach the Corps' forward positions sometime in the morning. The Corps' plan called for 1st Panzer Division to continue its advance toward Bulson, then turning west over Vendresse–Le Chesne toward Boutancourt with its left flank paralleling the Aisne River to Rethel. The 2nd Panzer Division would also turn west and advance toward Poix-Terron, then head southwest toward Rethel. Protection of the Corps' left flank fell to the 10th Panzer Division, which would advance south directly east of Bulson toward Stonne.[23]

By midnight the XIXth Panzer Corps had punched a salient six km deep and five km wide, with elements as far south as Chehery. Guderian, concerned with the imminent French counterattack, planned to use the rest of the night to strengthen the bridgehead. He therefore directed the infantry to prepare fighting positions along the forward edge of the bridgehead and ordered the movement of all available Panzer and antitank units across the Gaullier bridge as soon as possible. His intentions for May 14 included widening and protecting the bridge-head, exploiting the success of the Gaullier River crossing by securing crossing sites over the Ardennes Canal, and conducting a breakout toward Rethel.

Guderian's plans for May 13 had been realized, but the battle was not yet won. The Corps had taken heavy casualties in its infantry ranks, while the Panzer brigades were still unscathed. The French Army remained a force to be reckoned with, especially its armored forces.[24]

The Rolling Bombardment

During the "Phony War," German air reconnaissance systematically photographed the entire Sedan–Mézières sector. This aerial photograph aided 3rd Air Corps' pilots in locating their targets. Command posts, forward observer positions, bunkers, machine gun nests, and battery firing positions were caught in the hail of the Luftwaffe's bombs. The Luftwaffe flew unimpeded, and destroyed several villages around Sedan. This rolling air attack had a tremendously demoralizing effect on the French. The 55th Infantry Division's telephone lines were destroyed within 30 minutes, leaving only a limited number of radios and messengers to transmit information. The continued bombing and the Stuka sirens virtually paralyzed the French. Although later investigations revealed that fewer personnel were killed and equipment destroyed than originally anticipated, the demoralizing effect of the Stuka took its toll, severing the nerves of the defenders in 1st Panzer Division's sector, resulting in a panic by evening. The absence of any French antiaircraft guns or fighter aircraft certainly added to the psychological impact. The remnants of the 55th Infantry Division, the entire 71st Infantry Division, the majority of five artillery regiments, and rear services began to rout south on the Bulson–Maisoncelle and the Bulson–Chemery roads. Staffs, medical services, and anyone that could move joined this rout. Interestingly enough, many of these soldiers never sighted a single German other than the Luftwaffe airplanes unloading their ordnance. French general staff officers were out to restore order; however, many of these became caught in the chaos. Elements of this panic-stricken mass fled as far as Reims, 80 km behind the front before they could be stopped.[25]

TUESDAY, MAY 14, 1940

On the fifth day of the offensive, XIXth Panzer Corps' soldiers fought several major actions resulting in decisive consequences for both sides. For the German Army it resulted in its greatest victory since the Battle of Sedan some 70 years earlier, and for the French it marked the beginning of the end. The Corps enlarged the bridgehead south toward Stonne and crossed the Ardennes Canal in the west, while the French attempted throughout the day to crush Guderian's bridgehead. On this hot dry sunny Tuesday, both sides attacked and counterattacked in rapid succession, but Guderian maintained a clear vision of the General Staffs' Campaign Plan. Throughout the night German antiaircraft units came forward to defend those vital bridges, and at dawn the 102nd Flak Regiment (reinforced) assembled 81×20 mm, 54×3.7 cm, and 36×88 mm Flak guns to protect them. Above Sedan, Allied aircraft struggled the entire day to destroy the bridges. By nightfall they had suffered heavy losses and were incapable of eliminating them. The XIXth Panzer Corps' lifeline into the bridgehead remained open.[26]

The Corps systematically squeezed as many armored vehicles and artillery as possible across the bridge during the night. By early evening, nearly 300 armored vehicles of all types and a battalion of 105 mm howitzers passed over the Gaullier bridge. During the night, the 2nd Panzer Division managed to get one battalion of infantry across the river, but still was not able to construct a bridge of its own. The Division continued in this precarious situation until late in the day. During the night, Guderian directed 2nd Panzer Division to send one Panzer regiment with some infantry over the Gaullier bridge, to attempt rolling up the enemy's flank along the southern bank of the Meuse. Besides its difficulties at the crossing site, the 2nd Panzer Division also experienced tremendous traffic problems, with units still stretched beyond the Semois River. The assault bridge located at Vresse, damaged by enemy aircraft several times during the past day and a half, trapped units north of the Semois. In the wake of these continued air attacks, engineers struggled to repair the bridge in order to keep traffic flowing.[27]

Guderian, as usual, departed his command post at 0630 hours and drove directly to the lead elements of 1st Panzer Division south of the Bois de la Marfée. Concomitantly, air reconnaissance reported enemy motorized and tank columns heading toward 1st Panzer Division on the Rethel–Le Chesne–Chemery road. The French thus confirmed the intelligence estimate of the previous night. Guderian personally contacted his operations officer at 0850 hours, reporting enemy armor units heading towards Chemery and Bulson from the south, and directed the immediate dispatch of all available tanks and antitank units in that direction. Guderian recognized that a successful French counterattack meant the Allies could win the campaign.[28]

Expanding the Bridgehead

First Panzer Division demonstrated its tactical ability as a well-trained, superbly led fighting force on May 14, 1940. The Division, subjected to the brunt of the French counterattacks, withstood each crisis. General Kirchner, upon receipt of the 0630 hours air reconnaissance intelligence, ordered 2nd Panzer Regiment straight to Bulson. The Regiment arrived there at 0700 hours without infantry support, but decided to secure the village anyway. The French attacked shortly thereafter, and the violent engagement lasted until about 1000 hours, when they retreated to Chemery. The 2nd Panzer Regiment lost several armored vehicles to French tankers during this engagement. More important, although German tank armaments were inferior to French, superior tactics and up-to-date signal equipment provided the Germans with a clear advantage. Second Panzer Regiment outmaneuvered the French, struck in their flank, forced them to retreat, and wasted no time in giving chase to Chemery, where it became tangled with French infantry. Without their own infantry, the German tankers found it difficult combatting infantry, but a company of assault engineers from the 43rd Assault Engineer Battalion arrived at 1115 hours and cleared the village. The French counterattacked and nearly regained Chemery. When the situation became desperate for the Germans, the engineers began to use weapons more suited to their trade in an effort to repel the French tanks. Employing shaped charges, flame throwers, and smoke grenades, the engineers destroyed ten tanks in the streets of the village. At about 1215 hours the French finally had enough and retreated from the village leaving it under German control. During the fighting, the engineer company commander was killed. At 1230 hours elements of the antitank company of "Grossdeutschland" arrived with nine 5 cm antitank guns to reinforce the units at Chemery.[29]

Lieutenant-Colonel Balck's 1st Infantry Regiment also held off a French counterattack in his sector near Chehery. Without any heavy weapons, Balck watched French tanks supported by low-flying aircraft advance to within 30 meters of his position, until two 5 cm antitank guns pulled up. One of the guns took a direct hit while getting into action, the other one was luckier and engaged enemy tanks until the latter withdrew. Several of the low-flying aircraft fell prey to alert German machine gunners who had set up their MG 34's on the antiaircraft tripods. While the battle was in progress a lost field kitchen drove into Balck's position, providing the infantrymen with some badly needed humor. When the dust of the first engagements settled, a vast number of French tanks littered the battlefields of Bulson, Chemery, and Chehery. General Kirchner, recognizing the significance of capturing the Ardennes Canal bridges intact, ordered the Panzer Brigade to secure the crossings at Malmy and Omicourt immediately after the French attack. Colonel Keltsch directed one company of tanks to each bridge. They secured both bridges at 1230 hours and established small bridgeheads at each site. Capturing these bridges intact was extremely critical, because the Corps began to experience a shortage of bridging assets. It is questionable whether the Corps still possessed enough bridging equipment to support another two assault bridges. Then, for the second time in two days, the Luftwaffe attacked a target with German troops on it. Stukas accidentally bombed Chemery at 1300 hours, causing a number of casualties, including the commander of the 1st Panzer Brigade.[30]

In the meantime, elements of the 2nd Panzer Division advanced to the Baar Stream near Villers-sur-Baar; however, French defenders repulsed the first attempt to take the village. French armor and infantry also attempted a counterattack at Malmy, but the German tankers held firm. At 1430 hours, the commander at the Malmy bridgehead radioed 1st Panzer Division headquarters and reported that unless infantry reinforcements arrived soon, he would not be able to maintain his position much longer. The Division operations officer dispatched the 1st Motorcycle Battalion and 1st Battalion/73rd Field Artillery Regiment to support the Malmy bridgehead. As the battles raged on throughout the morning and early afternoon, the ammunition columns rearmed the tankers twice in their forward positions. For the first time since May 10, ammunition expenditure reached high rates, but French resistance began to soften later in the evening.[31]

Tenth Panzer Division, using the cover of darkness on the night of May 13 to 14, employed pneumatic boat ferries and transported 40 antitank guns into the bridgehead near Wadelincourt. At daybreak the infantry began to advance south, paralleling the Meuse. They reached Noyers–Pont-Maugis, Remilly, and Angecourt at noon. Along the edge of the forest near Haraucourt, their advance was checked by French defenders, primarily because the infantry had no heavy weapons or tank support. Since the assault bridge south of Sedan was not completed until 0645 hours, the infantry had to wait until early afternoon for armor support to continue the advance. The infantry's armored half tracks also moved forward, enabling the advance to pick up momentum. Tenth Panzer Division advanced on two axes, one on the road Angecourt–Haraucourt– Raucourt et Flaba, the other on the open grassy areas between the forest of Haraucourt and the Meuse River toward Muzon–Yoncq. By 1600 hours the Division broke through the French defenses at Haraucourt and captured 40 artillery pieces.[32] The Division continued south, seizing the heights southwest of Raucourt et Flaba at 1800 hours, finally stopping after reaching the edge of the Bois du Mont Dieu forest at midnight.[33]

While 10th Panzer Division conducted its advance south toward Le Besace-Flaba, "Grossdeutschland" paralleled the Division, seizing Maisoncelle-et-Villers around 1830 hours. By midnight "Grossdeutschland" linked with 10th Panzer's right flank south of Artaise-le Vivers north of the Bois du Mont Dieu. The 43rd assault engineers, the 4th Armored Reconnaissance Battalion, and the 37th Antitank Battalion supported "Gorssdeutschland's" right flank throughout the day, warding off several attempts by the French to penetrate the bridgehead south and southwest of Chemery. Chemery was a vital piece of terrain for XIXth Panzer Corps, because the east-west road to the Malmy bridge passed through the village. French forces again tried at 1700 and 1900 hours to break through at Chemery, but the Germans held firm. The actions of 10th Panzer Division, "Grossdeutschland," and the combat support elements secured the Corps' left flank (see Appendix A, Map 9).[34]

The Breakout

General Guderian, forcing himself not to lose sight of the ultimate objective, became concerned in the early afternoon that his forces, although expanding and protecting the bridgehead, were being diverted from the Corps' main goal. To the XIXth Panzer Corps commander, main goal meant reaching the English Channel. From 1330 to 1400 hours, while at the 1st Panzer Division's command post, Guderian discussed his proposed course of action with General Kirchner and Lieutenant-Colonel Wenck. Guderian wanted to hear their opinion on his very risky proposition. He expected 1st Panzer Division to turn west without delay and, using the crossing sites at Omicourt and Malmy, advance to Signy–Omont. Infantry Regiment "Grossdeutschland," reinforced with two heavy artillery battalions, would remain in the bridgehead and secure the Division's southern flank by advancing to Stonne. Second Panzer Division would continue its attempt to secure a crossing at Donchery and, once established, advance toward Flize–Hannogne. Tenth Panzer Division would continue south to Raucourt et Flaba–Mouzon, and thus protect the Corps' left flank.[35]

The risks of this concept of operation was that 1st Panzer Division would be initiating the right turn immediately while its flanks were not completely secured. Secondly, some of the raging battles had yet to be settled. Guderian, however, felt that in order to maintain the initiative, the Corps had to take advantage of the enemy's confusion and surprise him again by striking while the iron remained hot. When Guderian looked at Wenck for a reply, the operation officer simply stated, "The General taught us to hit with a fist and not to feel around with our fingers."[36] Guderian, confident in the soldiers and officers of his command, issued the necessary orders at 1400 hours from his command vehicle. His decision, truly operational in nature, was indicative of Guderian's type of leadership. The tremendous risk he undertook was bound to have far-reaching consequences, regardless of the outcome.[37]

First Infantry Regiment advanced west over Omicourt and Malmy at 1500 hours, and attacked its first intermediate objective, the key heights north of Vendresse, at 1530 hours. After the 1st Battalion captured the heights and the town, the French counterattacked with a reinforced tank battalion. As the short battle came to a close, at 1730 hours, between 30 and 40 enemy tanks were mired in the swampy low ground west of Vendresse. The 1st Company/1st Panzer Regiment and 4th Company/2nd Panzer Regiment also destroyed several French 35-ton tanks and numerous self-propelled antitank guns. North of Vendresse, the 2nd and 3rd Infantry Battalions advanced toward Signy. Third Battalion seized the town at midnight, thus reaching the objective set by Guderian at 1400 hours.[38]

Second Panzer Division's fortune changed late in the afternoon when it finally managed to get the remainder of its infantry regiment across the river near Donchery. With air attacks dwindling in the afternoon, and the assistance of the heavy artillery battalion, the Division neutralized a number of bunkers in its crossing sector. Engineers immediately constructed a 16-ton bridge, while simultaneously ferrying other light equipment. In the meantime, one of the Panzer regiments captured another crossing site over the Ardennes Canal at St. Aignan and drove north to link up with the infantry near Pont-a-Baar. Pont-a-Baar was the fourth bridge over the Ardennes Canal the Corps captured through a *coup de main*. At 1800 hours the 2nd Panzer Division assembled nearly 100 tanks near Pont-a-Baar to conduct a coordinated division attack on two axes. One axis advanced over Dom le Mesnil to capture Flize, the other over Hannogne to Signy. Supported by artillery and Stukas, the armor heavy force attacked along the Meuse River, completely surprising the French 3rd Battalion/

148th Fortress Regiment. Second Panzer Division struck them in the flank, and rolled up their defenses. The French also experienced a peculiar problem in that their bunkers were all oriented toward the north. Since the Germans attacked from the flank and rear, the bunkers' 2.5 cm antitank guns were useless. After reaching Dom le Mesnil at 2000 hours, the Division continued the advance striking the French 102nd Fortress Division's flank. French resistance crumbled, allowing 2nd Panzer Division to pass through Flize and right on to Boulzicourt. The advance along the southern axis also made excellent progress, linking up with the 1st Panzer Division at Sapogne just after 2100 hours. Thus, at 2400 hours on May 14, XIXth Panzer Corps stood on a line Boulzicourt–Signy–Omont (see Appendix A, Map 10).[39]

Guderian suspended all actions for the night, probably because the divisions were nearly out of fuel and ammunition. Fuel resupply was not at a critical stage yet. However, the supply officer for the 2nd Panzer Division complained late in the afternoon that he had no idea where half of his fuel columns were located. Supply and fuel columns were not authorized on tactical march routes, relegating the carriers of these vital commodities to secondary roads trying to locate fuel and ammunition distribution points. Guderian returned to his command post early in the evening to work out the next day's operation with his chief of staff. He planned to continue westward to Wasigny–Rethel, leaving 10th Panzer Division, reinforced with "Grossdeutschland," protecting the bridgehead's southern flank until relieved by infantry units from 12th Army. Von Kleist agreed with Guderian's aims during a 1830 hour radio conversation, but changed his mind at 2230 hours.[40]

General von Kleist, concerned about the threat from the south, wanted XIXth Panzer Corps to suspend movements westward until the bridgehead could be strengthened by follow-on infantry. Guderian, however, immediately opposed his commander and accused him of giving away the German victory to the French. Based on the latest intelligence reports, Guderian considered the flank threat minimal, and reminded von Kleist of the operational goal. Rather abrasive, Guderian suggested the Panzer Group misused uncommitted divisions by not employing them in the battle. Guderian further proposed the Panzer Group should have those uncommitted divisions following XIXth Panzer Corps providing more depth and flank security. He felt that by striking deep immediately, Allied counteroffensive plans would be spoiled and thus provide an additional measure of security. After a 30-minute conversation, von Kleist agreed with Guderian and authorized the advance to Wasigny–Rethel. At 2315 hours von Kleist called Nehring to impress upon him OKH's disapproval of the continued advance westward. However, at 0045 hours on May 15 the Panzer Group sent a teletype message confirming the day's objectives.[41]

The Panzer Group's operation order contained the previously outlined missions, but reflected needed task organization changes. Tenth Panzer Division and Infantry Regiment "Grossdeutschland" would be detached from XIXth Panzer Corps to XIVth Motorized Corps. XIXth Panzer Corps received the 2nd

Infantry Division (motorized) in return. The new command relationship would not take effect until noon on May 15, when Guderian would also turn over responsibility of the bridgehead to XIVth Motorized Corps. In the meantime he ordered 10th Panzer Division to advance to the line Ardennes Canal–Meuse River south of Villemontry.[42]

XIXth Panzer Corps engaged five and one-half French divisions throughout May 14. The enemy's counterattacks failed, resulting in the capture of over 3,000 prisoners of war, nearly 100 armored vehicles, numerous artillery pieces, and aircraft. Guderian's divisions proved themselves, breaking through the extended Maginot Line and opening the path to the English Channel. What many officers considered impossible, XIXth Panzer Corps achieved in 32 hours. The price was not cheap, since several units were considerably reduced in strength and many of the leaders were either wounded or dead. The Meuse River crossing operation, on the tactical level, was a major victory. However, in the overall concept of Halder's campaign plan it would only be decisive if it resulted in a pursuit to the Channel. Guderian, a true operational thinker, one of a select group of officers with the ability to focus beyond the tactical level during battle, never lost sight of Sedan as strictly a means to the greater end. It was also a doctrinal victory for the German Army. Outnumbered and outgunned at several engagements, the Germans executed their mobile warfare doctrine and outmaneuvered and defeated their enemy. The slow methodical manner in which the French advanced, lacking basic tactical maneuvers during the armor engagements, and repeatedly attacking the Germans frontally rather than in the flank, proved fatal. On numerous French counterattacks, German forces spoiled their plans by striking in the flank while they were preparing to attack.[43]

The remarkable achievements by Guderian's Panzer divisions have a tendency to cast a shadow on some rather obvious problems in German doctrine. Balck's overextended position on the morning of the 14th could have cost the Germans the battle. Since the Panzer divisions did not normally task organize, with the exception of the advance guards and forward detachments, the mechanized and tank forces remained pure. Thus Balck's infantry regiment had to advance without tank support or heavy artillery. German doctrine called for keeping the Panzer brigade intact, so that it was always available for the decisive blow. Had the French counterattacked an hour earlier, the situation at end of the day may have looked somewhat different. The Germans learned quickly from this lesson and formed Kampfgruppen (task forces) after Sedan, task organizing infantry and armor.[44]

For the first time since the offensive began, XIXth Panzer Corps required a massive resupply effort to sustain its forces in battle. As discussed earlier, ammunition and fuel were brought forward several times during the day. From all indications though, the logistics system functioned properly. On a larger scale, Panzer Group von Kleist requested Army Group A to establish a forward fuel and supply depot at Charleville because the lines of communication were badly stretched. The Army Group agreed, and designated forces began the movement of supplies and fuel trains on May 15. The Panzer Group also informed Army Group A to raise the ammunition priorities to the same level as fuel, reflecting the increased expenditure rates.[45]

OKH's intelligence experts busily analyzed reconnaissance reports on May 14 in an effort to determine whether the French were repositioning reserve forces, which would indicate a counteroffensive. Foreign Armies West reported no significant enemy movements toward Rethel or the bridgehead. This meant that, although resisting fiercely, French forces opposing the bridgehead would not be reinforced. For the fifth day in a row the French failed to detach reserves from the Maginot sector. The intelligence officers did identify a new infantry division, the 53rd, and several independent armored battalions during the tank battles. What amazed the intelligence analysts at OKH was the apparent paralysis of the French General Staff in not sending large reserves against the Sedan bridgehead. Five days passed and the French attempted no major counteroffensive. All indications led to the conclusion that the French could not alter the situation on the 15th. A movement of French reserves toward the breakthrough would take several days. Foreign Armies West's original analysis of French reactions and intentions remained unchanged.[46]

Victory in Sight

The breakthrough operation on May 15 developed in a classic manner and set the stage for the pursuit to the Channel. As a result the bridgehead was enlarged to a depth of 25 km and a width of 50 km. West of the Ardennes Canal, XIXth Panzer Corps operated with 1st and 2nd Panzer Divisions, advancing to Poix-Terron–La Bascule–La Horne–Bouvellemont before midnight, and to Montcornet by early morning the following day. French resistance, as predicted, remained fierce, and at La Horne the Spahi Brigade[47] put up an exceptionally valiant struggle hindering the German advance for several hours. The Spahis established a thorough defensive system around La Horne, depriving Balck's infantry regiment of an easy victory. Several attempts by the 3rd Battalion to roll up the enemy frontally failed. La Horne had thick woods bordering it to the north and flat open terrain in the south. Balck ordered the 2nd Battalion to maneuver through the dense forest in an effort to outflank the Spahis. He decided to accompany 2nd Battalion, and while making their way through the jungle-like dense underbrush, they surprised the regimental staff of the 2nd Spahi Regiment. After several minutes of hand-to-hand combat, the Spahi commander was killed and the remainder of the staff surrendered. Once on the far side of the forest, Balck decided to attack La Horne again, only this time employing a combined frontal and flank assault. The casualties in this engagement were indicative of the intensity of the battle and the Spahi's resolve not to give up easily. Twenty-seven Spahi officers were killed, another seven wounded, and with them died 610 brave soldiers. The Spahi Brigade ceased to exist, and 1st Infantry Regiment continued its advance toward Bouvellemont.[48]

The Panzer Brigade advanced south of 1st Infantry Regiment and had been stopped for hours at Chagny, located southeast of Bouvellemont. The defenders there also refused to yield, grinding 1st Panzer Brigade's advance to a standstill. Balck's regiment reached a small hilly area northeast of Bouvellemont as twilight fell upon the battlefield. First Infantry Regiment's soldiers were completely exhausted and unable to go any further; the day had been extremely hot and combat fatigue was making the men weary. The soldiers were without food all day, since rations could not be brought forward and what little water they carried was consumed hours ago. To make matters worse, they were nearly out of ammunition. Casualties, although minor at each separate engagement over the past few days, began to add up. Balck knew of the tanker's predicament at Chagny, and recognized the importance of Bouvellemont. If he captured Bouvellemont, the French at Chagny would be cut off. Realizing what was at stake, Balck gathered his commanders and issued the necessary orders for the attack. For the first time the officers expressed reservation about attacking an objective in light of the soldiers' condition, and pleaded for a night's rest. Balck refused to accept their arguments. However, he found himself in a serious leadership dilemma since no one moved to implement his orders. Raised in the old tradition, unable to take no for an answer, and realizing that all the orders in the world would not motivate his officers and men to attack, Balck simply stood up and proclaimed that, "If you do not want to, then I will take the village myself,"[49] and began walking toward Bouvellemont. The French 15th Legere Mechanique Regiment defended the town and had been engaging the Germans with sporadic machine gun fire. Balck walked no further than 100 meters when the officers and men, realizing the seriousness of their commander's proclamation, jumped up and joined him. The artillery battalion already in position provided fire support. The French fought ferociously, requiring Balck's men to capture the village house by house. The defenders refused to yield and thus had to be annihilated. Balck's men captured eight tanks during the process. Lieutenant-Colonel Balck received the Knight's Cross for his actions on May 15, 1940. At Chagny, the French probably recognized the hopelessness of their situation, and retreated under the cover of darkness. Their retreat signaled the collapse of the last organized resistance by French forces in the breakout sector. Second Panzer Division captured Poix-Terron and La Bascule earlier in the day, hoping to link up with elements of the XLIst Panzer Corps advancing from Charleville-Mézières. Throughout the night of 15 to 16 May, both Panzer divisions reorganized, resupplied, and continued the advance which rapidly developed into a pursuit (see Appendix A, Map 11).[50]

During the night Panzer Group von Kleist received orders from OKH to suspend all westward movements. OKH worried that the Panzer Group, penetrating too deep behind the enemy's rear, may be cut off and defeated in detail. They wanted to wait for 12th and 16th Armies' infantry to effectively strengthen the bridgehead and protect the southern flank before commencing west. Guderian and Reinhardt promptly protested to von Kleist. XIXth Panzer Corps' commander went so far as to threaten disobedience in face of any restraint order. Guderian repeatedly explained his concept, first to Zeitzler, then to von Kleist, emphasizing the importance of continued pressure on the French. Only a pursuit, Guderian argued, would deny the Allies time to rest, regroup, or counterattack. Furthermore, he underscored the Panzer Group's freedom of action, which would be threatened if it were entangled in an infantry battle. General von Kleist successfully argued the Panzer Group's case with OKH, and in view of the strong protest by the Corps and Group commanders, Halder agreed to retract the order. With this decision von Kleist ended a particularly good day, since Colonel Schmundt, Hitler's Wehrmacht Adjutant, delivered the Führer's personal greetings with the Knight's Cross during the afternoon.[51]

Guderian spurred on his division commanders throughout the night, driving first to the headquarters of the 2nd Panzer Division, followed by a visit to the 1st Panzer Division. Later, to the amazement of his tankers, he passed lead elements of the 1st Panzer Division on their way to Montcornet, where he met with the commander of the 6th Panzer Division, of Reinhardt's XLIst Panzer Corps. The link up at Montcornet established a two-corps front for the Panzer Group. Guderian and the 6th Panzer Division's commander coordinated the boundaries established in the Panzer Group order and commenced the pursuit to the Channel Coast. Enemy actions on May 16 demonstrated just how decisive the victory at the Meuse River had been. As the Panzer columns advanced westward unimpeded, they passed streams of retreating French soldiers. Not organized to handle prisoners of war (POW), the German tankers simply disarmed them, piled their weapons along the side of the road, drove over the weapons, and directed the French to the nearest POW collection center. The Panzer Group reached Abbeville on May 19 and the mouth of the Somme River the following day. General Halder's campaign plan unfolded as scheduled and the Allied armies were cut in half. Confidence levels at OKH, after the successful Meuse crossings and the breakout, were summed up by Halder when he confided in Colonel Wagner on May 18 that he felt like the blue forces leader in a war game, fully cognizant of the red team's actions in advance.[52]

Logistics burdened the forces in the bridgehead and breakout sectors on May 15, because ground transportation columns could not get to combat units. The Luftwaffe flew several resupply missions air-dropping both fuel and ammunition into forward lines. Taxed to its maximum capabilities, the Luftwaffe requested Army Group A to remind its units that aerial resupply missions should only be called for in emergencies. Traffic problems probably were the main cause for transportation units failing to resupply combat units with ammunition and fuel. Infantry armies hastened to reinforce the bridgehead and the flanks of the break-through blocked all roads into the Sedan sector. A very limited road network between the Semois and Meuse Rivers compounded the Panzer Group's problems, because both supply and combat units needed to cross the bridges at the same time. Von Kleist became so infuriated that he contacted von Rundstedt's headquarters, demanding that a responsible officer be flown to the crossing sites to reestablish control. Traffic problems, although annoying, did not hinder forward combat units from accomplishing their missions.[53]

On the morning of May 16, General Guderian was elated. His XIXth Panzer Corps achieved in six days what the German Army of 1914 could not accomplish in four years. As far as he was concerned, a westward drive to the Channel was all that remained to defeat France and her Allies. Hitler queried Guderian during a briefing on February 14, 1940, about his intentions, should a river crossing and a breakthrough at Sedan succeed. Guderian then simply replied, "I intend on the next day to continue my advance westward. The supreme leadership must decide whether my objective is to be Amiens or Paris. In my opinion the correct course is to drive past Amiens to the English Channel."[54] On the morning of May 16, 1940, XIXth Panzer Corps had successfully accomplished what Guderian predicted 90 days earlier.

5

Efficiency Mania

Viel leisten, wenig hervortreten, mehr sein als scheinen,
muss sich jeder Generalstabsoffizier zum Walhspruch nehmen.
(Work relentlessly, accomplish much, remain in the background, and be more
than you seem, must be the guiding motto of every General Staff officer.)
Feldmarschall Graf Schlieffen, April 1, 1930

XIXth Panzer Corps' success during the first five days of the Battle of France
can not be attributed to any one single factor or event, but rather a combination
of planning and training executed under the guidance of the German Army
General Staff. The roots of the operation emerged in the latter part of September
1939 when Hitler confronted the service chiefs with his decision to attack
France. A reluctant Army General Staff, led by General Franz Halder,
attempted for two months to dissuade the Führer from this venture, because the
officers felt it was not in the best interest of the German Army, nor the German
nation to attack France. When, however, Hitler left them no alternative, they
conceded and planned "Fall Gelb," establishing a clear goal of defeating
France. The officers on the General Staff and those occupying command and
general staff positions within the Field Army were the driving force in the
success of the May 1940 offensive. Who then were these men?

Every key position on the General Staff and in the Field Army was occupied
by officers from the original 4,000-officer Reichsheer cadre.[1] The creators of
the Reichswehr trained its officers in the tradition of von Schlieffen and von
Moltke. Captain Truman Smith, the U.S. Military Attaché in Berlin and an
analyst of Reichswehr and Wehrmacht conditions, noted in 1936 "that the

Reichswehr officer corps was, in the opinion of all competent foreign observers, the most highly trained, efficient, and forward looking officer corps in the world."[2] They were officers rooted and educated in the traditions of the old Imperial Army, living for the day when Germany would again be a major power. In many respects, they lived in the past and the future, but not in the present.[3]

The Versailles Treaty reduced Germany's officer corps to 4,000 active army officers. With a pool of ten times as many to chose from, the creator of the new post-war army, General Hans von Seeckt, retained only the very best. The limitations of the treaty forced von Seeckt to stress quality and performance in the officer corps. These virtues in turn attracted men yearning for elitism, tradition, and the idealism of the military profession. The requirements of the Abitur further narrowed the selection and ensured that only men with a good general educational background would join the officer ranks. In its training, however, the Reichswehr stressed technical and tactical proficiency rather than generalities. Von Seeckt introduced an Officer Evaluation Report (OER) system that served to identify weak officers and those with potential for advancement. Promotions and dismissals were handed out as a result of this OER system.[4] Competition in the small officer corps was therefore extremely intense, since only one bad OER surely meant dismissal from the Army. Besides technical and tactical qualities, another even more important component of the OER was the officers' character evaluation. Officers raised under von Seeckt's system quickly learned to conform because "everything from curfew violations to substandard performance in the field"[5] fell under the category of character failures. Officers incapable of meeting the expectations of the new Army found themselves without a profession, their vacancy filled quickly, since equally qualified ex-officers were waiting for the chance to prove their qualities. In such a fierce competitive atmosphere only the cream of the crop survived, thus producing a military culture feeding on "efficiency mania." It was this selected corps of officers that planned, trained, and led the German Army of 1939 and 1940.[6]

The General Staff's efforts after September 1939 revolved around two major issues simultaneously, the deployment plan for France and Army reforms as a result of the recently completed Polish Campaign. The Army's campaign in Poland revealed problems that most armies experience when they enter the field of battle after an extended period of peace. The most critical of these deficiencies were faulty junior leadership and improper divisional tables of organization and equipment. More important was the ability and the willingness within the officer corps to identify specific problems and to initiate proper action to ameliorate them.[7] One would have expected very little criticism after the Army's impressive victory in Poland. However, this is another example of the officer corps trained in the "efficiency oriented" Reichsheer of the Weimar Republic. As a result both problems received the necessary attention, the resulting solutions being instrumental in the Army's success in France, but particularly in XIXth Panzer Corps' advance across the Meuse River.[8]

Junior leaders raised under the new National Socialist regime were full of faith and idealism, but lacked training and experience. Von Brauchitsch recognized this deficiency and elected junior leadership as his number one priority over the winter-spring period of 1939-40. Two week courses were established to train young officers and noncommissioned officers on the fundamentals of leadership, tactics, and the caring for their soldiers. These courses were vital to solidifying the tactical backbone of the Army. Concomitantly, battalion and regimental commanders trained to lead battalions and regiments. Schools disseminated a common doctrine and fostered an offensive spirit. Senior commanders, like General von Bock who desired more aggressive leadership, were in no way advocating a blind interpretation of orders that would lead to the "attack-mania" experienced in the officer corps of the late nineteenth century.[9] Training exercises conducted from battalion to divisional levels emphasized officers and NCOs employing initiative within the constraints of the commander's aim. Commanders, in their orders, which used verbal and written statements of intent, provided subordinates with the operational concept and an idea of the big picture. The training period served two purposes. Commanders educated and trained subordinates on what we label Auftragstaktik today, and secondly, to familiarize units with the new TO&Es and weapon systems. Thus, by May 1940, they had a relatively good idea of the limitations of the new equipment, but also enjoyed an opportunity to train their soldiers to overcome those deficiencies. Additionally, commanders could rely on subordinates to comprehend the scope of an order, especially in the midst of a battle. The senior officer knew that his subordinate understood the mission and, aware of his subordinates' strengths and weaknesses, had an approximate idea of how his directives would be executed.

Initially planned as a long-range project after the Polish Campaign, the reorganization of light divisions into Panzer divisions had to be executed at a much faster pace because of Hitler's insistence on an early offensive in the West. The end result provided the Army with ten Panzer and three motorized divisions for "Fall Gelb." It was not the ideal structure, since it incorporated numerous expedients; however, it provided the largest mechanized strike force the world had yet seen.

The German General Staff always planned with a clear perception of main effort. Hitler, though, wrestled with von Brauchitsch and Halder continuously, beginning in October 1939, introducing almost daily changes in an attempt to force his will on military operations. General Halder, however, shielded his officers from these daily annoyances, to allow his staff to conduct the necessary theoretical, operational, and strategic planning, and war gaming required to formulate a campaign plan. It was in essence the General Staff, those trained officers operating under the tutelage of Halder, who finally refined the operation plan executed on May 10, 1940.

Since its creation, the Prusso-German General Staff always enjoyed relative independence in its internal affairs. Throughout the winter and spring period of 1939-40, the General Staff continued to function under the illusion that nothing had changed in the relationship between the political and military leadership. It was, however, during this period that the rift between these two institutions widened significantly. Hitler's meeting with von Brauchitsch on November 5,

1939, followed by the public denunciation of him during the assembly of the senior Wehrmacht commanders on November 20, 1939, must be viewed as a significant turning point between Hitler and the Army. General Halder, however, adhered to the old rules of General Staff independence and provided his staff with the time and freedom to develop a campaign plan based on solid intelligence and tested for its feasibility. Halder disseminated his intentions to field commanders, ensured complete understanding of the concept, and linked air and land combat elements into a highly mobile and flexible combat-experienced force. He designated a Panzer Group as main effort and assumed a calculated risk by launching it against the weakest sector on the Allied line.[10]

The most important aspect of this plan, however, was its link to the Field Army through a thorough understanding of the operational goals. The doctrinal concept of leaders leading from the front further enhanced the plan's chances for success, because leaders were in a position to take full advantage of unforeseen opportunities, rather than relying on subjective and garbled reports from the front. The Army, during its developmental stages, recognized the need for communication in its doctrine of mobile warfare and provided commanders at all levels with the necessary means to accomplish their tasks. Thus, commanders were free to command by positioning themselves at the perceived critical point. The chief of staff, as the commanders' deputy and technical expert, guided the staff through its routine of running the organization. Commanders and chiefs of staff were a very close knit team since the chief of staff, sometimes able to focus on a much broader scale than the commander, had the prerogative of issuing orders contrary to the commander.[11] It is not by mistake that the relationship between a commander and his chief of staff was labeled a marriage.

During the offensive operations, adherence to fundamental rules, doctrinal concepts, and a solid plan significantly contributed to the German Army's success. The command and control structure, well in hand, enabled OKH to control its armies in a taut manner rather than allowing them to operate on loose reins as was the case in 1914. Actions at operational and tactical levels resulted from commanders clearly understanding von Brauchitsch's intent. The Army General Staff profited from the lessons of the initial phases of the Western Campaign in World War I where commanders, unaware of changes to the operational concept because of a lack of communications, conducted isolated tactical actions that spoiled the campaign plan. This campaign is probably the last opportunity to study the German Army's General Staff as an independent instrument, enjoying relatively little interference from Hitler. Wilhelm Weiss, chief editor of *Der Völkische Beobachter*,[12] noted in his 1941 book *Triumph der Kriegskunst* that "the calm atmosphere in which the officers of the General Staff conducted themselves was reminiscent of an institution rooted in the knowledge and experience of generations before them."[13] As such the General Staff evaluated situations and maneuvered its armies to an unprecedented success. It would lose this luxury in another year and a half. Unfortunately, General von Brauchitsch and his General Staff did not receive the proper credit for their actions. The label of greatest military genius went to Adolf Hitler.[14]

Commanders down to battalion level in Guderian's Panzer divisions understood the operational concept in 1940, and thus were able to take full advantage of unexpected circumstances. Intense training during the winter and spring period, at all levels, prepared commanders for the mental challenges of making those critical decisions. The numerous war games conducted at army group, army, and corps provided them with the opportunity to study all aspects of the upcoming battle. At the unit level, repeated river crossings at locations closely resembling the actual crossing sites, leaders rehearsed their tasks until they became second nature. At the training centers, mechanized infantry units practiced attacking fortified locations, tankers refined their armor movement techniques, and both incorporated the Luftwaffe into combined arms warfare. Through this rigorous training period, leaders perfected the mobile warfare doctrine that ultimately led them to victory in France.

Armament, discussed earlier, presented notable problems to German tankers. However, a thorough understanding of doctrine aided in overcoming the shortfalls. Guderian instilled in his tankers the idea that the engines of their vehicles were just as important as their weapons. Thus, through flexibility, tactical mobility, and employment of combined arms the Germans negated their deficiencies. The German Army's training doctrine during the winter and spring period further instilled the necessary offensive spirit and linked the Luftwaffe more closely to the ground commander. Guderian's close coordination with von Stutterheim throughout spring facilitated the planning effort of both commanders for the Meuse River operation. Von Stutterheim, also a product of the Weimar Republic's Reichswehr, knew what the ground force commander expected from the Luftwaffe, and thus concentrated the available time to plan properly and train for the most effective support possible. Guderian, on the other hand, could rely on von Stutterheim's pilots to supplement his lack of artillery. The close working relationship between the two commanders and their staffs resulted in von Stutterheim providing the support for the river crossings that he and Guderian coordinated, rather than what von Kleist and Sperrle demanded. The German Army was also able to exploit the failures of the Allied General Staffs, since the advance through the Ardennes, a calculated risk, would probably have taken on a different course had the French known in advance of the intended Belgian withdrawal, or had they employed stronger forces along the Sedan–Mézières sector.

While the German Army, through a rigorous training program, incorporated lessons learned from the Polish Campaign, the French failed to suitably evaluate the massed use of tanks and aircraft. Although recognizing the potential threat, French doctrine was not changed. OKH always worked with a clear understanding of main effort, while the French, falling for the German deception plan, positioned and oriented their main effort at the wrong location. Once the offensive commenced, they failed to evaluate properly German intentions, and even after the Meuse crossings, remained idle and incapable of mounting a significant counteroffensive. The French High Command neglected to recognize the value of combining motorization and mechanization with the Luftwaffe into a combined arms doctrine. The French failed to organize their armored forces for mass employment, engaging them piecemeal over the entire front, and thus incapable of providing the penetration effect of a massed armored formation. A lack of mobile doctrine, command and control, and combined arms warfare further resulted in the failure of their only massed armored attack, on May 14, by the 3rd Armored and 3rd Mechanized Divisions. Concomitantly, the French General Staff miscalculated its ability to move reserves by 75 percent on transit times alone, failing to plan both for roads congested with civilian refugees, and the Luftwaffe's bombing campaign.

The most essential lesson is that the German Army was not a myth, but was rather very similar to most other Western armies. It faced the same problems that other armies faced. However, what made the German Army different was its ability and willingness to evaluate itself and undertake the necessary changes to improve in both personnel and training. Through years of "efficiency aimed" training and a common doctrine, staffs were able to dispense with lengthy operation orders during the actual campaign and simply operate with fragmentary orders. The concept of commanders at the front ensured more face to face discussion between commanders and subordinates, contributing not only to higher confidence levels in the command, but also furnishing a clear understanding of the leaders' aims. Like the United States Army, dedicated officers and NCOs enabled the German Army to overcome inherent friction. Numerous General Staff officers like the Wagners, Zeitzlers, and Nehrings, folloiwng Field Marshal Count von Schlieffen's principle that "staff officers should work relentlessly, accomplish much, remain in the background, and be more than they seem," contributed as much if not more to the success in May 1940 than the flamboyant Guderians and Rommels. Since corps staffs organized on tactical lines were rather small, logistics, for example, remained largely the function of divisional and army staffs. As chief logistician in the Army High Command, Wagner deserves much of the credit for the logistics plan during the Battle of France. Without his pioneering of aerial resupply, the Panzer divisions could not have maintained their momentum. He engineered a logistics effort, establishing intermediate depots, and resupplying 300 km beyond the rail heads on May 18, 1940. Such innovative concepts were unheard of in 1940. When Guderian did not receive his new Mark III's and IV's on time to conduct a detailed training program, dedicated officers and NCOs ensured crews' and units' readiness on May 10, 1940. Von Manstein's insistence of shifting the main effort in the winter of 1939, Zeitzler's traffic control plan, and Liss' intelligence preparation of the battlefield all accumulatively contributed to the success in 1940. We must also not lose sight of the fact that the new generation of officers and NCOs, although instilled with National Socialist faith and ideals, were in fact raised to think and lead themselves. These young men, through the intense training effort, were molded into leaders by the older traditional generation by May 1940.[15]

XIXth Panzer Corps' advance through the Ardennes was a remarkable achievement, but it also provided the German General Staff with a fair amount of lessons learned. Most notably was the need for better traffic control. Without the Panzer Groups' traffic control plan the entire operation in the Ardennes would probably have resulted in a disaster. Zeitzler, however, in his after-action report was very critical of the allocation of forces to traffic control. Additionally, he emphasized the need for a traffic control staff at army headquarters, organized under a separate TO&E, to include airborne traffic control. The traffic control staff, he explained, should have not only the responsibility to plan and carry out all functions, but also be provided with the authority to enforce the plan.[16]

The absolutely sterling planning of both Guderian's and von Kleist's staffs, and the series of war games specifically conducted to analyze the engineer tasks, clearly identified the main effort for the engineers and allowed them to plan and prepare accordingly. The numerous rivers and streams made it a necessity to have as many engineer bridging assets as far forward as possible in the march columns. The campaign also identified a need for more bridging assets since on May 14 Guderian's corps would have had serious problems crossing the Ardennes Canal had it not taken the bridges by a *coup de main*. All of XIXth Panzer Corps' and Panzer Group von Kleist's bridging equipment had been committed. The General Staff's plan to train infantrymen as assault engineers became a key factor, since the unexpectedly vast numbers of barriers and mine-fields in the Ardennes, along with its rivers and streams, could not have been supported by engineers alone. The war games, conducted at all staff levels, served as a tool to identify problems that would not have to be confronted in the heat of battle. General von Brauchitsch, interviewed by a reporter in late 1940, was questioned on whether rivers present significant obstacles in modern warfare. The Army Commander in Chief replied that "the rivers by themselves are not significant obstacles anymore, but rather of greater importance is who attacks and defends them."[17] Without the thorough preparation of the Army, and its modern outlook on combined arms warfare, the Battle of France may well have had a different outcome.

In the final analysis then, it is plain to see that the German Army General Staff planned while the French Army's staff slept. The planning and training combined with the leadership of a dedicated officer corps provided the basis for success. General Guderian simply took advantage of the modern technical equipment and, with an almost reckless daredevil attitude amongst the commanders and officers of his corps, coupled to a complete understanding of the operational concept, led XIXth Panzer Corps through the successful operations from May 10 to 15, 1940.

1. Field Marshal Ewald von Kleist. Photograph courtesy of the National Archives.

2. General Heinz Guderian with the commander of the Corps Reconnaissance Battalion (directly behind Guderian) and engineers in Bouillon, Belgium, May 2, 1940. Guderian's aide de camp, Captain Kriebel, stands to his left. Photograph courtesy of the National Archives.

3. OKH field headquarters, Fontainebleau, France, September 1940. Field Marshal Walter von Brauchitsch faces the camera and General Halder is second from right. Photograph courtesy of the National Archives.

4. General Friedrich Kirchner issues orders to his staff on the evening of May 11, 1940. His G3, Lieutenant-Colonel Walther Wenck is to Kirchner's right. Photograph courtesy of the National Archives.

5. Fortifications at Bodange, Belgium, May 10, 1940. Photograph courtesy of the National Archives.

6. Elements of 1st Panzer Regiment on the advance between Bouillon and Sedan, May 13, 1940. Photograph courtesy of the National Archives.

7. A German lieutenant interrogates a French prisoner of war near Mouzaive, Belgium, May 11, 1940. Photograph courtesy of the National Archives.

8. Traffic jam in Bouillon, Belgium, May 12, 1940. Photograph courtesy of the National Archives.

9. Advancing armored reconnaissance vehicles, passing traffic, on the road to Martelange, May 11, 1940. Note the 20 mm anti-aircraft half-tracks. Photograph courtesy of the National Archives.

10. German engineers quickly bridged this cratered road near Brisy, Belgium, May 11, 1940. Photograph courtesy of the National Archives.

11. In a gorge in the Our Valley, May 11, 1940. German engineers hastily bridged a cratered section of a mountain for advancing German troops. Photograph courtesy of the National Archives.

12. Camouflaged elements of the 1st Panzer Regiment in a forward assembly area, May 13, 1940. Photograph courtesy of the National Archives.

13. Along the Semois River near Mouzaive, Belgium, May 12, 1940, engineers begin to build a bridge in the foreground, while armored elements cross a ford site down stream. Photograph courtesy of the National Archives.

14. A bridge column and mechanized infantry vehicles in the traffic jam in Bouillon, Belgium, May 13, 1940. Photograph courtesy of the National Archives.

15. 1st Panzer Division bridge column on the road to Martelange, May 10, 1940. Note the "K" on some of the vehicles. Photograph courtesy of the National Archives.

16. 1st Panzer Regiment's trains on the road to Bertrix, May 11, 1940. Photograph courtesy of the National Archives.

17. Ferry operations across the Semois River, May 12, 1940. Photograph courtesy of the National Archives.

18. A Panzer Mark III slipped into an obstacle in Cheveuges, France, May 14, 1940. Photograph courtesy of the National Archives.

19. A typical infantry company trains during the Battle of France. Note the multiple modes of transportation. Photograph courtesy of the National Archives.

20. Infantry prepares for the Meuse River crossing, May 13, 1940. Photograph courtesy of the National Archives.

21. Infantry crossing a makeshift bridge, May 12, 1940. Photograph courtesy of the National Archives.

Appendices

Appendix A: Situation Maps

Maps Legend

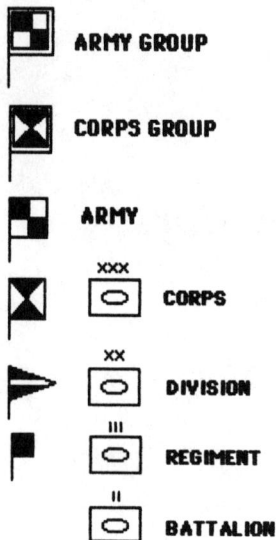

ARMY GROUP

CORPS GROUP

ARMY

CORPS

DIVISION

REGIMENT

BATTALION

BOUNDARIES:

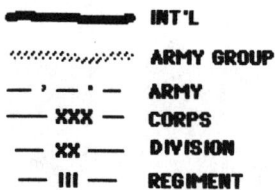

INT'L

ARMY GROUP

ARMY

CORPS

DIVISION

REGIMENT

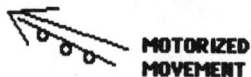

MOTORIZED MOVEMENT

 Assembly area

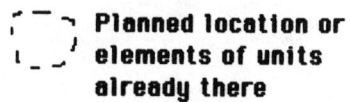 Planned location or elements of units already there

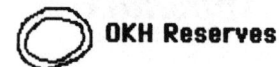 OKH Reserves

Armies are designated with numbers

Corps' are designated with Roman numerals

 PARACHUTE OPERATION

 MAIN EFFORT

 GLIDER OPERATIONS

 FIXED WING AIR ASSAULT

 RAILROAD TRACKS

 DEFENSIVE POSITION

100

Map 1
NIWI Landing Zones

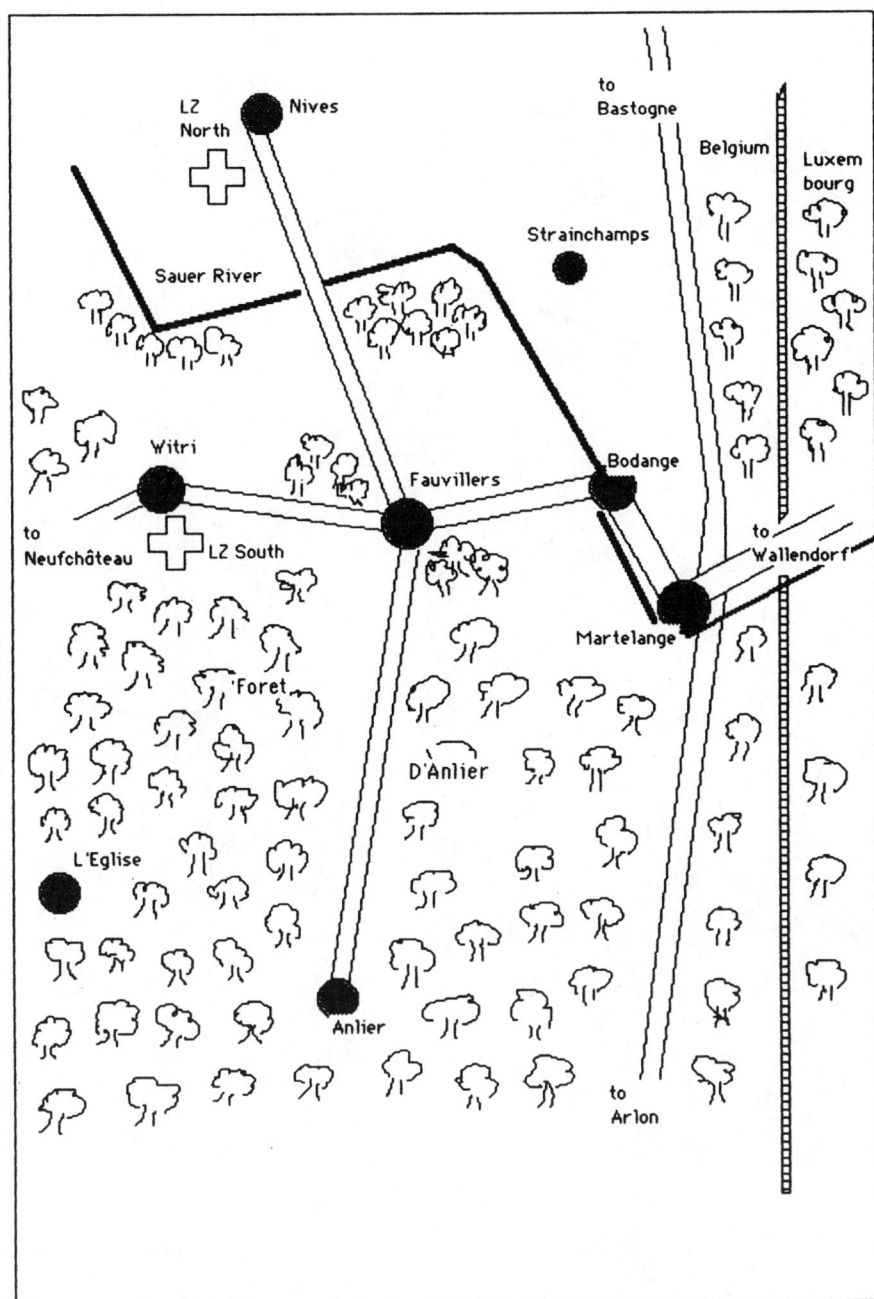

Map 2
Operation NIWI

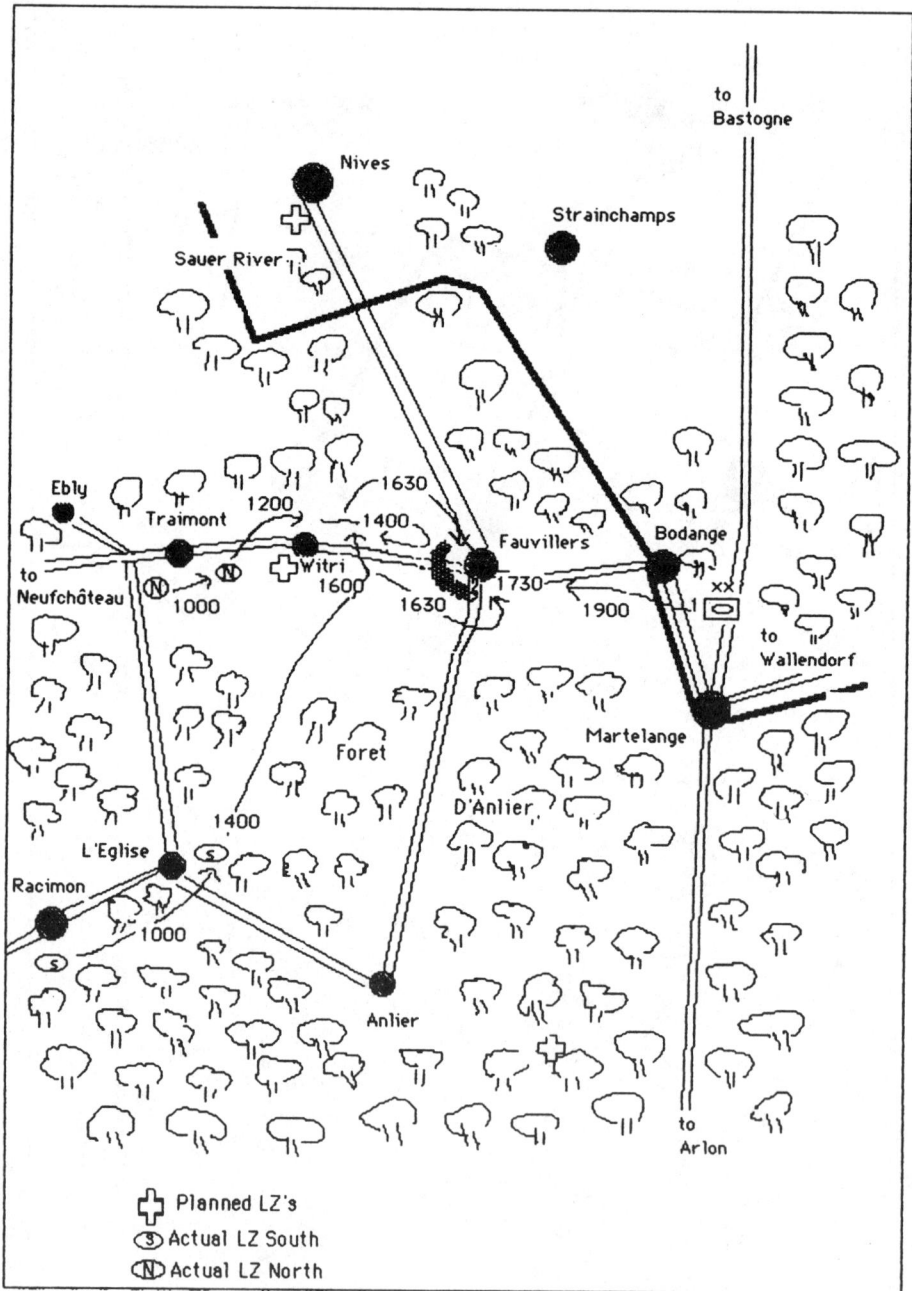

to
Bastogne

Nives

Strainchamps

Sauer River

Ebly

Traimont

1200

1630

1400

Fauvillers

Bodange

to
Neufchâteau

1000

Witri
1600

1630

1730

1900

xx

to
Wallendorf

Foret

Martelange

1400

D'Anlier

L'Eglise

Racimon

1000

Anlier

to
Arlon

Planned LZ's
Ⓢ Actual LZ South
Ⓝ Actual LZ North

102

Map 3
May 10, 1940

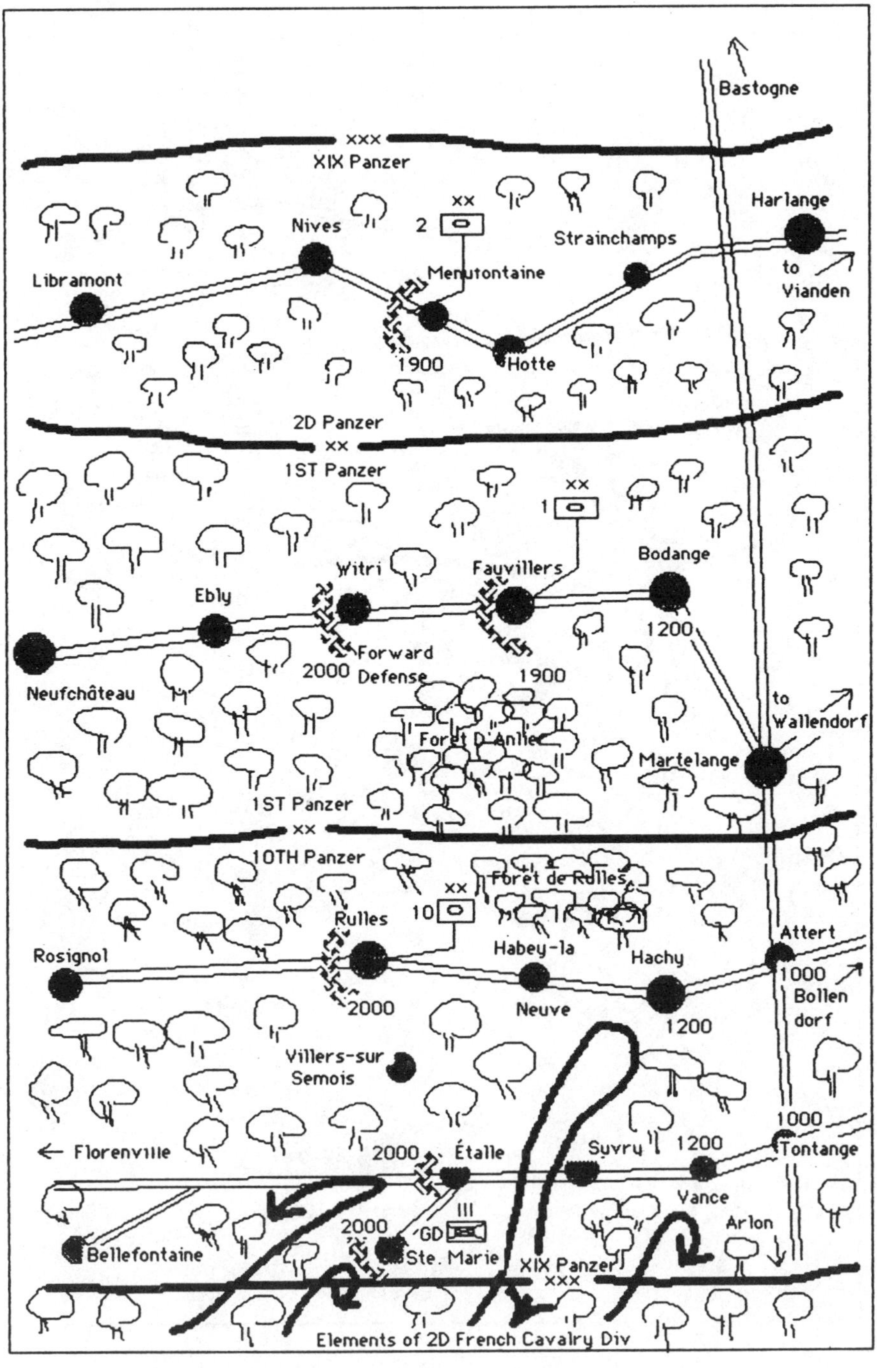

Bastogne

xxx
XIX Panzer

Harlange

Nives

xx
2

Strainchamps

to
Vianden

Libramont

Menutontaine

1900   Hotte

2D Panzer

xx
1ST Panzer

xx
1

Bodange

Witri   Fauvillers

Ebly

1200

Neufchâteau

Forward
2000 Defense   1900

Forêt D'Anlie

to
Wallendorf

Martelange

1ST Panzer

xx
10TH Panzer

Forêt de Rulles

xx
Rulles   10

Attert

Rosignol

Habey-la   Hachy

1000
Bollen
dorf

2000

Neuve   1200

Villers-sur
Semois

1000

← Florenville

2000   Étalle   Suvru   1200   Tontange

Vance

III
2000   GD

Arlon

Bellefontaine   Ste. Marie   XIX Panzer
xxx

Elements of 2D French Cavalry Div

103

Map 4
May 11, 1940

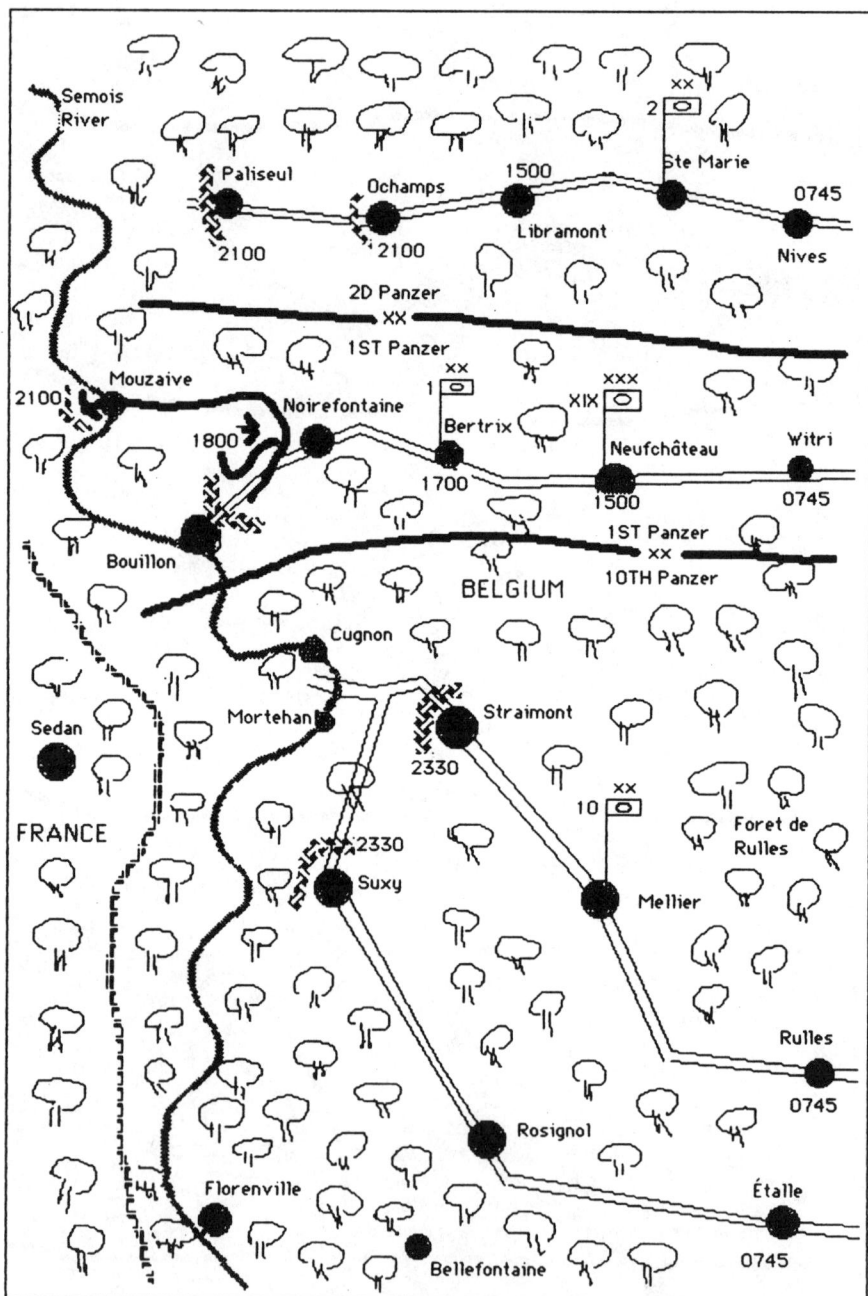

Map 4
May 11, 1940

Map 5
May 12, 1940

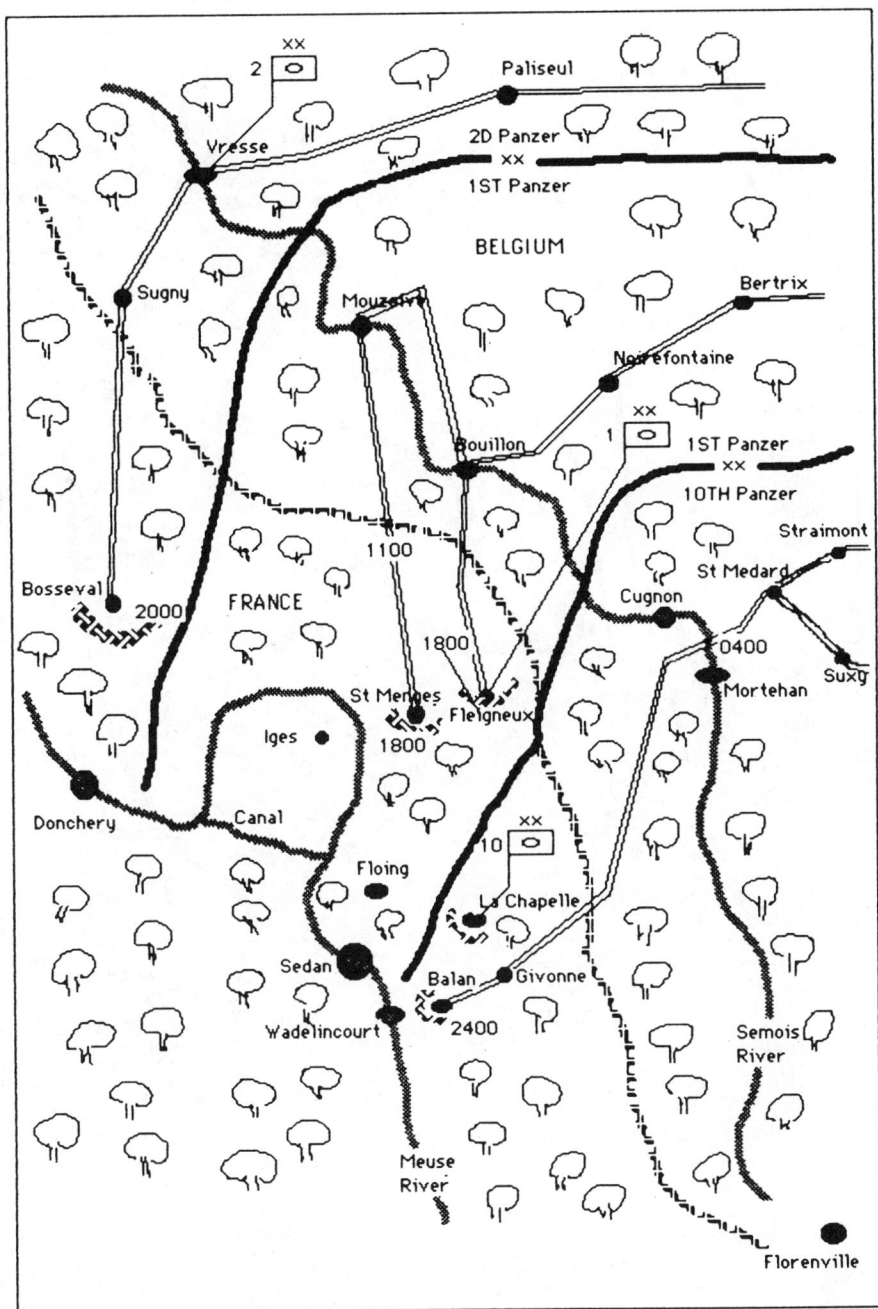

Paliseul

2 | XX | o |

Vresse

2D Panzer
XX
1ST Panzer

BELGIUM

Sugny

Mouzaive

Bertrix

Noirefontaine

Bouillon

1 | XX | o |

1ST Panzer
XX
10TH Panzer

Straimont

St Medard

1100

Cugnon

Bosseval

2000

FRANCE

1800

0400

Suxg

Mortehan

St Menges

1800

Fleigneux

Iges

Donchery

Canal

Floing

10 | XX | o |

La Chapelle

Sedan

Balan

Givonne

Wadelincourt

2400

Semois
River

Meuse
River

Florenville

Map 6
May 13, 1940 (1600 hours)

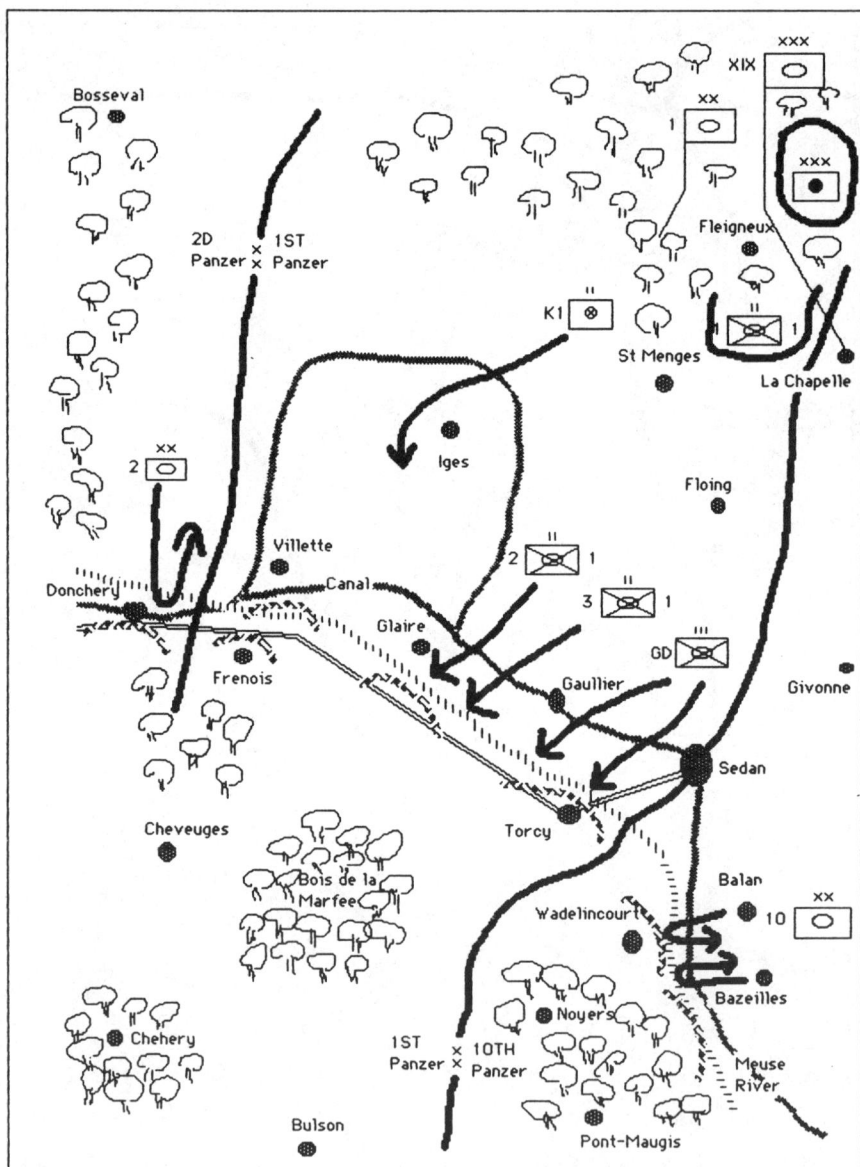

Map 7
May 13, 1940 (1900 hours)

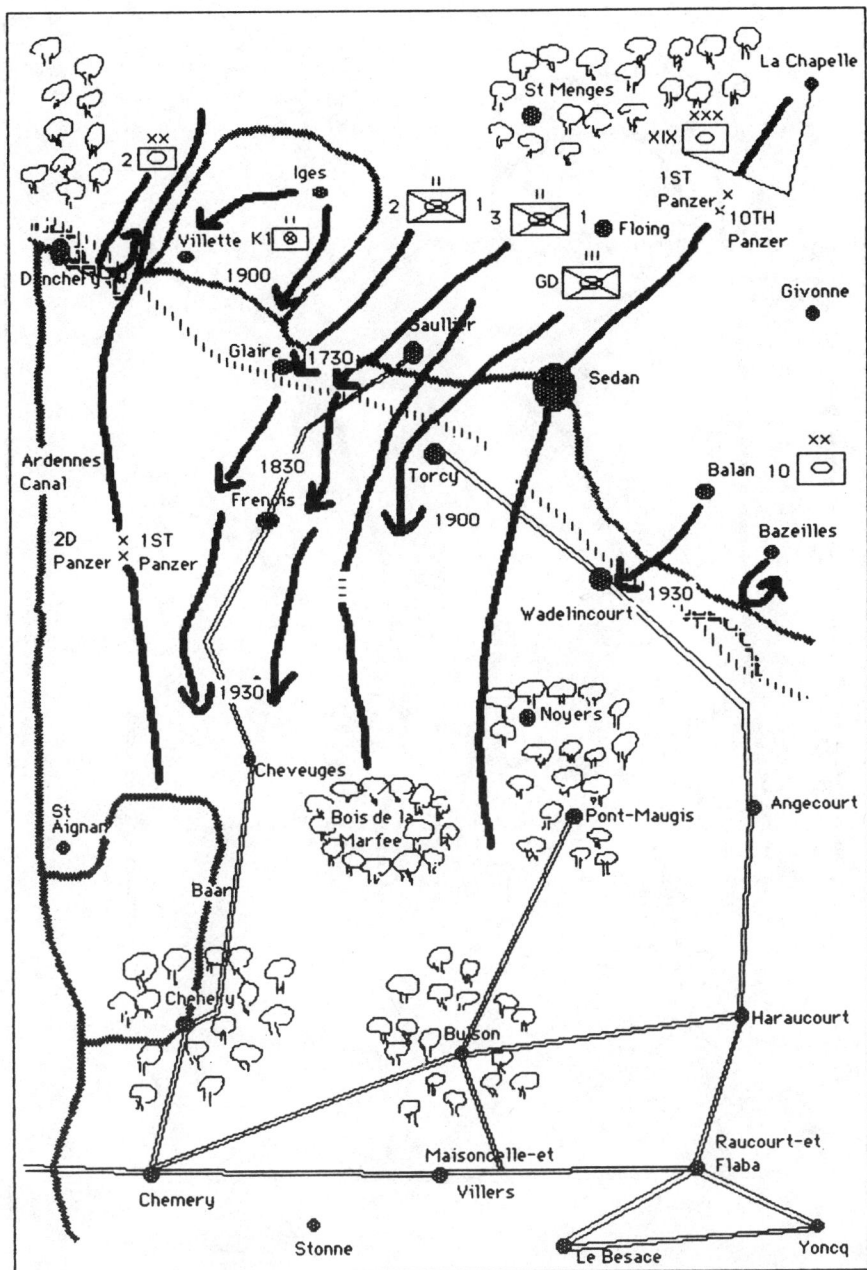

La Chapelle

St Menges

XIX

2

Iges

Villette K1

Dincher?

1900

2 1 3 1

Floing

GD

1ST Panzer

10TH Panzer

Givonne

Glaire 1730

Saullier

Sedan

Ardennes Canal

1830

Freńois

Torcy

1900

Balan 10

Bazeilles

2D Panzer 1ST Panzer

1930

Wadelincourt

1930

Cheveuges

Noyers

St Aignan

Bois de la Marfee

Pont-Maugis

Angecourt

Baan

Chehery

Bulson

Haraucourt

Raucourt-et Flaba

Chemery

Maisoncelle-et Villers

Stonne

Le Besace

Yoncq

107

Map 8
May 13, 1940 (2400 hours)

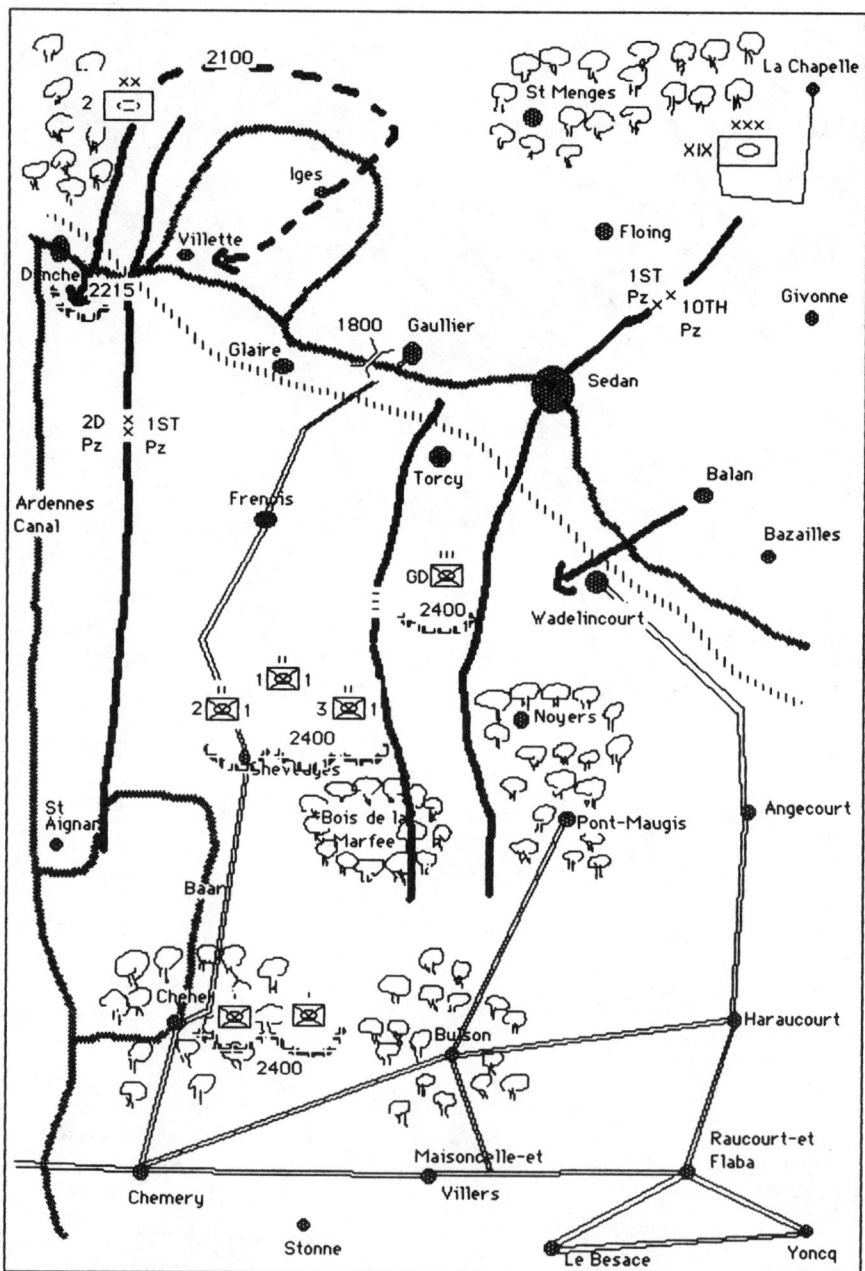

Map 9
May 14, 1940 (Bridgehead action)

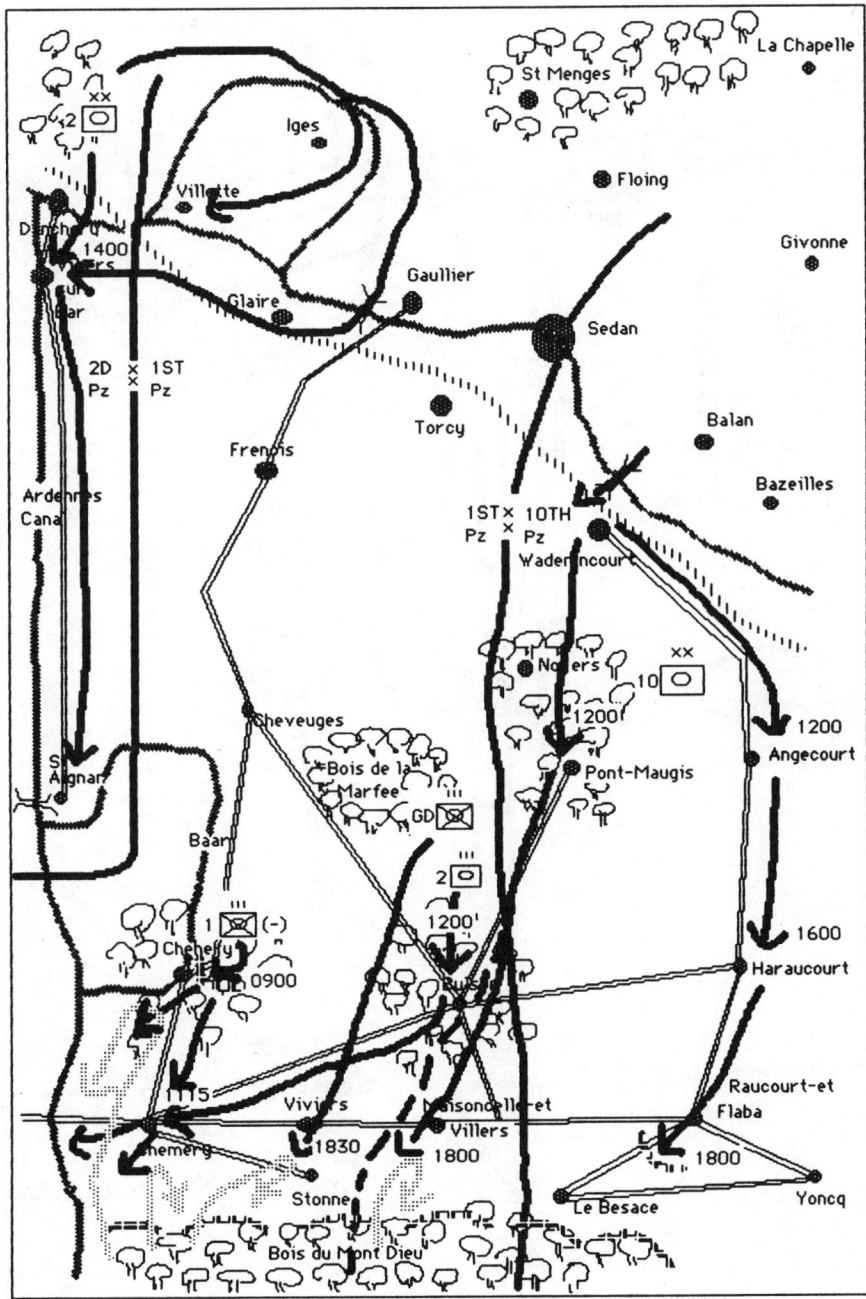

May 10
May 14, 1940 (The Breakout)

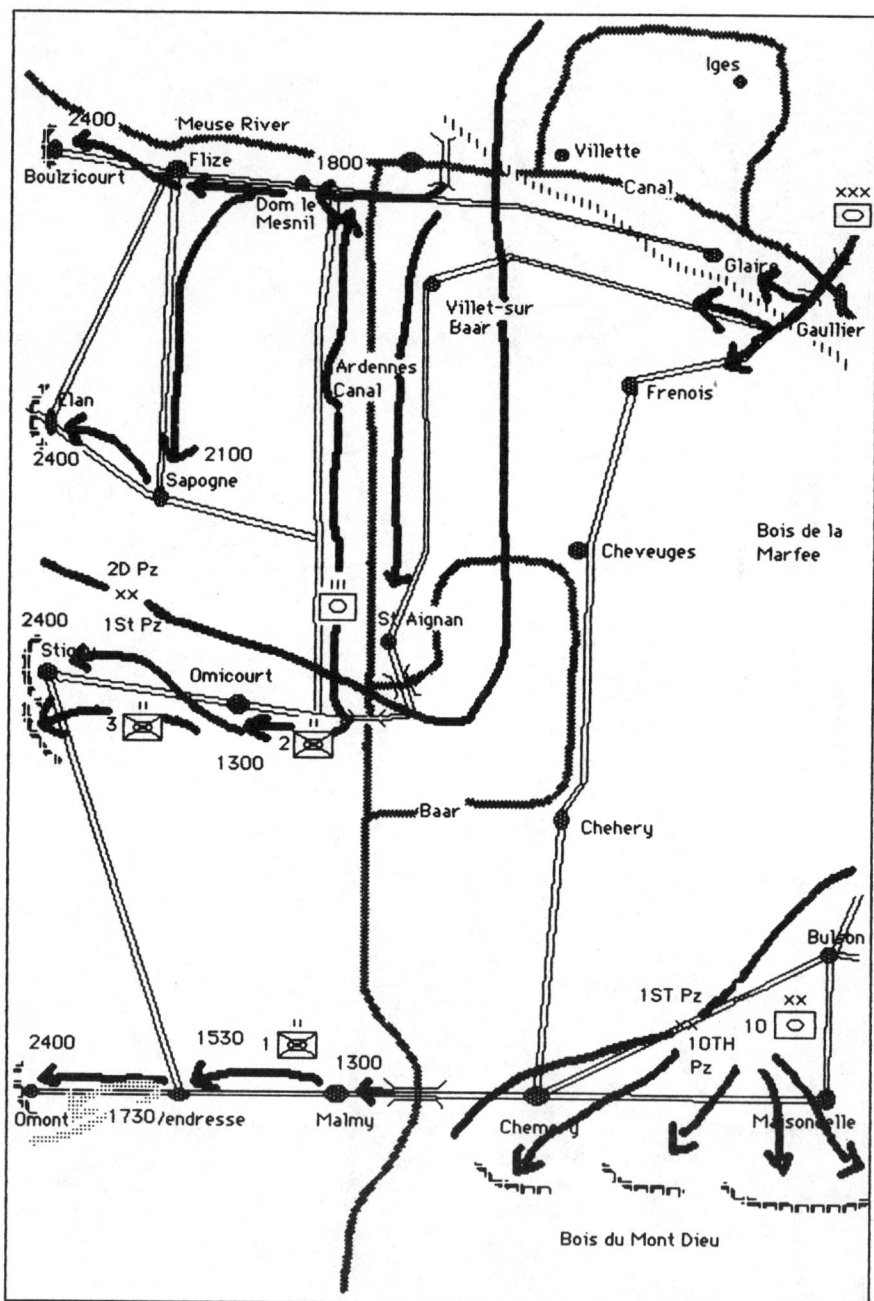

Map 11
May 15 to 16, 1940

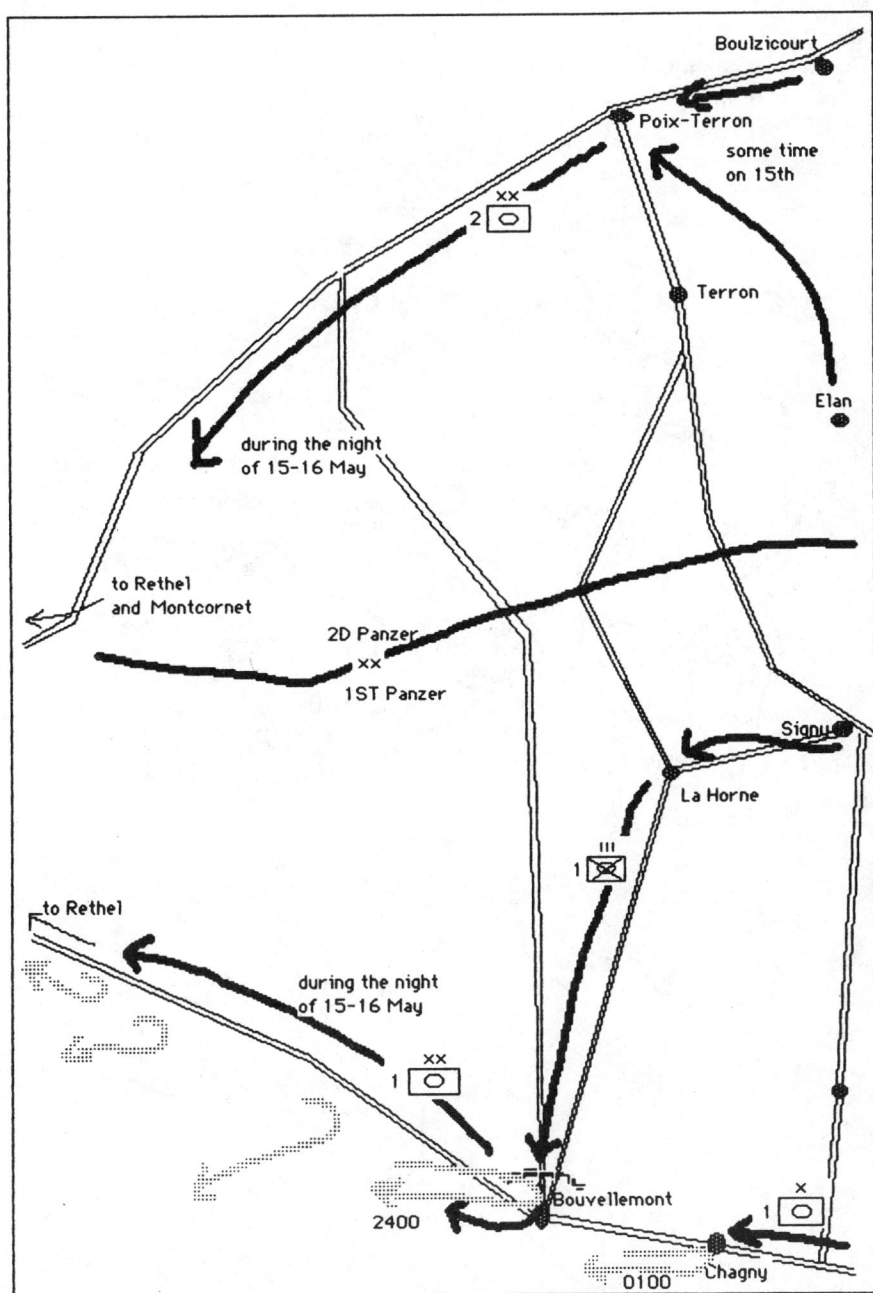

Map 12
German Situation in the West, September 1939[1]

Map 12
German Situation in the West, September 1939[1]

Holland

G.16
G.6
VI.

XXX Duisburg
254.
269.
Rhine
253.
XXVII
267.
A
226.
Aachen
Koeln
263.
Ahr
1/3 76
1/3 76
Meuse Liege
Malmedy
1/3 76
Wetzlar
Namur Belgium
22.
268.
87.
5
Our
216.
XVI
Koblenz
C
211. Kyllbg.
69.
Mosel
River
Germany
IR
58.
Mainz
16. 366 Eifel
Frankfurt
227.
26.
223.
1.
Sedan
Kreuznach
209.
Luxemburg
Trier
231.
Gr Div
XII
IX
Longwy
Saar 86.
45.
175.
Manheim
79. 34.
15. 52.
France
6. 9.
25.
33.
Saarpf
215.
Neckar
2/3 78.
Karlsruhe
Metz
Strasburg
35. Oberrh.
V
Nancy
7.
260.
Colmar
Stuttgart
1/3
78.
212.
14. Lw.
1/3 260.
Muelhausen
1/3 260.
1/3 260.
Basel

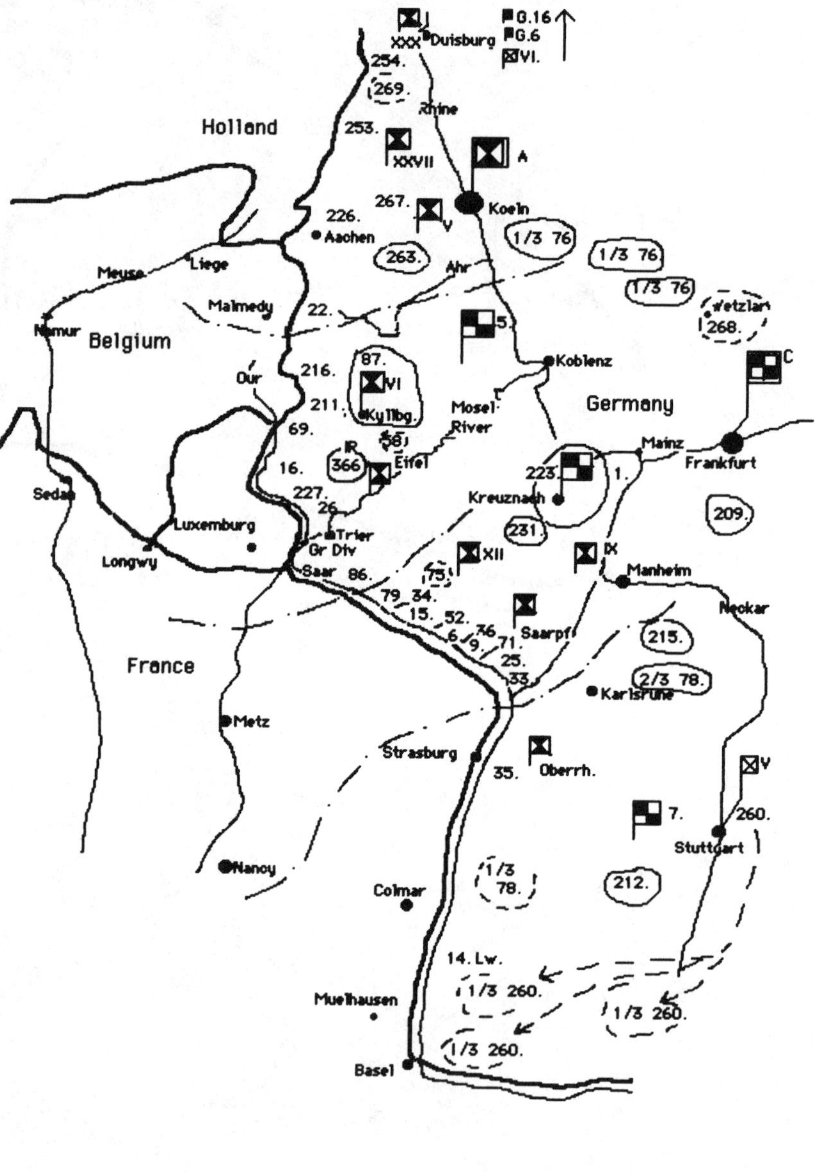

Map 13
German Situation in the West, Mid-October 1939[2]

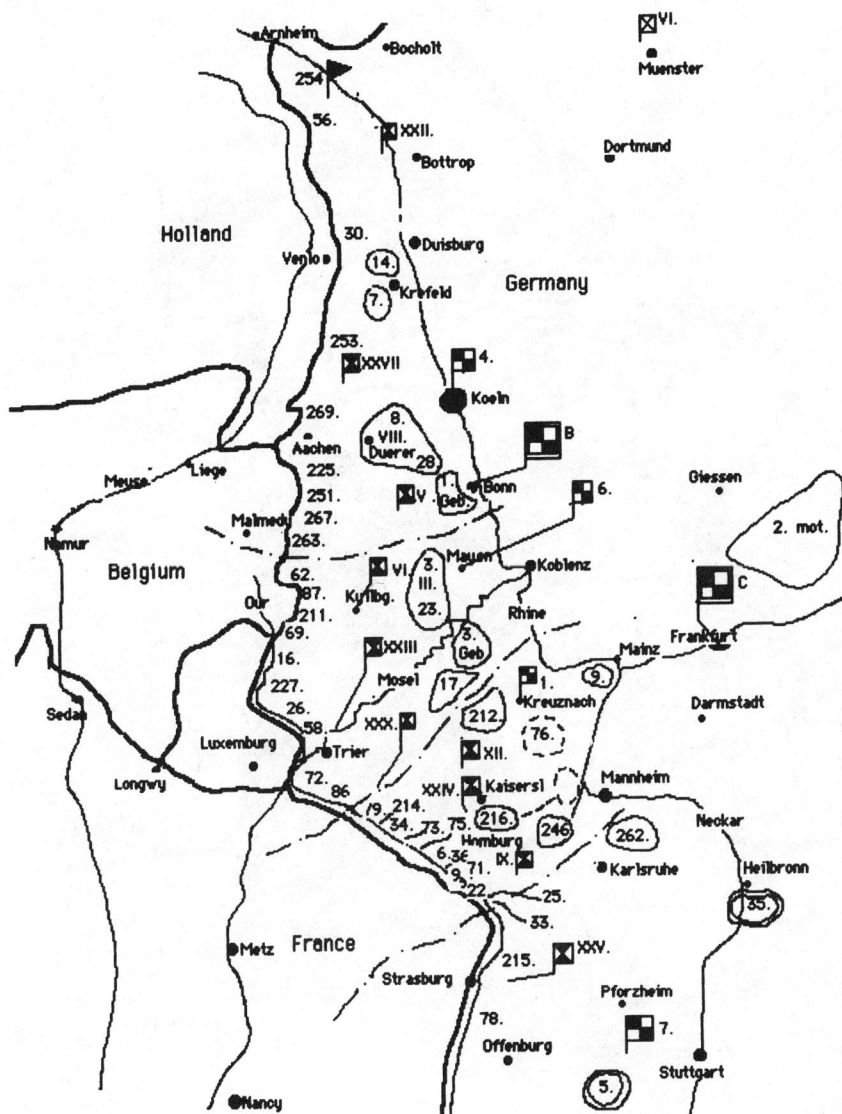

Map 14
"Fall Gelb" Operational Plan, October 19, 1939[3]

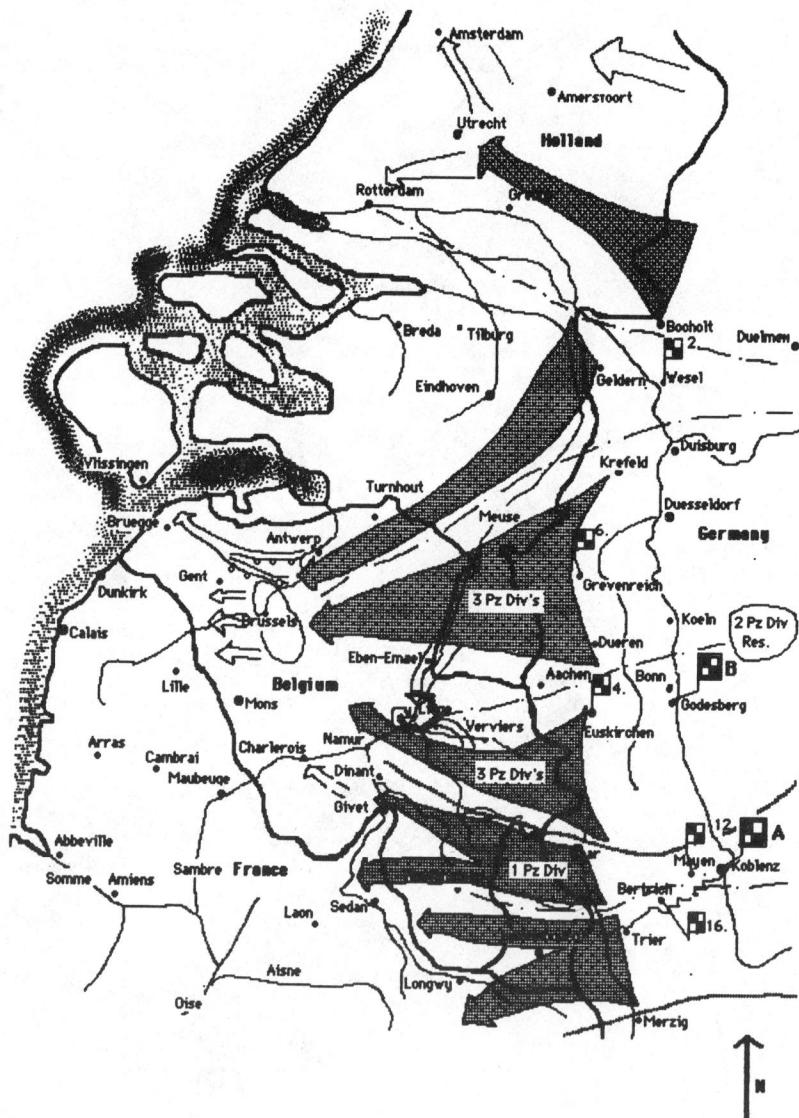

Map 15
"Fall Gelb" Operational Plan, October 29, 1939[4]

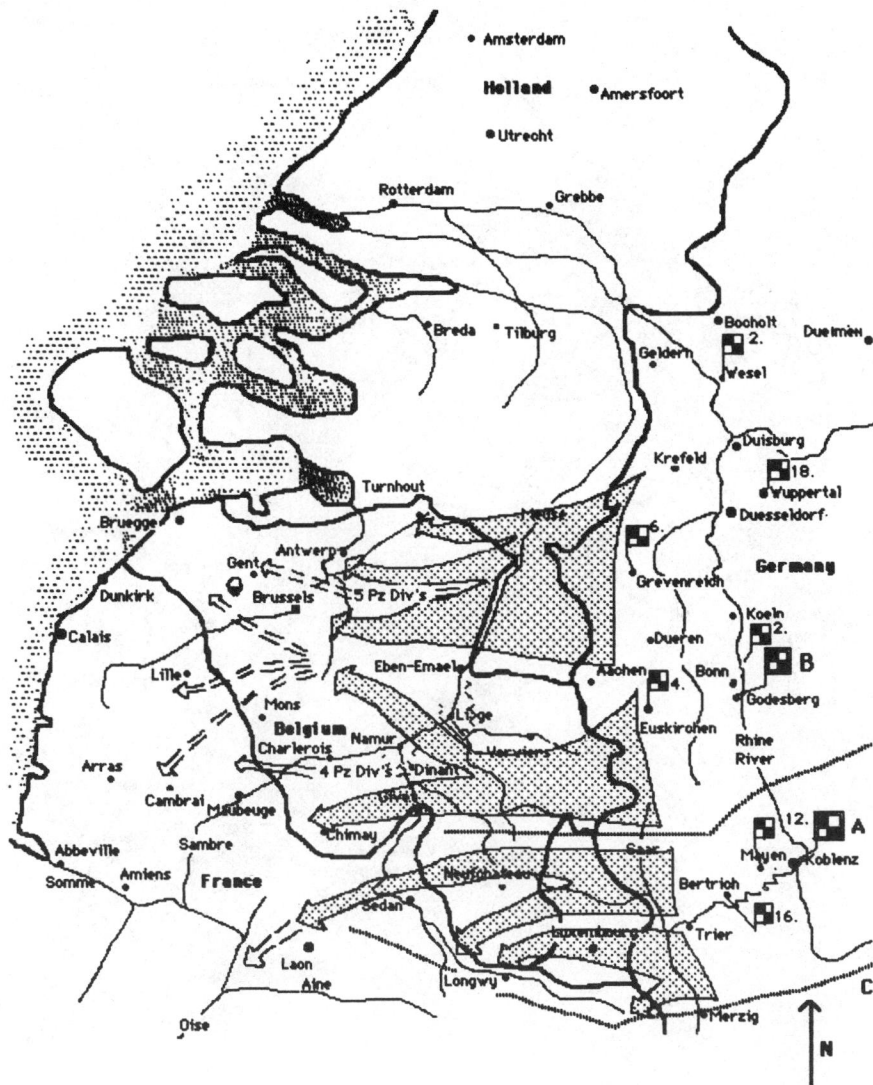

Map 16
"Fall Gelb" Operational Plan, January 17, 1940[5]

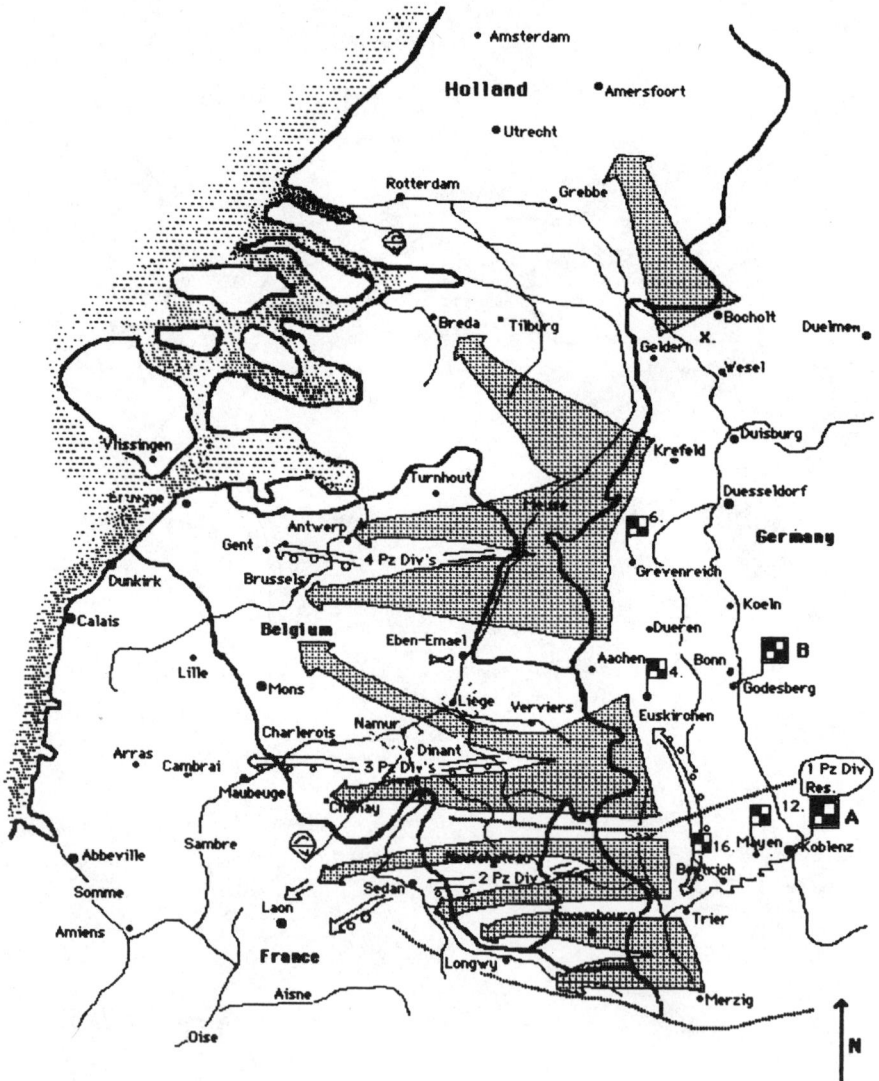

Map 17
"Fall Gelb" Operational Plan, February 24, 1940[6]

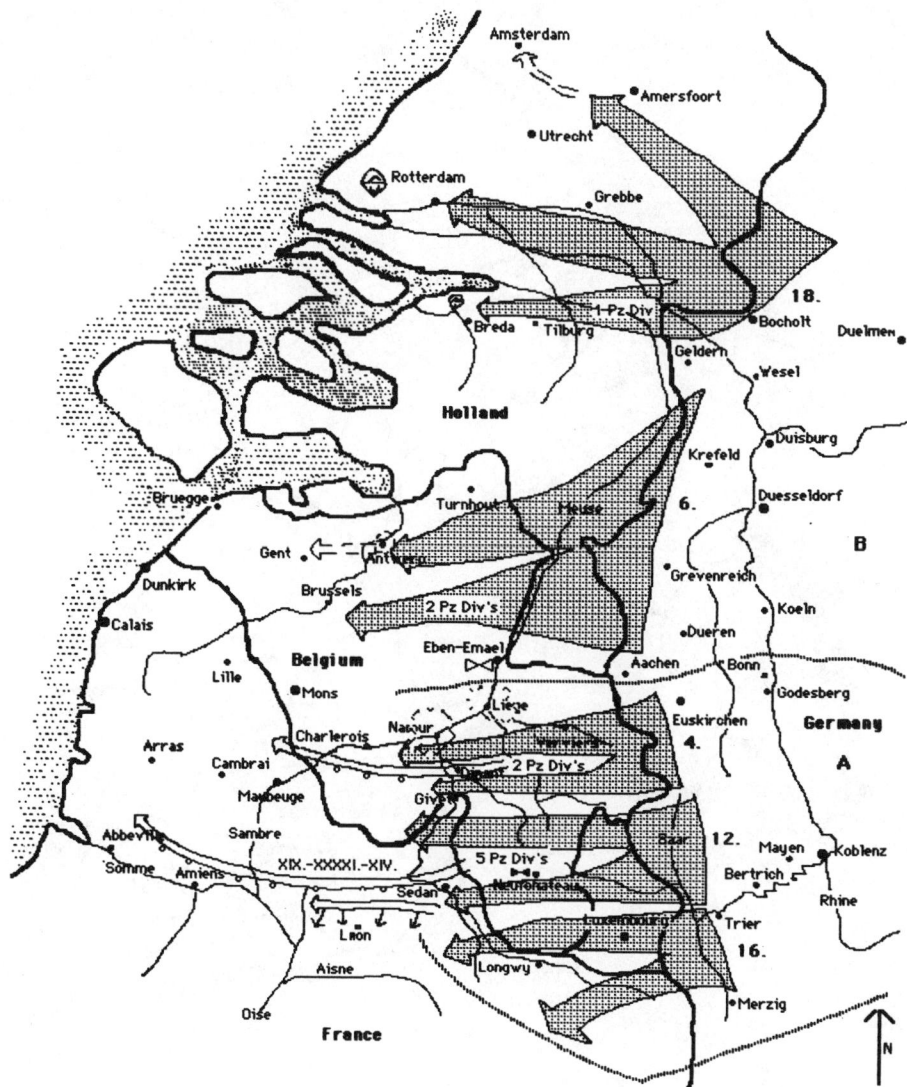

Map 18
Von Manstein's Proposal[7]

Appendix B: Movement Orders

**SPECIAL MOVEMENT ORDERS TO PANZER GROUP
VON KLEIST**

First Echelon XIXth Panzer Corps:

a. 2nd Panzer Division: TMR A, controls all roads within its deployment area and feeds directly into TMR A.

b. 1st Panzer Division: TMR B, controls all roads within its deployment area and feeds directly into TMR B.

c. 10th Panzer Division: ½ TMR C and ½ TMR D, controls all roads within its deployment area, must use the following feeder roads, at times specified in timetable, to feed into TMRs C and D.

(1) Hermeskeil-Erhang, cross Moselle at Pfalzel.

(2) Bernkastel, Naviand, Osann, Klausen, Hetzerath.

(3) Traben-Trabach, Wolf, Kinheim, Urzig, Bombogen.

(10th Panzer Division can only use feeder roads between H-7 and H+5).

d. XIXth Panzer Corps, Corps troops and Flak Regiment 102: as per XIXth Corps operation order.

Second Echelon:

a. XLIth Panzer Corps: 6th Panzer Division, XLIst Panzer Corps, Corps troops, and ½ 8th Panzer Division on TMR A. 6th and 8th Panzer Divisions use designated feeder roads to TMR.

b. XLIth Panzer Corps: 2nd Infantry Division (mot), XLIst Panzer Corps, Corps troops, and ½ 8th Panzer Division on TMR B. 2nd Infantry Division (mot) and 8th Panzer Divisions use designated feeder roads to TMR.

c. XIXth Corps: Logistics/resupply on TMR C.

d. XIVth Motorized Corps: 29th Infantry Division (mot) on TMR D. 29th uses designated feeder roads to TMR.

Third Echelon:

a. XIVth Motorized Corps main Tactical Operation Center (TOC) with Corps troops and 13th Infantry Division (mot) follow on TMRs B and C.

Once the second echelon crosses the international border, TMR A and D (within Germany) revert to 12th and 16th Armies respectively. [1]

MOVEMENT ORDERS ISSUED TO PANZER GROUP
VON KLEIST ON MAY 3, 1940

1. *XIXth Panzer Corps:*

a. Begin movement at H-8 (D-1) from start line (Seinsfeld–Eisenschmitt–Wittlich–Bernkastel) to just short of the international border. Elements of 10th Panzer Division can only use feeder roads from H-7 to H+5. While resting and refueling during H-4 and H-2, road intersections at Kordel must be cleared for VIIth Corps, and road from Ruwer–Pfalzel–Biewer must be cleared for XIIIth Corps.

b. 102nd Flak Regiment and 1st Flak Battalion/3rd Flak Regiment must be organized into corps movement for the duration. 1st Battalion/3rd Flak Regiment and Balloon Battery/1st Observer Battalion, must cross the Rhine River no later than H-hour. 1st Battalion/3rd Flak Regiment will be alerted by the Panzer Group.

c. Once clearance has been provided to cross the international border, the following must remain open for General Headquarters Troops and the second echelon:

along TMR A:	Mosbruch prior to H+4
	Daun prior to H+6
	Seinsfeld prior to H+10
	Rittersdorf prior to H+14
	Roth prior to H+18
along TMR B:	Monreal prior to H+6
	Manderscheid prior to H+11
	Eisenschmitt prior to H+14
	Bitburg prior to H+15
	Wallendorf prior to H+20
along TMR C:	Polch prior to H+3
	Wittlich prior to H+7
	Irrel prior to H+11
	Bollendorf prior to H+12
along TMR D:	Cochem prior to H−2
	Alf prior to H+2
	Wittlich prior to H+5
	Eisenach prior to H+11
	Ralingen prior to H+12

2. *XLI Panzer Corps:* Be prepared to initially move to a line Seinsfeld–Badem–Niederkail. The following roads are available:

a. 6th Panzer Division: Feeder road Wallendorf to Horperath, change to TMR A. Cross Rhine bridge at Neuwied no earlier than H + 9. When lead elements reach Seinsfeld, rest and close the rest of the division to Oberelz. Tracked vehicles may move past Monreal after H + 8.

b. 2nd Infantry Division (mot): Feeder road Bollendorf and TMR C to Wittlich. At Wittlich take Wittlich–Eisenschmitt road, proceed on TMR B. Cross bridge at Koblenz no earlier than H + 7; bridge is only available for 10 hours. When lead elements pass Badem, close division to Kaisersesch.

c. Corps troops: Begin movement on feeder road Echternach no earlier than H + 4½ from Nassau. Cross Rhine bridge at Niederlahnstein no earlier than H + 5, continue to Cochem behind the General Headquarters Troops of March Serial C. At Cochem take Route 259 to Ulmen.

d. 8th Panzer Division: Assemble in deployment area at dusk on D-Day (about H + 15). Until assembly, east-west roads must remain open for 16th Army. No later than noon on D + 1 the division must be across the Moselle River, waiting in rest areas. Use designated feeder roads for the division. The division must clear TMR D for 29th Infantry Division (mot) from Alf after H + 26, and from Wittlich after H + 27½. 8th Panzer Division then follows 6th Panzer Division and 2nd Infantry Division (mot) on their respective TMRs. The division may use TMR C (up to Röhl and the stretch Röhl–Bitburg) for the purpose of feeding in to TMRs A and B.

3. *XIVth Panzer Corps:* Be prepared to conduct road movement on D-Day no earlier than H + 15.

a. 13th Infantry Division (mot): Conduct tactical road march on feeder road Herborn–Wölferlingen to east shore of Rhine River. Close and rest the division. On order cross Rhine at Neuwied bridge, and be prepared to conduct movement on TMC B or C.

b. 29th Infantry Division (mot): Conduct tactical road march on feeder road Heuchel-heim–Limburg and feeder road Bollendorf to Koblenz. Cross Rhine no earlier than H + 19. Continue on feeder road Echternach to Alf. Close division and rest. Be prepared to continue on or about noon on D + 1, follow southern element of 10th Panzer Division on TMR D.

c. XIVth Panzer Corps, Corps troops: incorporated with 13th Infantry Division (mot).

4. *Tactical Command Post Group von Kleist* depart Niederlahnstein at 1500 hours on D-1 initially on feeder road Bollendorf, then TMR C to main TOC at Masholder. The last March serial pass through Wittlich at 2100 hours prior to XIXth Panzer Corps assembly. XIXth Panzer Corps ensures that TMRs in its deployment area remain open.

5. *General Headquarters Troop of Panzer Group von Kleist* follows behind 10th Panzer Division on D-Day to vicinity of international border. March serials consist of:

March Serial A:	49th Artillery Regiment
	passtime 35 minutes
	assemble and depart no earlier than H + 1 at Niederlahnstein; use use feeder road Echternach to Welschbillig
March Serial B:	1st Security Regiment
	(rear services)
	passtime 70 minutes

assemble and depart no earlier than H + 1 at Niederlahnstein; use feeder road Echternach to Wittlich, change to TMR C and use until Niederweis, change to MSR

March Serial C: 1st *Nebelwerfer* Regiment[2]

passtime 80 minutes

assemble and depart no earlier than H+2½ at Niederlahnstein; follow March serial B to Welschbillig; then elements to Masholder and Stahl

6. *Main Supply Routes:* See "Special Instructions for Logistics and Resupply for Panzer Group von Kleist," (O. Qu/Qu 1 Nr. 175/40 g. Kdos, 1.4.40).

7. *Non-Panzer Group von Kleist units:* Designated units on the distribution list not attached to Group von Kleist are requested to notify their subunits of reference and road movements. Direct coordination with TMR users is authorized.

8. *Air Reconnaissance Groups of Group von Kleist:* Ground elements of the Air Recon Groups of the various corps and divisions must coordinate movements of TOCs and airfields with their respective ground headquarters for TMR usage. Ground HQs will only allow small elements on the TMRs.

9. *Road march speed:* Corps Headquarters and March Serial commanders designate march speeds according to the situation. They will ensure that serials and vehicles maintain proper distances.

10. *Traffic control:* As per traffic control order (see traffic control in Chapter Two).

11. *Code words for traffic control:*

2nd Panzer Division	Apfel (apple)
1st Panzer Division	Birne (pear)
10th Panzer Division	Traube (grape)
XIXth Corps troops	Pflaume (plum)
Group von Kleist General Headquarters Troops	Tomate (tomato) (add A, B, C, D for each march serial)
6th Panzer Division	Hirsch (stag)
8th Panzer Division	Reh (deer)
2nd Infantry Division (mot)	Fuchs (fox)
XLIth Motorized Corps troops	Hase (rabbit)
13th Infantry Division (mot)	Habicht (hawk)
29th Infantry Division (mot)	Falke (falcon)
XIVth Panzer Corps troops	Sperber (sparrowhawk)
Non-Panzer Group road users	Tanne (fir)
Ground elements of Air Recon units	Eiche (oak)

12. *Rest areas:* All villages along Group von Kleist TMRs may be used as rest areas. Units must coordinate with VIth and VIIth Corps for rest areas along feeder roads.

13. *Movements of Infantry divisions remaining in Germany:*

   a. 21st Infantry Division/XVIIIth Corps will clear the following roads on D-Day:

     (1) Polch–Kehrig after 0800 hrs

     (2) Neuwied–Monreal 0800 hrs to 1000 hrs, off and on after 1300 hrs

     (3) Koblenz–Ochtendung–Mayen 0800 hrs to 1000 hrs, and after 1300 hrs

   b. 9th Infantry Division/XL Corps as much as possible refrains from road movements in the area north of Dierdorf–Selters–Freilingen road on D-Day until H+7 to facilitate passing of 6th Panzer Division's rear elements.[3]

MOVEMENT TIMETABLE FOR PANZER GROUP VON KLEIST

    D-Day = May 10, 1940
    H-Hour = 0530
    Dusk: 2100 = H+15

XIXth Panzer Corps

D-1

H-18	Start assembly
H-8	Cross start line
H-2	Cochem cleared (start point TMR D)

D-Day

H-4 to H-2	Rest, refuel
H-hour	Begin Operation NIWI XIXth Corps crosses international border
H+1	Border barricades removed; roads clear for movement
H+2	Bridge at Wallendorf ready for crossing
H+3	Kolberg and Polch cleared
H+4	Bridge at Vianden and south of Weilerbach ready for crossing
H+5	At Belgian border; occupy assault position, close combat forces for strike; Wittlich cleared (TMR D)
H+6	Monreal cleared
H+7	Earliest attack (probably not before H+9)
H+8	Wittlich cleared (TMR C)
H+10	Field expedient bridge at Minden complete; construction of structural bridge begins; Seinsfeld cleared
H+12	Structural bridge at Minden complete; 41st Engineer Battalion freed for other missions
H+14	Eisenschmitt cleared
H+15	Lead elements at railway line Libramont–Neufchâteau–Hachy; tail of Corps has crossed Bitburg–Trier line

Panzer Group von Kleist Army Troops

D-1

H-11	Alert

D-Day

H-3	Prepared to depart in deployment areas
	Marching orders issued
	Begin assembly on highway 42
H-hour	March serial A begins movement from Niederlahnstein
H+35 minutes	March serial A has passed through Niederlahnstein
H+1	March serial B begins movement from Niederlahnstein
H+2	March serial B has passed through Niederlahnstein
H+2½	March serial C begins movement from Niederlahnstein
H+4	March serial C has passed through Niederlahnstein; Koblenz bridge is available for XLIst Motorized Corps
H+8	March serial A lead elements at Hetzerath; march serial B lead elements at Wittlich, reaches tail of 10th Panzer Division; march serial C lead elements at Bremm
H+11	March serial B lead elements at Irrel (behind 10th Panzer Division); rests
H+12	March serial A lead elements at Welschbillig; rests; march serial C at Röhl; rests (with the exception of Command group and Signal Regiment)
H+12½	Group Adjutant and Signal Regiment arrive at Masholder

Tactical Command Post

D-1

H-15	Prepared to depart; truck column departs; cars depart about H-14
H-11	Cars pass columns of VIIth Corps at Speicher
H-10	Cars arrive at Main Tactical Operation Center in Masholder
H-9	Truck column clears Wittlich; has passed through XIXth Panzer Corps area
H-6 (2400 hrs)	Truck column arrives in Masholder
	Decision to cross international border must be received and issued!!

XLI Panzer Corps

D-1

1330 hrs	Alert notification to Flak (to XIXth Panzer Corps) Group will notify

D-Day

H-4	Alert corps (only after receiving border crossing decision)
H+4	Prepared to depart (excluding 8th Panzer Division)
H+5	2nd Infantry Division (mot) begins movement from Limburg; Corps troops are authorized to cross Rhine at Koblenz

H+7	Lead elements of 21st Infantry Division (mot) cross the Rhine at Koblenz; 6th Panzer Division begins movement from Freilingen
H+9	Lead elements of 6th Panzer Division cross Rhine at Neuwied (21st Infantry Division (mot) cleared Neuwied–Monreal road at H+7); 8th Panzer Division prepared for movement in deployment area
H+13	Lead elements of 21st Infantry Division (mot) in Wittlich; rest for 1 hour while closing tail end of division to Kaisersesch; Lead elements of 6th Panzer Division in Daun
H+15 (or dusk)	8th Panzer Division begins its movement from the deployment area; 2nd Infantry Division (mot) continues to move; at Eisenschmitt switch to TMR B
H+16	Lead elements of 6th Panzer Division (mot) at Seinsfeld; closes division to Oberelz and rests for the night
H+17	Lead elements of 2nd Infantry Division (mot) at Badem; rests for the night; tail end of 2nd Infantry Division (mot) has crossed Rhine at Koblenz; bridge clear for 29th Infantry Division (mot); tail end of 6th Panzer Division has crossed Rhine at Neuwied; clear for 13th Infantry Division (mot)
H+17½	Lead elements left march serial of 8th Panzer Division at Bernkastel
H+18½	Lead elements right march serial of 8th Panzer Division at Zell

D+1

H+19	Led elements right march serial of 8th Panzer Division at Bullay; crossing TMR D; TMR D blocked for 5 hours
H+20	Tail end of 8th Panzer Division clears deployment area
H+21	Lead elements left march serial of 8th Panzer Division at Niederkail; rests for night
H+22	Lead elements right march serial of 8th Panzer Division at Lutzerath
H+22½	Tail end left march serial of 8th Panzer Division has crossed Moselle River at Bernkastel
H+24	Tail end right march serial of 8th Panzer Division has crossed Moselle River at Bullay; TMR D open again
H+27	If Libramont is taken, 6th Panzer Division and 2nd Infantry Division (mot) continue their march from Seinsfeld–Badem
H+37	6th Panzer Division and 2nd Infantry Division (mot) at international border (start line)
H+39	Earliest start time for 8th Panzer Division to continue (not before dusk); each march serial has a passtime of 5 hours

XIVth Corps

D-Day

	Alerted
H+15	13th and 29th Infantry Division (mot) begin movement

D+1

H+19   Lead elements at Rhine River, 13th Infantry Division (mot) rests
                    and closes division, 29th Infantry Division (mot) crosses Rhine at
                    Koblenz and continues on feeder road Echternach and TMR D to
                    Alf

H+26   Lead elements of 29th Infantry Division (mot) at Alf; 8th Panzer
                    Division cleared Alf at H+24; rest and close tail elements

H+29   Trail elements of 29th Infantry Division (mot) has crossed the Rhine
                    at Koblenz; bridge is cleared; on order continue on TMR D behind
                    10th Panzer Division

Be prepared to cross Rhine at Neuwied; ½ division on feeder road Wallendorf and TMR
B behind 8th Panzer Division; ½ division on feeder road Bollendorf, TMR C, and MSR
behind 8th Panzer Division.

All times for XIVth Corps are situation dependent![4]

Appendix C: Organizational Charts

Oberkommando der Wehrmacht, May 1940

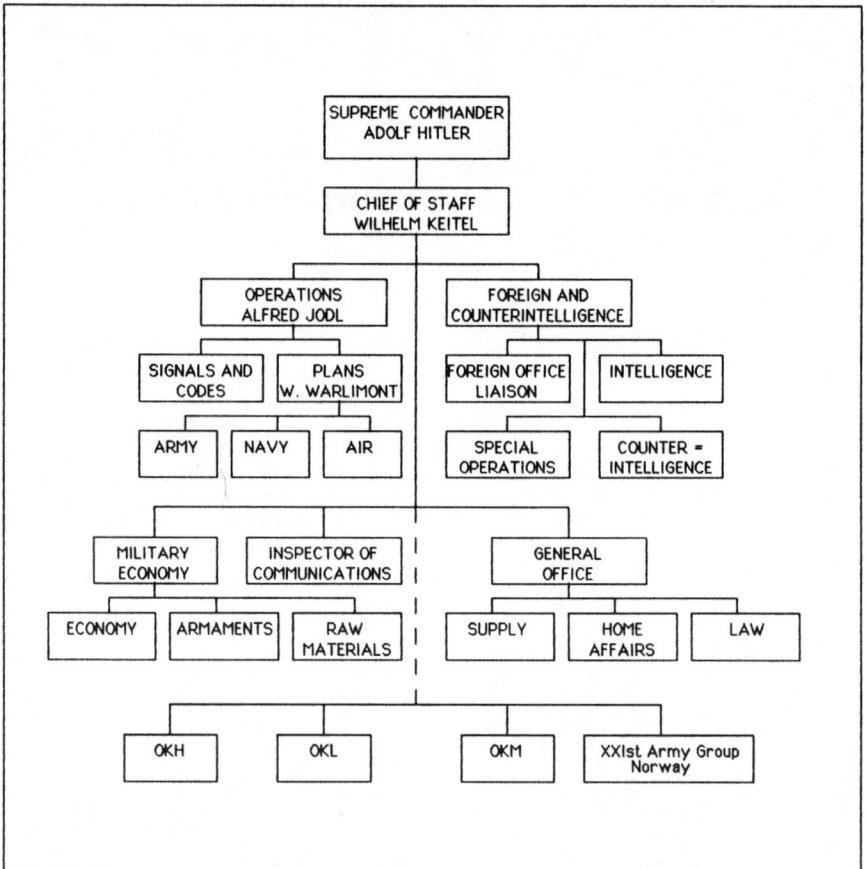

```
                        ┌──────────────────────┐
                        │  SUPREME COMMANDER   │
                        │     ADOLF HITLER     │
                        └──────────────────────┘
                                   │
                        ┌──────────────────────┐
                        │   CHIEF OF STAFF     │
                        │   WILHELM KEITEL     │
                        └──────────────────────┘
```

| OPERATIONS ALFRED JODL | FOREIGN AND COUNTERINTELLIGENCE |

| SIGNALS AND CODES | PLANS W. WARLIMONT | FOREIGN OFFICE LIAISON | INTELLIGENCE |

| ARMY | NAVY | AIR | SPECIAL OPERATIONS | COUNTER = INTELLIGENCE |

| MILITARY ECONOMY | INSPECTOR OF COMMUNICATIONS | GENERAL OFFICE |

| ECONOMY | ARMAMENTS | RAW MATERIALS | SUPPLY | HOME AFFAIRS | LAW |

| OKH | OKL | OKM | XXIst Army Group Norway |

Oberkommando des Heeres, 1939-40

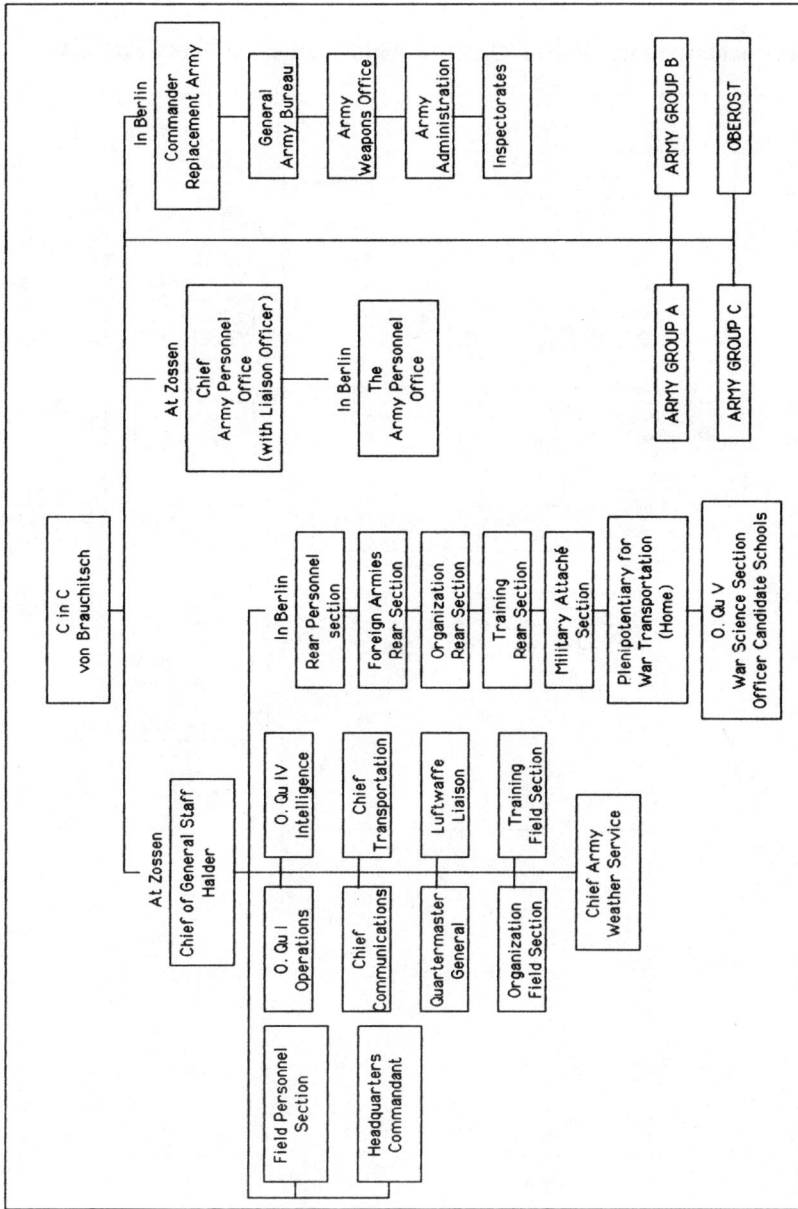

C in C
von Brauchitsch

At Zossen
Chief of General Staff
Halder

In Berlin
Commander
Replacement Army

- General Army Bureau
- Army Weapons Office
- Army Administration
- Inspectorates

At Zossen
Chief Army Personnel
Office
(with Liaison Officer)

In Berlin
The Army Personnel
Office

In Berlin
- Rear Personnel Section
- Foreign Armies Rear Section
- Organization Rear Section
- Training Rear Section
- Military Attaché Section

Plenipotentiary for War Transportation (Home)

O. Qu V
War Science Section
Officer Candidate Schools

O. Qu IV
Intelligence

Chief Transportation

Luftwaffe Liaison

Training Field Section

O. Qu I
Operations

Chief Communications

Quartermaster General

Organization Field Section

Field Personnel Section

Headquarters Commandant

Chief Army Weather Service

ARMY GROUP A

ARMY GROUP B

ARMY GROUP C

OBEROST

Oberkommando des Heeres, Order of Battle for the Battle of France: May 1940

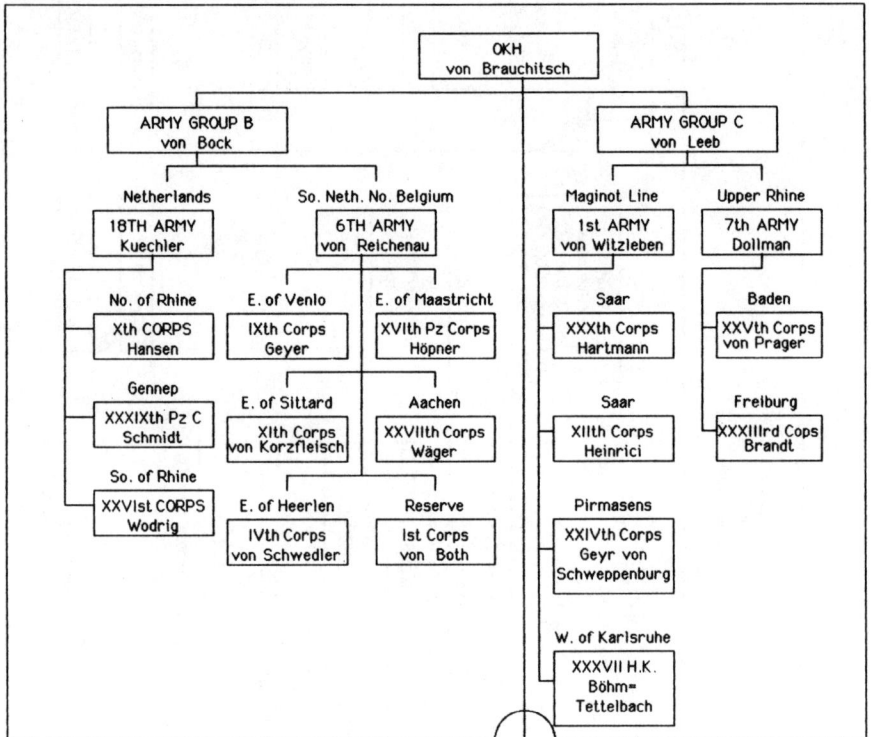

```
                              OKH
                         von Brauchitsch

        ARMY GROUP B                              ARMY GROUP C
         von Bock                                   von Leeb

  Netherlands    So. Neth. No. Belgium      Maginot Line    Upper Rhine
  18TH ARMY         6TH ARMY                 1st ARMY         7th ARMY
   Kuechler       von Reichenau            von Witzleben      Dollman

 No. of Rhine   E. of Venlo   E. of Maastricht     Saar           Baden
  Xth CORPS     IXth Corps    XVIth Pz Corps    XXXth Corps    XXVth Corps
   Hansen         Geyer          Höpner          Hartmann       von Prager

  Gennep        E. of Sittard     Aachen            Saar          Freiburg
 XXXIXth Pz C    XIth Corps    XXVIIth Corps     XIIth Corps    XXXIIIrd Cops
   Schmidt     von Korzfleisch    Wäger           Heinrici        Brandt

 So. of Rhine   E. of Heerlen    Reserve         Pirmasens
 XXVIst CORPS    IVth Corps      Ist Corps      XXIVth Corps
   Wodrig      von Schwedler     von Both         Geyr von
                                               Schweppenburg

                                            W. of Karlsruhe
                                             XXXVII H.K.
                                               Böhm=
                                             Tettelbach
```

Order of Battle for the Battle of France (continued)

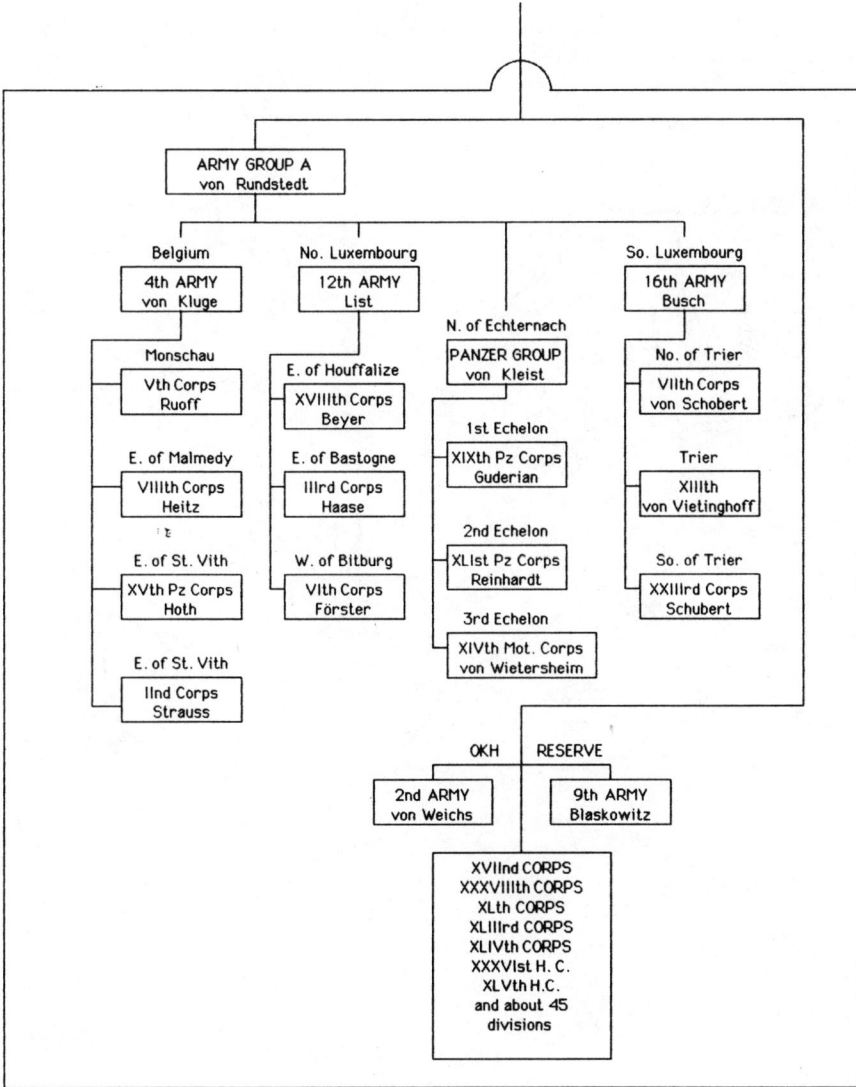

```
                                              │
                                             ╱‾╲
        ┌──────────────────────────────────────────────────────────────────┐
        │           ┌─────────────────────┐                                 │
        │           │   ARMY GROUP A      │                                 │
        │           │   von Rundstedt     │                                 │
        │           └─────────────────────┘                                 │
        │                                                                    │
        │     Belgium          No. Luxembourg                 So. Luxembourg │
        │  ┌───────────┐      ┌───────────┐                  ┌───────────┐   │
        │  │ 4th ARMY  │      │ 12th ARMY │                  │ 16th ARMY │   │
        │  │ von Kluge │      │   List    │                  │   Busch   │   │
        │  └───────────┘      └───────────┘  N. of Echternach└───────────┘   │
        │                                   ┌─────────────┐                  │
        │    Monschau                       │PANZER GROUP │   No. of Trier   │
        │  ┌───────────┐      E. of Houffalize│ von Kleist │ ┌─────────────┐ │
        │  │ Vth Corps │     ┌─────────────┐ └─────────────┘ │ VIIth Corps │ │
        │  │  Ruoff    │     │XVIIIth Corps│                 │von Schobert │ │
        │  └───────────┘     │   Beyer     │  1st Echelon    └─────────────┘ │
        │                    └─────────────┘ ┌─────────────┐                 │
        │  E. of Malmedy      E. of Bastogne │XIXth Pz Corps│     Trier      │
        │  ┌───────────┐     ┌───────────┐   │  Guderian   │  ┌───────────┐  │
        │  │VIIIth Corps│    │ IIIrd Corps│  └─────────────┘  │  XIIIth   │  │
        │  │   Heitz   │     │   Haase    │   2nd Echelon     │von Vietinghoff│
        │  └───────────┘     └───────────┘   ┌─────────────┐  └───────────┘  │
        │  E. of St. Vith     W. of Bitburg  │XLIst Pz Corps│   So. of Trier │
        │  ┌───────────┐     ┌───────────┐   │  Reinhardt  │  ┌───────────┐  │
        │  │XVth Pz Corps│   │ VIth Corps │  └─────────────┘  │XXIIIrd Corps│ │
        │  │   Hoth    │     │  Förster   │   3rd Echelon     │  Schubert  │  │
        │  └───────────┘     └───────────┘   ┌─────────────┐  └───────────┘  │
        │  E. of St. Vith                    │XIVth Mot. Corps│               │
        │  ┌───────────┐                     │von Wietersheim│               │
        │  │ IInd Corps│                     └─────────────┘                 │
        │  │  Strauss  │                                                     │
        │  └───────────┘       OKH    RESERVE                                │
        │                    ┌───────────┐  ┌───────────┐                    │
        │                    │ 2nd ARMY  │  │ 9th ARMY  │                    │
        │                    │von Weichs │  │Blaskowitz │                    │
        │                    └───────────┘  └───────────┘                    │
        │                    ┌─────────────┐                                 │
        │                    │ XVIInd CORPS │                                │
        │                    │XXXVIIIth CORPS│                               │
        │                    │  XLth CORPS  │                                │
        │                    │ XLIIIrd CORPS │                               │
        │                    │ XLIVth CORPS │                                │
        │                    │ XXXVIst H. C. │                               │
        │                    │  XLVth H.C.  │                                │
        │                    │ and about 45 │                                │
        │                    │  divisions   │                                │
        │                    └─────────────┘                                 │
        └──────────────────────────────────────────────────────────────────┘
```

Artillery Fire Plan Sector Sketch

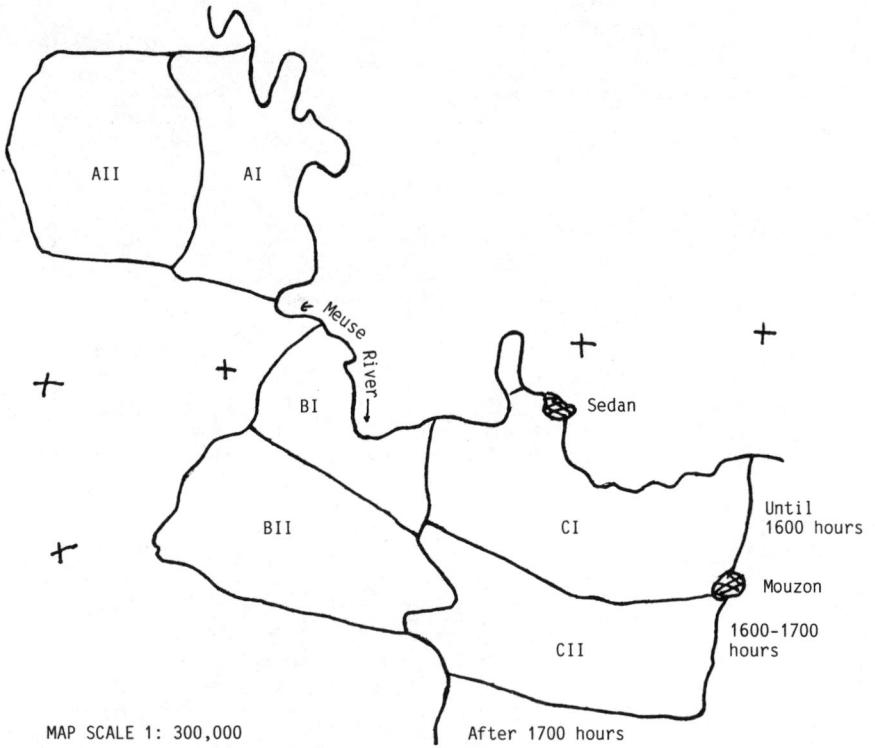

AII

AI

← Meuse River →

BI

Sedan

+

+

BII

CI

Until
1600 hours

Mouzon

CII

1600-1700
hours

MAP SCALE 1: 300,000

After 1700 hours

Appendix D: Comparison of Ranks

German Army/Luftwaffe	U.S. Army	As Used in This Book
Generalfeldmarschall	General of the Army	Field Marshal
Generaloberst	General	Colonel-General
General (der Inf, etc.)	Lt. General	General (of the Inf, etc.)
General (der Flieger, etc.)		General (of Fliers, etc.)
Generalleutnant	Major General	Major-General
Generalmajor	Brig. General	Brigadier-General
Oberst	Colonel	Colonel
Oberstleutnant	Lt. Colonel	Lieutenant-Colonel
Major	Major	Major
Hauptmann	Captain	Captain
Rittmeister	Captain	Captain
Oberleutnant	Lieutenant	Lieutenant
Leutnant	Second Lieutenant	Second Lieutenant

Appendix E: Tables of Organization and Equipment (TO&E)

PANZER DIVISION OF MAY 1940

Type Unit

Equipment

Panzer Troops:
1st, 2nd, & 10th Panzer Divisions
one Panzer brigade headquarters

The division's tank force consisted of Mark I's, III's, and IV's, however mainly of III's and IV's. Total number of tanks in the division: 300

two Panzer regiments
(each consisting of:)
  two Panzer battalions
  (each consisting of:)
    command group

Mark III's

    one headquarters company
    two light tank companies

Mark I, II, and III's

    one med. tank company

Mark IV's

    one trans. company

$1 \times \frac{1}{2}$ ton all-terrain vehicle, $2 \times 1\frac{1}{2}$ ton trucks, 15×3 ton trucks, 4 motorcycles (2 with side car)

    one maint. company

$4 \times \frac{1}{2}$ ton all-terrain vehicles, $10 \times 1\frac{1}{2}$ ton trucks, 16×3 ton trucks, 10 double axle trailers, and 3 single axle trailers

6th and 8th Panzer Divisions:
  one Panzer regiment headquarters
    three Panzer battalions

same as above, except that the number of tanks were reduced to 210 per division

Type Unit   **Equipment**

Infantry Troops:
  1st and 2nd Panzer Divisions:

  one infantry brigade staff
  one infantry regiment (mot) (consisting of:)

    three battalions of:
      three rifle companies (each with:)   9 light machine guns, 2 heavy machine
                                             guns, 3 light mortars (5 cm)

      one machine gun company   8 heavy machine guns, 6 med. mortars (8
                                             cm)

      one heavy company   2 light infantry guns (7.5 cm), 3×3.7 cm
                                             antitank guns

      one light trans. company (mot)   1 × ½ ton all-terrain vehicle, 1 × ½ ton
                                             troop transporter, 4 motorcycles (1 with
                                             side car), 16×1½ ton trucks

  6th and 8th Panzer Divisions:

  one infantry brigade staff
  one infantry regiment (mot) (consisting of:)

    three battalions of:
      three rifles companies (each with:)   18 light machine guns, 2 heavy machine
                                             guns, 3 light mortars

      one heavy company   8 heavy machine guns, 6 med. mortars,
                                             3×3.7 cm antitank guns

      one infantry gun company   8 light infantry guns (7.5 cm)

  10th Panzer Division:

  one brigade staff
  two regiments (each consisting of:)
    two battalions of:
      three rifle companies (each with:)   9 light machine guns, 2 heavy machine
                                             guns, 3 light mortars

      one heavy company   8 heavy machine guns, 6 med. mortars
      one motorcyle platoon   24 motorcycles (9 with side car), 3 light
                                             machine guns

      one infantry gun company   8 light infantry guns (7.5 cm)
      one antitank company   12×3.7 cm antitank guns
      one light trans. company (mot)   same as above

Reconnaissance Squadron: 1st, 2nd, 6th, 8th, and 10th Panzer Divisions

  two armored car troops (each with:)   3 × ½ ton troop transporters, 8×1½ ton
                                             trucks, 10 armored scout vehicles, 14
                                             motorcycles (8 with side car), 25 light
                                             machine guns, 10×3.7 cm antitank guns

  one motorcycle troop   56 motorcycles (46 with side car), 9 × ½

Type Unit   **Equipment**

                                                        troop transporters, $6 \times 1\frac{1}{2}$ ton trucks, 9 light machine guns, 2 heavy machine guns, 3 light mortars

one heavy troop (mot)
   one engineer platoon $3 \times \frac{1}{2}$ ton trucks, $6 \times 1\frac{1}{2}$ ton trucks, 3 light machine guns

   one antitank platoon 3×3.7 cm antitank guns
   one infantry gun platoon   2 light infantry guns (7.5 cm)
   one type B engineer bridge platoon
one light trans. company (mot)   same as above

Motorcycle Reconnaissance Battalion: 1st, 2nd, 6th, and 8th Panzer Divisions

  two motorcycle companies (each with:)   56 motorcycles (46 with side car), 9 light machine guns, 2 heavy machine guns, 3 light mortars

  one heavy company (mot)   same as above
  one heavy motorcycle company   6 med. mortars, 8 heavy machine guns, $10 \times \frac{1}{2}$ ton trucks, $15 \times 1\frac{1}{2}$ ton trucks, 44 motorcycles (38 with side car)

Artillery:

one artillery regiment (mot)
  one observation platoon $6 \times \frac{1}{2}$ ton all-terrain vehicles, $1 \times \frac{1}{2}$ ton troop transporter, $2 \times 1\frac{1}{2}$ ton trucks

  one meteorological section 1×3 ton truck
one printing section $1 \times \frac{1}{2}$ ton all-terrain vehicle, $1 \times 1\frac{1}{2}$ ton truck, 1×3 ton truck

  one regimental band
two light artillery battalions (each consisting of:)

  three batteries (with:)   4 light 105 mm howitzers, 2 light machine guns, $4 \times \frac{1}{2}$ ton all-terrain vehicles, $6 \times \frac{1}{2}$ ton troop transporters, $13 \times 1\frac{1}{2}$ ton all-terrain trucks, 6×3 ton trucks, 4 double axle trailers, 4 single axle trailers, 11 motorcycles (2 with side car)

  one signal platoon $4 \times \frac{1}{2}$ ton all-terrain vehicles, $5 \times \frac{1}{2}$ton troops transporters, $2 \times 1\frac{1}{2}$ ton trucks, 1×3 ton truck

  one survey section $1 \times \frac{1}{2}$ ton all-terrain vehicle, $1 \times 1\frac{1}{2}$ ton truck, 2 motorcycles

Antitank Battalion: 1st, 2nd, and 10th Panzer Divisions:

  one signal platoon   same as above
  three antitank companies (each with:) 6 light machine guns, 12×3.7 mm antitank guns

Type Unit   **Equipment**

6th and 8th Panzer Divisions:

only two antitank companies, the remainder is the same

Engineer Battalion (mot):

two engineer companies (mot) (each with:)
6×½ ton trucks, 2×1½ ton trucks, 13×3 ton trucks, 12 motorcycles (7 with side car), 9 large (trailer-mounted) air compressors, 20 power saws, 6 welding sets, 9 flame throwers, 10 search lights

one engineer company (mech.)
35 light machine guns

one bridge company (type B) (heavy pontoon and trestle equipment)
16 half pontoons, 24 large pneumatic boats,* 48 small pneumatic boats (used to transport troops and to construct ferries), 12×2 ton pneumatic boat ferries, 6×4 ton pneumatic boat ferries, steel rails and wooden planks for road surface, 2 light machine guns

one bridge company (type K) (fixed bridge, small box girder)
one engineer trans. company
18 assorted ½ ton, 1½ ton, and 3 ton trucks, 2 light machine guns

Signal Battalion (divisional):

one radio company
21 submachine guns, 13 light machine guns, 23 assorted wheeled vehicles, 21 armored half tracks, 13 motorcycles, (1 with side car)

one field telephone company
6 submachine guns, 2 light machine guns, 38 assorted wheeled vehicles 6 armored half tracks, 13 motorcycles (1 with side car)

one light signal trans. company
4×1½ ton trucks, 7×3 ton trucks, 1 single axle trailer, 2 motorcycles (1 with side car)

Flak Battalion (mot):

three Flak batteries (each with:)
12×20 mm antiaircraft guns

Logistics:
Supply Battalion Commander and Staff (divisional) with:

7 small trans. companies
(30 ton capacity per platoon)
(each with:)
3 motorcycles (2 with side car), 1×½ ton all-terrain vehicle, 1×1½ ton truck, 10×4.5 ton trucks

Type Unit	Equipment
three large fuel tanker companies (13,000 gallon capacity per platoon) (each with:)	$1 \times \frac{1}{2}$ ton all-terrain vehicle, $2 \times 1\frac{1}{2}$ ton trucks, 20×4.5 ton trucks, 3 motorcycles (2 with side car)
one supply company	7 motorcycles (6 with side car), $1 \times \frac{1}{2}$ truck, $2 \times 1\frac{1}{2}$ ton trucks, 12×3 ton trucks
two maint. companies (each with:)	40 med. half track prime movers, 4 med. fully tracked prime movers, 44 double axle trailers, 23 assorted wheeled trucks
Administrative services:	
one bakery company	19 assorted wheeled vehicles, 5 mobile bakeries, 6 motorcycles (2 with side car)
one butcher company	7 assorted wheeled vehicles, 2 motorcycles (1 with side car)
one commissary office	4 assorted wheeled vehicles, 1 motorcycle
Medical services:	
two medical companies (each with:)	19 assorted wheeled vehicles, 4 motorcycles (3 with side car)
three ambulance platoons	$18 \times 1\frac{1}{2}$ ton ambulances, 4 motorcycles with side car
Military Police:	
one military police section	$7 \times \frac{1}{2}$ ton all-terrain vehicles, 8 motorcycles (2 with side car)
Postal services:	
one field post office	3 assorted wheeled vehicles
Division headquarters:	
one motorcycle platoon	24 motorcycles (9 with side car), 3 light machine guns
map section (divisional)	$1 \times 1\frac{1}{2}$ ton truck, 1 motorcycle
machine gun section	2 heavy machine guns[1]

INFANTRY DIVISION (MOTORIZED) OF MAY 1940

Infantry Troops

two infantry regiments (mot) (each with:) one signal platoon	$6 \times \frac{1}{2}$ ton trucks, $5 \times 1\frac{1}{2}$ ton trucks, 1×3 ton truck

Type Unit   **Equipment**

   one regimental band
   three battalions (each with:)
      three rifle companies (each with:)   9 light machine guns, 2 heavy machine guns, 3 light mortars, 13 × 1½ ton troop transporters, 4 × 1 ton trucks, 3 × ½ ton all-terrain vehicles

      one machine gun company   8 heavy machine guns, 6 med. mortars, 11 × 1½ ton troop transporters, 4 × 1 ton trucks, 10 × ½ ton all-terrain vehicles

   one motorcycle platoon   see Panzer division
   one infantry gun company   8 light infantry guns (7.5 cm), light half track as prime mover for guns

   one antitank company   12 × 3.5 cm antitank guns, light half track as prime mover for guns

   one light trans. company (mot)   see Panzer division (infantry troops)

Reconnaissance Battalion:

   one motorcycle troop   see Panzer division
   one armored car troop   see Panzer division

Artillery:

one artillery regiment (mot) consisting of:
   one signal platoon   6 × ½ ton trucks, 5 × 1½ ton trucks, 1 × 3 ton truck

   one regimental band
   two light battalions (each with:)
      one signal platoon   4 × ½ ton all-terrain vehicles, 5 × ½ ton troops transporters, 2 × 1½ ton trucks, 1 × 3 ton truck

      one survey section   1 × ½ ton all-terrain vehicle, 1 × ½ ton truck, 2 motorcycles

      three batteries (each with:)   4 × 105 mm howitzers
      one heavy battery   4 × 150 mm howitzers

one observation battalion (consisting of:)
   one signal platoon   4 × ½ ton all-terrain vehicles, 5 × ½ ton troops transporters, 1 × 3 ton truck

   one meteorological section   3 × ½ ton trucks, 2 × 1½ ton trucks
   one printing section   1 × ½ ton truck, 1 × 1½ ton truck, 1 × 3 ton truck

   one survey battery   33 assorted wheeled vehicles, 4 motorcycles (1 with side car), 2 light machine guns

   one sound ranging battery   33 assorted wheeled vehicles, 4

Type Unit	Equipment
	motorcycles (1 with side car), 2 light machine guns
one flash ranging battery	33 assorted wheeled vehicles 4 motorcycles (1 with side car), 2 light machine guns

Antitank battalion:

two antitank companies (each with:)	12×3.5 cm antitank guns, half tracks as prime mover of guns

Engineer Battalion:

three engineer companies (each with:)	see Panzer Division
one bridging company (type B)	see Panzer Division
one engineer trans. company	see Panzer Division

Flak Battalion (mot):

three Flak batteries (each with:)	12×20 mm antiaircraft guns

Signal Battalion (divisional):

one radio company	21 submachine guns, 23 assorted wheeled vehicles, 21 armored half tracks, 13 motorcycles (1 with side car)
one field telephone company	6 submachine guns, 38 assorted wheeled vehicles, 6 armored half tracks, 13 motorcycles (1 with side car)
one light signal trans. company	4×1½ ton trucks, 7×3 ton trucks, 1 single axle trailer 2 motorcycles (1 with side car)

Logistics:

Supply battalion commander and staff (divisional):

six small trans. companies (30 ton capacity per platoon) (each with:)	3 motorcycles (2 with side car), 1×½ ton all terrain vehicle, 1×1½ ton truck, 10×4.5 ton trucks
two large fuel tanker companies (13,000 gallon capacity per platoon) (each with:)	1×½ ton all terrain vehicle, 2×1½ ton trucks, 20×4.5 ton trucks, 3 motorcycles (2 with side car)
one supply company	7 motorcycles (6 with side car), 1×½ ton truck, 2×1½ ton trucks, 12×3 ton trucks
two maint. companies (each with:)	40 med. half track prime movers, 4 med. fully tracked prime movers, 44 double

Type Unit	Equipment
	axle trailers, 23 assorted wheeled trucks
Administrative services:	
one bakery company	19 assorted wheeled vehicles, 5 mobile bakeries, 6 motorcycles (2 with side car)
one butcher company	7 assorted wheeled vehicles, 2 motorcycles (1 with side car)
one commissary office	4 assorted wheeled vehicles, 1 motorcycle
Medical services:	
two medical companies (each with:)	19 assorted wheeled vehicles, 4 motorcycles (3 with side car)
three ambulance platoons	$18 \times 1\frac{1}{2}$ ton ambulances, 4 motorcycles with side car
one field hospital	14 assorted wheeled vehicles, 2 motorcycles with side car, plus specialized equipment and tentage
Military Police:	
one military police section	$7 \times \frac{1}{2}$ ton all-terrain vehicles, 8 motorcycles (2 with side car)
Postal services:	
one field post office	3 assorted wheeled vehicles
Division headquarters:	
one motorcycle platoon	same as Panzer division headquarters
map section (divisional)	$1 \times 1\frac{1}{2}$ ton truck, 1 motorcycle
machine gun section	2 heavy machine guns[2]

INFANTRY COMPANY (MOTORIZED)

Headquarters platoon:	
one headquarters section	$1 \times \frac{1}{2}$ ton all-terrain vehicle
supply section	$3 \times 1\frac{1}{2}$ ton trucks (ammunition, food stores, fuel)
two machine gun sections (each with:)	1 heavy machine gun
Three rifle platoons: (each with:)	
one platoon headquarters	$1 \times 1\frac{1}{2}$ ton troop transporter
three rifle squads (each with:)	1 squad leader (submachine gun), three man machine gun section (1 light machine gun, gunner and assistant gunner carried 9 mm pistols, ammunition bearer a 7.92 mm rifle), six infantry men (armed with 7.92 mm rifle), $1 \times 1\frac{1}{2}$ ton troop transporter

Type Unit	Equipment
one mortar section	3 men, 1×50 mm mortar, 1×1½ ton troop transporter[3]

INFANTRY REGIMENT "GROSSDEUTSCHLAND" (MOTORIZED)

Regimental headquarters and staff:

same as motorized infantry regiment of a motorized infantry division
three battalions (each with:)

three rifle companies (each with:)	12 light machine guns, 3 light mortars
one machine gun company	8 heavy machine guns, 6 med. mortars, 10×½ ton trucks, 4×1½ ton trucks, 11×3 ton trucks, 9 motorcycles (5 with side car)

one heavy battalion

one motorcycle platoon	see Panzer division
one antitank company	12×3.5 cm antitank guns, half tracks as prime movers for guns
two heavy infantry gun companies (each with:)	one company with 4 and one with 6 heavy infantry guns (15 cm), half track as prime mover of guns
one assault gun battery	6 assault guns
one small trans. company (30 tons)	see Panzer division (logistics)[4]

STANDARD CORPS HEADQUARTERS (MOTORIZED)

Corps Headquarters:

two light machine gun sections	light machine gun (see infantry company (mot.))
one motorcycle messenger platoon	1×½ ton all-terrain vehicle, 2×1½ ton trucks, 38 motorcycles
one corps map section (mot)	1×½ ton truck, 1×1½ ton truck, special equipment

Corps Troops:

Engineers:

one engineer battalion

three engineer companies	see Panzer division
two bridging companies (type B)	see Panzer division
one bridging company (type K)	see Panzer division
one engineer trans. company	see Panzer division

Type Unit	Equipment

Signal:

one signal battalion (corps)
  one radio company (mot).

40 assorted wheeled vehicles, 13 motorcycles (1 with side car)

one field telephone company (mot)

31 assorted wheeled vehicles, 11 motorcycles (1 with side car)

one light signal trans. company (mot)

$1 \times$ ½ ton half track, 14×1½ ton trucks, 7×3 ton trucks

Rear Services:

one supply battalion commander and staff
  two small trans. companies (30 ton) — see Panzer division
  one large fuel tanker company
  (13,000 gallons) — see Panzer division
  one main. company — see Panzer division

Military Police:

  one military police section — see Panzer division

Postal Services:

  one field post office — see Panzer division[5]

FLAK CORPS (LUFTWAFFE)

Headquarters:

Corps staff — unknown

Flak Units:

three Flak regiments (consisting of:)
  three heavy Flak battalions (each with:)
    three heavy batteries (each with:)

4×88 mm Flak guns, 6×3.7 cm Flak guns, 3×20 mm Flak guns, 3 search lights (60 mm), 3 searchlights (150 mm), 3 sound locating devices

    two med. batteries (each with:)

9×3.7 cm Flak guns, 4 searchlights (60 mm)

    one searchlight battery

9 searchlights (150 mm), 9 sound locating devices

  one light Flak battalion (consisting of:)
    two light Flak batteries (each with:) — 12×20 mm Flak guns
two heavy Flak battalions — same as above
one signal regiment (consisting of:)
  two signal battalions (each with:) — similar to Panzer division signal battalion
one corps support element — similar to standard motorized corps[6]

Appendix F: The Meuse River Crossing

XIXTH PANZER CORPS ATTACK ORDER

I. Panzer Group von Kleist will attack across the Meuse on 13 May in the Charleville–Sedan sector. The attack will be conducted with the extraordinarily heavy support of the Luftwaffe, which has now become free for commitment in Belgium. In a continuing eight-hour attack, the Luftwaffe will destroy the enemy's Meuse defenses. The infantry attack will commence at 1600 hours and under all circumstances force a crossing of the Meuse River.

II. Aims:

XIXth Panzer Corps will cross the Meuse at 1600 hours on May 13 on both sides of Sedan (between the Baar Stream and Bazeilles) and will form a bridgehead on the following line: Boutancourt–Sapogne–Chehery–Noyers–Pont-Maugis.

III. Orders

A. Right Attack Group:

Commander: Major-General Veil

Units: 2nd Panzer Division, one engineer battalion to assist in the river crossing, one assault engineer company for bunker reduction, and two light artillery battalions.

Command Post: Sugny

Crossing Site: Between the mouth of the Baar Stream and the Iges Peninsula (exclusive).

Attack Frontage: Five km

Mission: Commence the attack at 1600 hours and capture the heights south of Donchery and its lower woods. The Division immediately turns to the west and crosses the Ardennes Canal prior to the Baar Stream and rolls up the Meuse defenses; right flank advances to Boutancourt, left flank to Sapogne et Feucheres.

B. Center Attack Group:

Commander: Brigadier-General Kirchner

Units: 1st Panzer Division, Infantry Regiment ''GD,'' one engineer battalion for the river crossing, one assault engineer battalion (43rd) for bunker reduction, the Corps' reinforced artillery regiment, and the heavy artillery battalions from the 2nd and 10th Panzer Divisions.

Command Post: St. Menges

Crossing Site: Between the Iges Peninsula (inclusive) and Torcy (inclusive).

Attack Frontage: Six km

Mission: Commence the attack at 1600 hours between Glaire and Torcy. Clear the Meuse curve and advance initially to the road Bellevue–Torcy. Then continue the attack to the Bois de la Marfee heights and advance to the line Chehery–Chaumont.

C. Left Attack Group:

Commander: Major-General Schaal

Units: 10th Panzer Division, one engineer battalion for the river crossing, one assault engineer company for bunker reduction, and two light artillery battalions.

Command Post: Givonne

Crossing Site: Between Sedan (inclusive) and Bazeilles (inclusive).

Attack Frontage: Seven km

Mission: no later than 1600 hours, in coordination with 1st Panzer Division, secure positions on the east side of Sedan and simultaneously occupy the line of departure along the line Sedan–Bazeilles. At 1600 hours commence the attack across the Meuse, capture Wadelincourt, and secure the heights along the line Noyers–Pont–Maugis.

IV. Assault Troops:

1. Attack simultaneously with all three Panzer divisions on line. Attack will be late afternoon.

2. After a short artillery preparation the infantry will cross the Meuse on a narrow front and build a bridgehead. Crossing materials: pneumatic boats and assault boats.[1]

3. Install ferries and transport antitank guns during the daylight, in order to consolidate the bridgehead.

4. A bridge will be constructed during the cover of darkness and tanks will be driven across.

5. On the following day the tanks will break out of the bridgehead in a westerly direction.

V. Luftwaffe:

1. The main body of IIIrd Air Corps (General Sperrle) will support the attack of the Corps throughout May 13 (910 aircraft).

2. This will not be one single bombing attack, but rather the aircraft are to conduct support throughout the crossing. From 0800 hours until nightfall the Luftwaffe will provide a continuous attack to subdue the enemy's artillery and stop traffic, isolating the battlefield.

3. On May 14 only limited air support can be expected, since the Luftwaffe will be required elsewhere. For air defense of the bridgehead, one fighter squadron (90 aircraft) will be available.

VI. Flak:

1. Protection of the assembly areas of assault forces, and firing positions of supporting weapons have priority. Designated elements of Flak will be called forward to combat bunkers and ground positions.

2. Beginning May 14 the main effort will be the protection of the bridges, since they undoubtedly will become the primary targets of the enemy.

VII. Artillery:
    1. Annex A: Fire Support Plan
    2. In the second phase of the artillery preparation, the artillery will overlap the Luftwaffe.
    3. The artillery's main effort is with 1st Panzer Division.
VIII. Cooperation with the Luftwaffe:
    1. Artillery and Luftwaffe will fire according to timetable in Annex B.
    2. All Luftwaffe coordination will be conducted through 2nd Close Air Support Group.
IX. Signal: omitted
X. The Corps Command Post will be located at Bellevaux, after 1200 at La Chapelle.
Corps Troops
One reinforced artillery regiment
One heavy mortar detachment (210 mm)
One Nebelwerfer (rocket projector) battalion
One assault engineer battalion
101st Flak Regiment (reinforced with one Flak battalion)[2]

CORPS ARTILLERY ORGANIZATION FOR THE MEUSE RIVER CROSSING

To support non-main effort divisional attacks	48 guns
To support the main effort and counter battery fire	236 guns

Artillery assets were reorganized for the Meuse River crossing operation. The divisional support groups of 2nd and 10th Panzer Divisions consisted mainly of assets not taken from them. Maximum support was directed to 1st Panzer Division since it again became designated the main effort. Control of the artillery preparation was the responsibility of the Corps Artillery Commander (ARKO 101), Brigadier-General Wilhelm Berlin.[3] The artillery organization consisted of the following forces:
    1st Panzer Division: (ARKO 101)

To combat infantry:	
73rd Artillery Regiment	24 × 105 mm howitzers
For main effort and counter battery:	12 × 150 mm howitzers
49th Artillery Regiment (reinforced with:)	24 × 105 mm howitzers
	12 × 150 mm howitzers
2nd Battalion/45th Artillery Regiment	12 × 150 mm howitzers
2nd Battalion/69th Artillery Regiment	12 × 150 mm howitzers
3rd Battalion/90th Artillery Regiment	8 × 105 mm howitzers
	4 × 100 mm field guns
3rd Battalion/74th Artillery Regiment	8 × 105 mm howitzers
	4 × 100 mm field guns
616th Heavy Artillery Battalion (separate)	8 × 210 mm mortars
one Nebelwerfer (rocket projectile) Battalion	108 × 210 mm rocket launchers

  1st Observation Battalion (reinforced by two artillery observation aircraft)
Total 236 tubes of artillery for 1st Panzer Division.

2nd Panzer Division:

74th Artillery Regiment	
(minus 3rd Battalion {heavy battalion})	24 × 105 mm howitzers

10th Panzer Division:

90th Artillery Regiment	
(minus 3rd Battalion {heavy battalion})	24 × 105 mm howitzers

The observation points for 2nd and 10th Panzer Divisions were required to set up at locations where they could also observe the 1st Panzer Division's sector. Likewise, one of each of the 2nd and 10th Panzer Divisions' artillery battalions were required to occupy firing points that supported 1st Panzer Division's sector, should the need to support have arisen.[4]

ENGINEERS

A. In the area west of Donchery, Sedan, Balan, and Bazeilles.

1. The technical control of the river crossing in 1st Panzer Division's sector of advance was provided by the staff of 511th Engineer Regiment (commander: Colonel Müller), also designated the main effort of the attack.

2. The technical control of the river crossing in 2nd Panzer Division's sector was provided by commander 38th Engineer Battalion (Major Wassung).

3. The technical control of the river crossing in 10th Panzer Division's sector was provided by commander 41st Engineer Battalion (Lieutenant-Colonel Warmuth).

B. Available Engineer Units:

1.	1st Panzer Division	37th Engineer Battalion
		505th Engineer Battalion
2.	2nd Panzer Division	38th Engineer Battalion
		70th Engineer Battalion
3.	10th Panzer Division	49th Engineer Battalion
		41st Engineer Battalion

The divisions were also tasked to employ all available infantry trained as assault engineers in assault engineer roles.

C. Available Equipment:

1. All pneumatic assault boats of bridging companies, including those that built bridges over the Semois, engineer battalions, and infantry assault engineers were made available to the Panzer divisions.

2. The 43rd Assault Engineer Battalion provided nine Sturmboote (assault boats) to 1st Panzer Division for the crossing.

3. Bridging equipment installed over the Semois River was unavailable for the Meuse River crossings.

D. XIXth Panzer Corps planned to establish a reserve of engineer assets.

Divisions were responsible for conducting reconnaissance of the river crossing sites well in advance. Crossing points and planned locations for bridges had to be reported to XIXth Panzer Corps. Building materials for emergency bridges, a unit responsibility, also had to be located and pre-positioned prior to the commencement of the operation. Bridging companies shifting laterally along the Meuse River were given priority (after the attack started) on the following roads: Vrigne aux Bois, St. Albert, St. Menges, and Fleigneux.[5]

FIRST PANZER DIVISION FIRE SUPPORT PLAN

The 1st Panzer Division's fire support was a four phase operation, aimed at a division frontage of five km with the actual crossing site's width only 2.5 km. Phase one encompassed the time from 0800 hours to 1550 hours and called for heavy infantry weapons[6] to engage targets of opportunity, while other weapons designated for direct engagements of bunkers[7] targeted those along the far bank and in the villages of Glaire and Torcy. The artillery's[8] mission was to protect the movement forward of assault groups by engaging targets on the far bank, blow tracks through river bank obstacles, shift fire to the heights above the banks, and finally, between 1500 and 1550 hours, mass its fires onto the narrow crossing sector.

Phase two, shortly before the assault crossings, from 1550 to 1600 hours, combined the heavy infantry weapons' fires onto the narrow crossing sector, while the designated direct fire weapons and the artillery continued the same functions as in phase one. Phase three, commencing with the assault crossings from 1600 hours on, envisioned heavy infantry weapons supporting the infantry and engineers in their crossing sector, while designated direct fire weapons engaged bunkers nearest the crossing site[9] and the artillery supported the infantry.

TIMETABLE FOR THE MEUSE RIVER CROSSINGS ON MAY 13, 1940

Time	Luftwaffe	Ground Forces
until 0800		Prepare for river crossings. Artillery prepares fire plan.
0800-1200	Harassing fire on sectors BI and CI.	Preparations for the crossings under the protection of the Luftwaffe harassing fires. Artillery continues to prepare for its fire support plan.
1200-1600	Combined bombing attack on sectors AI, BI, and CI.	Continuation and completion of all preparations. Artillery ready to execute fire support plan.
1600-1730	Shift harassing fires to sectors AII, BII, CII, and to gun emplacements near Mouzon. Stukas commence attack on sectors BI and CI.	Surprise river crossing.
1730 to evening nautical twilight	Attack targets of opportunity in the direction of the enemy in sectors AII, BII, and CII.	Secure bridgeheads.
Hours of darkness	Harass all movement directly north and east of the roads coming from Hirson, Laon, Rethel, Vouziers, and Stenay.[10]	Building of bridges, Panzer and artillery crosses the river.

The Luftwaffe placed 61 percent of its total air assets at the disposal of Panzer Group von Kleist on May 13. This reflects the importance placed upon forcing a crossing of the

Meuse River. Not all of the aircraft were committed at Sedan, since Reinhardt's XLIst Panzer Corps was also forcing a crossing further north in the Montherme–Mézières sector.

Panzer Group von Kleist	Sedan Sector	Montherme–Mézières Sector
420 ME 109	280 ME 109	140 ME 109
180 ME 110	90 ME 110	90 ME 110
270 JU 87 Stuka	180 JU 87	90 JU 87
900 HE 111 and Do 17 bombers	360 HE 111	540 HE 111 & Do 17
1,770	910	860[11]

FIRST PANZER DIVISION'S TASK ORGANIZATION

Infantry Brigade (reinforced)

First Infantry Regiment (reinforced) (corps and division main effort)
  one artillery regiment
  one engineer battalion to operate the boats for the crossing
  one assault engineer company to neutralize bunkers
  one antitank battalion for direct fire on bunkers
  one 88 mm Flak battery for direct fire on bunkers

Infantry Regiment "Grossdeutschland" (mot) (reinforced) (adjacent sector)
  one 105 mm howitzer battalion
  one engineer company to operate boats for the crossing
  two assault engineer platoons to neutralize bunkers[12]

Regimental Organizations for the River Crossing

1st Infantry Regiment (reinforced)
  Assault forces
    Against infantry outside bunkers
    three infantry battalions

    Against bunkers
    one assault engineer company
    (minus one platoon)

  Fire Support
    Against ground targets
    24×105 mm/12×150 mm howitzers
    9 heavy infantry guns (15 cm)

    Against Bunkers
    36×3.7 cm antitank guns
    4×88 mm Flak guns

  Technical Support
    one engineer battalion (reinforced (with)
    12 assault boats
    60 small pneumatic boats
    45 large pneumatic boats[13]

Infantry Regiment "Grossdeutschland" (reinforced)
  Assault forces
    Against infantry outside bunkers
    three infantry battalions

    Against bunkers
    one assault engineer platoon

Fire Support
   Against ground targets
   12×105 mm howitzers
   3 heavy infantry guns (15 cm)
   6 light infantry guns (7.5 cm)

Technical Support
one engineer company (with)
   9 assault boats
   30 small pneumatic boats
   15 large pneumatic boats[14]

Against Bunkers
18×3.7 cm antitank guns
6×5 cm antitank guns
6 armored assault guns (7.5 cm)

Appendix G: Order of Battle

PANZER GROUP VON KLEIST (MAY 10, 1940)

Panzer Group von Kleist

General Headquarters Troops (GHT):[1]
  General Headquarters Regimental Signal Staff
    425th Signal Battalion (corps-construction)
    422nd Signal Battalion
  Nebelwerfer Regiment (rocket projectile)
  2nd Nebelwerfer Battalion
  511th Engineer Regiment headquarters
  41st Engineer Battalion
  85th Engineer Battalion with one type B bridging company
  1st Company/407th Engineer Battalion (type B bridge)
  49th Artillery Regiment (staff only)
  2nd Battalion (heavy)/69th Artillery Regiment (mot) (100 mm Field Gun)
  3rd Battalion (heavy)/111th Artillery Regiment (mot) 100 mm Field Gun)
  4th Battalion (heavy)/259th Artillery Battalion (mot) (150 mm Howitzer)
  29th Observation Battalion
  521st Antitank Battalion
  General Headquarters Regimental Supply Staff
  422nd Supply Battalion (corps)
  Luftwaffe Support Group
    3rd Flight/31st Air Reconnaissance Squadron (Flak)
    Luftwaffe Signal Battalion (mot)

XIXth Panzer Corps
  1st Panzer Division
    1st Panzer Brigade

1st Infantry Brigade (mech)
73rd Artillery Regiment (mot)[2]
1st Motorcycle Reconnaissance Battalion
37th Engineer Battalion
2nd Company/406 Engineer Battalion (type B bridge)
37th Antitank Battalion
2nd Flight/23rd Air Reconnaissance Squadron (Army)
93rd Flak Battalion (Army-light)
4th Armored Reconnaissance Battalion
37th Signal Battalion (divisional)
81st Supply Battalion (divisional)
1st Battalion/18th Flak Regiment (Luftwaffe) (GHT)

2nd Panzer Division
  2nd Panzer Brigade
  2nd Infantry Brigade (mech)
  74th Artillery Regiment (mot)
  2nd Motorcycle Reconnaissance Battalion
  38th Engineer Battalion
  1st Company/406th Engineer Battalion (type B bridge)
  38th Antitank Battalion (Army)
  92nd Flak Battalion (Army-light)
  5th Armored Reconnaissance Battalion
  38th Signal Battalion (divisional)
  82nd Supply Battalion (divisional)
  2nd Battalion/38th Flak Regiment (Luftwaffe) (GHT)
  1st Flight/71st Air Reconnaissance Squadron (Army)

10th Panzer Division
  4th Panzer Brigade
  10th Infantry Brigade (mech.)
  6th Motorcycle Reconnaissance Company/69th Infantry Regiment (mech.)
  90th Artillery Regiment (mot)
  49th Engineer Battalion
  1st Company/430th Engineer Battalion (type B bridge)
  90th Antitank Battalion (Army)
  71st Flak Battalion (Army-light)
  1st Armored Reconnaissance Battalion/8th Regiment
  90th Signal Battalion (divisional)
  90th Supply Battalion (divisional)
  1st Battalion/36th Flak Regiment (Luftwaffe) (GHT)
  3rd Flight/41st Air Reconnaissance Squadron (Army)

Under Corps control:
  Infantry Regiment Grossdeutschland (mot)
    1st through 4th Infantry Battalions
  43rd Assault Engineer Battalion (GHT)
  101st Artillery Command and Staff (corps artillery commander)
    2nd Battalion (heavy)/45th Artillery Regiment (150 mm Howitzer)
    616th heavy Artillery Battalion (210 mm Mortars) (GHT)
    1st Observation Battalion

102nd Flak Regiment (−) (Luftwaffe) (GHT)
  91st Flak Battalion (light)
  1st Battalion/3rd Flak Regiment (medium)
  1st Battalion/8th Flak Regiment (hvy)
505th Engineer Battalion
70th Engineer Battalion
one Bridge Construction Company
419th Supply Battalion (divisional)
80th Signal Battalion (divisional)
Reconnaissance School Battalion
4th Flight/31st Air Reconnaissance Squadron (Army)

XLI Panzer Corps
  6th Panzer Division
    11th Panzer Regiment
    4th Infantry Regiment (mech.)
    76th Artillery Regiment (mot)[3]
    6th Motorcycle Reconnaissance Battalion
    57th Engineer Battalion
    41st Antitank Battalion
    76th Flak Battalion (Army)
    6th Armored Reconnaissance Battalion
    82nd Signal Battalion (divisional)
    57th Supply Battalion (divisional)
    3rd Flight/12th Air Reconnaissance Squadron (Army)

  8th Panzer Division
    10th Panzer Regiment
    9th Infantry Regiment (mech)
    80th Artillery Regiment (mot)[4]
    2nd Motorcycle Reconnaissance Battalion/9th Infantry Regiment
    59th Engineer Battalion
    2nd Armored Reconnaissance Battalion/8th Cavalry Regiment
    43rd Antitank Battalion
    84th Flak Battalion (Army)
    84th Signal Battalion (divisional)
    69th Supply Battalion (divisional)
    3rd Flight/41st Air Reconnaissance Squadron (Army)

  2nd Infantry Division (mot)
    25th Infantry Regiment (mot)
    5th Infantry Regiment (mot)
    2nd Artillery Regiment (mot)[5]
    2nd Armored Reconnaissance Battalion
    2nd Engineer Battalion
    32nd Signal Battalion (divisional)
    2nd Antitank Battalion

Under Corps control:
  1st Battalion/3rd Flak Regiment (GHT) (Luftwaffe)
  441st Signal Battalion (corps)
  441st Supply Battalion (corps)

XIVth Motorized Corps:
  13th Infantry Division (mot)
    93rd Infantry Regiment (mot)
    66th Infantry Regiment (mot)
    13th Artillery Regiment (mot)
    13th Antitank Battalion
    4th Engineer Battalion
    13th Signal Battalion (divisional)
    13th Armored Reconnaissance Battalion
    13th Supply Battalion (divisional)

  29th Infantry Division (mot)
    71st Infantry Regiment (mot)
    15th Infantry Regiment (mot)
    29th Artillery Regiment (mot)
    29th Antitank Battalion
    29th Armored Reconnaissance Battalion
    29th Signal Battalion (divisional)
    29th Engineer Battalion
    29th Supply Battalion (divisional)

  Under Corps control:
    60th Engineer Battalion
    60th Signal Battalion (corps)
    414th Supply Battalion (corps)[6]

First Flak Corps
  101st Flak Regiment
    1st Battalion/12th Flak Regiment
    1st Battalion/22nd Flak Regiment
    1st Battalion/51st Flak Regiment
    85th light Flak Battalion

  102nd Flak Regiment
    1st Battalion/18th Flak Regiment
    1st Battalion/36th Flak Regiment
    2nd Battalion/38th Flak Regiment
    91st light Flak Battalion

  104th Flak Regiment
    1st Battalion/8th Flak Regiment
    1st Battalion/11th Flak Regiment
    2nd Battalion/11th Flak Regiment
    75th light Flak Regiment
  3rd Battalion (heavy)/General Göring Flak Regiment
  3rd Battalion/9th Flak Regiment
  101st Air Signal Regiment
    1st and 2nd Battalions
  1st Corps Supply Element[7]

Appendix H:
German Military Documents

The narrative is largely based on documentary evidence from the National Archives (NARS) in Washington, D.C. All German Army documents originated from National Archives microfilmed records. The documents in this work are cited based on German Army document filing procedures. Documents are cited according to their office of origin, registry number, title (when applicable), and signature. Document headers are abbreviated, beginning with the office of origin, descending in hierarchical order. An example is as follows:

Der Oberbefehlshaber des Heeres, Gen St d H/Ausb. (Ia), Nr. 400/39g. 13.10.39, Betr. "Ausbildung des Feldheeres."

This document originated with the Commander in Chief of the Army, General Staff, Training Section of the Operations Branch, the 400th document issued in 1939, classified secret, dated October 13, 1939, and subject: "Training of the Field Army."

Notes

CHAPTER 1

1. Hans-Adolf Jacobsen, *Fall Gelb: Der Kampf um den Deutschen Operationsplan zur Westoffensive 1940* (Wiesbaden: Franz Steiner Verlag, GmbH, 1957), p. 9.

2. Rudolf Schmundt was born on August 13, 1896, in Metz. He entered the 35th Rifle Regiment in 1914 and later obtained General Staff training. Schmundt replaced Hossbach as Hitler's Army adjutant in 1938, serving in this position until seriously wounded during the assassination attempt on Hitler on July 20, 1944. In 1942 he assumed the additional role of Chief, Army Personnel Office. General of the Infantry, Rudolf Schmundt died from his wounds on October 10, 1944, in a field hospital at Ratzeburg. Wolf Keilig, *Das Deutsche Heer,* 1939-1945, *Die Generalität des Heeres im 2. Weltkrieg.* Vol. III (Bad Neuheim: Podzun-Pallas Verlag, 1957), p. 301.

3. Nicolaus von Below attempted to enter 12th Infantry Regiment (Halberstadt) as an officer candidate in 1925, but was rejected because of slight shortsightedness. An uncle, General a. D. Otto von Below, provided assistance and Nicolaus joined the training battalion of the Regiment in April 1926. To his dismay, before completing basic training, Nicolaus and 19 of his comrades were sent to the Deutsche Verkehrsfliegerschule (German Commercial Pilot School) in Schleissheim. Below demonstrated a talent for aviation, thus the Reichsheer transferred him to Lipezk, USSR, for pilot training from May to September 1929. He returned to the 12th Infantry Regiment on October 1, 1929, serving in the Regiment until separating from the Reichsheer on July 1, 1933, to enter the secret Luftwaffe. On June 16, 1937 he assumed the duties as Hitler's Luftwaffe aide-de-camp, remaining in the position until the conclusion of the war. Nicolaus von Below became one of Hitler's most trusted adjutants, with whom he discussed many details of the previous years. Nicolaus von Below, *Als Hitlers Adjutant 1937-1945* (Mainz: von Hase & Köhler Verlag, 1980), pp. 13-14, 431.

4. Nicolaus von Below, *Als Hitlers Adjutant,* pp. 210-11.

5. Oberbefehlshaber des Heeres (ObdH); Army Commander in Chief. Colonel-General Freiherr von Fritsch occupied the position from 1934 until 1938, thereafter Field Marshal Walter von Brauchitsch until December 1941, when Hitler personally assumed command of the Army. Baron Werner von Fritsch was born in Bernrath near Düsseldorf on August 4, 1880. He joined the 25th Hessian Light Field Artillery Regiment on September 21, 1898. Early on young von Fritsch earned himself a posting to the Kriegsakademie, or Staff College. During World War I, he served on the General Staff and as general staff officer (operations) of the 1st Guards Division. After the war he remained in the Reichsheer commanding an artillery regiment, a cavalry division, and an infantry division. Concomitantly, with his promotion to General of the Artillery, he assumed the position of Chef der Heeresleitung (Army chief of staff) on February 1, 1934. Von Fritsch became ObdH during the reorganization of the Armed Forces in 1935 and was promoted to Colonel-General in 1936. Accused of being a homosexual, Baron von Fritsch resigned from the Army in 1938. Subsequently exonerated by a military Court of Honor, von Fritsch was not reinstated as ObdH, but merely made honorary Colonel of the 12th Artillery Regiment. General von Fritsch, not called to active duty when war broke out in 1939, elected to join his artillery regiment in Poland. Baron Werner von Fritsch died a soldier's death while leading a reconnaissance patrol in Poland on September 22, 1939. He is credited with the organized expansion of the German Army from 1934 through 1938. Keilig, *Das Deutsche Heer*, p. 43; F. W. von Mellenthin, *German Generals of World War II As I Saw Them* (Norman: University of Oklahoma Press, 1977), pp. 3-4; also see Adolf Graf von Kielmansegg's book, *Der Fritsch Prozess* (Hamburg: Hoffman und Campe Verlag, 1949).

6. Walter von Brauchitsch was born in Berlin on October 4, 1881. After serving as a cadet, he became an officer in the 3rd Prussian Guard Regiment. Originally an infantry officer, he later transferred to the artillery. During World War I he earned a reputation as a capable officer. In 1932 he became Inspector of Artillery, and in 1935 Commander of Wehrkreis I (Corps Area I). In early February 1938, Hitler chose him as von Fritsch's successor for the position of ObdH. He was promoted to the rank of Field Marshal on July 19, 1940. After being replaced by Hitler in 1941, he saw no further service in the German Army. Field Marshal von Brauchitsch died in Hamburg in 1948. Keilig, *Das Deutsche Heer*, p. 91; F. W. von Mellenthin, *German Generals*, pp. 16-17; Lewis, *Forgotten Legions* (New York: Praeger Publishers, 1985), p. 18; and Below, *Als Hitlers Adjutant*, p. 65-73.

7. Hermann Wilhelm Göring was born in Rosenheim, Bavaria on January 12, 1893. The son of a colonial official, he entered cadet school at Karlsruhe. During World War I he served as an infantry officer, later transferring to the Air Force and making a name for himself commanding Richthofen's famous Flying Circus. Göring received the much coveted Pour le Merite and the Iron Cross First Class. Finding it difficult to adjust to civilian life after the war, Göring worked in several fields: initially in the Fokker Aircraft Works, then as advisor to the Danish government, as a stunt pilot, and a commercial pilot for Svenska Lufttraffik in Sweden. He met Hitler in 1922 through his first wife, the Swedish-born Carin von Kantzow. After the Beer Hall Putsch in 1923, Göring, although arrested, managed to escape to Austria, subsequently living in Italy and Sweden. He returned to Germany in 1926 after the German government granted political amnesty, reestablishing his contacts with Hitler. In 1928, Göring became one of the first National Socialists (Nazis) elected to the Reichstag. Göring was reelected in 1930. After the

overwhelming victory by the Nazis in the 1932 Reichstag election, Göring played a key role in the negotiations for Hitler's appointment to Reichskanzler. In the new government, Göring held a number of important positions: Reich Minister without Portfolio, Reich Commissioner for Air, Prussian Minister President, Prussian Minister of the Interior. In the latter position Göring harnessed control over all Prussian police forces, subsequently establishing the Geheime Staatspolizei (Gestapo). Göring quickly rose to the number two position in the Reich. On March 1, 1935, Göring became Oberbefehlshaber der Luftwaffe (ObdL), Air Force Commander in Chief, subsequently promoted to full General in 1936. Hitler also appointed Göring as plenipotentiary for the implementation of the Four-Year Plan in 1936, giving him vast powers over the state economy and rearmament program. In 1938, Göring engineered the removal of the War Minister, von Blomberg and the Commander in Chief of the Army, von Fritsch, in hopes of being elevated to the position of War Minister himself. In the latter days just before the outbreak of war, Göring attempted to negotiate with Prime Minister Neville Chamberlain through Birger Dahlerus, a Swedish intermediary. After the Battle of France, on July 19, 1940, while Field Marshal's batons were handed to Army generals, Göring received a promotion to Reichsmarschall. Toward the end of the war Göring tried to seize power from Hitler. At hearing the news Hitler deprived him of all his offices and ordered him shot. Göring, captured by the U.S. Army on May 9, 1945, stood trial before the Nürnberg War Tribunal, receiving the death penalty. Two hours before his execution, on October 15, 1946, Hermann Wilhelm Göring committed suicide by taking a vial of poison. Louis C. Snyder, *Encyclopedia of the Third Reich* (New York: McGraw Hill, 1976), pp. 122-24; and Hans Otto Meisner, *Die Machtergreifung* (Esslingen: Bechtle Verlag, 1983), pp. 232-35; also, for a more indepth biography of Herman Göring, see Willi Frischauer's book *The Rise and Fall of Hermann Göring* (Boston: Houghton Mifflin, 1951).

8. Erich Raeder was born to a north German middle-class family in Wandsbeck, near Hamburg, on April 24, 1876. He attended the Naval Academy at Kiel. As a young officer he made a cruise to the Orient with a flotilla of warships, and served on the Emperor's yacht "Hohenzollern." During World War I, Raeder served in the Battle of Jutland. After the war he remained in the Navy and in 1928 became Chef der Marineleitung (Chief of the Naval Command). In 1935, Hitler named Raeder Oberbefehlshaber der Marine (ObdM), a position he held until 1943. In this capacity, Raeder played a key role in the rearmament of the Navy. Early 1939 marked his last promotion to Grand Admiral. Raeder recommended an invasion of Norway in the first months of the war. The admiral opposed Hitler's ambitions for war against the Soviet Union. However, once the decision was made he supported the effort. The differences between Hitler and Raeder became strong enough by 1943 to warrant his retirement. On the Führer's orders, Raeder retired on January 30, 1943. After the war, Admiral Raeder was prosecuted at the Nürnberg War Tribunal and received a sentence of life imprisonment. In late September 1955 he was released because of ill health. Admiral Raeder died in Kiel on November 6, 1960. Snyder, *Encyclopedia of the Third Reich,* pp. 279-80; also see Erich Raeder's autobiography, *My Life* (Annapolis: United States Naval Institute, 1960).

9. Colonel-General Franz Halder, *The Halder Diaries: The Private War Journals of Colonel General Franz Halder,* vol. 2 (Boulder, Colo.: Westview Press, 1976), p. 15.

10. Oberkommando des Heeres (OKH), Army High Command, established along with the Luftwaffe and Navy High Commands in 1935 as separate services under the Oberkommando der Wehrmacht (OKW), Armed Forces.

11. Casualties suffered in the Army were: 8,082 killed, 27,278 wounded, and 5,029 soldiers missing in action. Officers represented 4.6 percent (dead) of these figures, which is quite high. Lewis, *Forgotten Legions,* p. 81.

12. Below, *Als Hitlers Adjutant,* p. 211.

13. Jacobsen, *Fall Gelb,* pp. 8, 10 and 29; and Halder, *The Halder Diaries,* vol. 2, p. 18; and Alistair Horne, *To Lose a Battle: France 1940* (Boston: Little, Brown and Company, 1969), p. 139; and Below, *Als Hitlers Adjutant,* p. 210.

14. Main effort; Schwerpunkt. The context in which the German military used the term Schwerpunkt during World War II signifies the point of main effort. Clausewitz, in his writings, calls it the center of gravity, the source from which the enemy derives his power or energy to fight.

15. Below, *Als Hitlers Adjutant,* p. 211; and Jacobsen, *Fall Gelb,* p. 9.

16. Franz Halder was born in Würzburg, Bavaria, on June 6, 1884. In 1902 he entered the 3rd Bavarian Field Artillery Regiment. After the war he remained in the Reichsheer. In 1935 he took command of the 7th Infantry Division, and in late 1936 transferred to the Army General Staff as the Oberquartiermeister I (Deputy Chief of Staff for Operations). After the Blomberg-Fritsch crisis, Halder became the Army Chief of Staff. He was an anti-Nazi, extremely gifted, and able to outthink and outperform any of his OKW counterparts. Although at odds with the Nazi philosophy and the route on which it had placed Germany, Halder's religious convictions and conservative nature prevented him from undertaking any murderous act. He maintained occasional contacts with the resistance, but never participated in any covert or overt act. As a methodical staff officer, Halder became infuriated with interventions by Hitler and OKW. After Hitler relieved Colonel-General Halder on September 24, 1942, he saw no further service during the war. Occasionally he appeared in public at official functions, especially military funerals. He finally retired on January 31, 1945. After the war he lived in Karlsruhe. Keilig, *Das Deutsche Heer,* p. 117; Telford Taylor, *The March of Conquest* (New York: Simon & Schuster, 1958), pp. 14-15; and Halder, *The Halder Diaries,* p. XXVI.

17. President (Field Marshal) Paul von Hindenburg died on August 1, 1934. The following day Hitler ordered the entire Reichswehr to swear an oath of allegiance to him. Oaths were not taken lightly by the German Army. This new oath, in particular, was sworn to Hitler and not to a constitution and had a special significance since all members of the Armed Forces swore the same unconditional obedience to the Führer. The oath was not void until Hitler's death.

18. Jacobsen, *Fall Gelb,* p. 26; Lewis, *Forgotten Legions,* p. 43; Harold C. Deutsch, *The Conspiracy against Hitler in the Twilight War* (Minneapolis: The University of Minnesota Press, 1968), pp. 34-35; and Walter Warlimont, *Inside Hitler's Headquarters 1939-1945,* trans. R. H. Barry (New York: Praeger Publishers, 1964), p. 61.

19. Lewis, *Forgotten Legions,* pp. 8-11; Halder, *The Halder Diaries,* pp. 5 and 22; and Below, *Als Hitlers Adjutant,* p. 211.

20. Zossen is a town about 20 miles south of Berlin where OKH maintained its field headquarters from October 1939 to May 1940. Subsequently, the headquarters displaced to Münstereifel, closer to the German–Belgian frontier, for the Battle of France. After the Battle of France it was relocated at Fontainebleau, France. Hitler used the name Zossen in a derogatory manner, often referring to the OKH leadership as the ''Spirit of Zossen'' (defeatists). Taylor, *The March of Conquest,* p. 15.

21. Jacobsen, *Fall Gelb,* p. 32; for additional information on opposition to Hitler's plans see Edgar Röhricht's *Pflicht und Gewissen: Erinnerungen eines deutschen Generals,*

pp. 151-55; and Walter Warlimont's *Inside Hitler's Headquarters 1939-1945.*

22. General von Bock took command of Army Group B on October 10, 1939; Franz Halder, *The Halder Diaries,* p. 100; Max Domarus, *Hitler, Reden und Proklamationen 1932-1945: Kommentiert von einem deutschen Zeitgenossen,* vol. 2, *Untergang Erster Halbband 1939-1940* (Wiesbaden: R. Löwitt, 1973), pp. 1378-93; also see Chapter 3, "Hitler Elects to Attack in the West," in Harold C. Deutsch, *The Conspiracy against Hitler in the Twilight War.*

23. Fedor von Bock was born on December 3, 1880 in the town of Kustrin. He entered the 5th Prussian Foot Guard Regiment in March 1898. Von Bock distinguished himself as a staff officer during World War I. He was promoted to the rank of Field Marshal on July 19, 1940. Von Bock saw no further service after 1942 and on May 4, 1945, died of wounds suffered during an RAF strafing attack. Lewis, *Forgotten Legions,* p. 90; and Taylor, *The March of Conquest,* p. 405.

24. Wilhelm Ritter von Leeb was born on September 5, 1876, in Passau and became an officer in the 4th Bavarian Artillery Regiment. In the Reichsheer he commanded the 7th Infantry Division. After his retirement in 1938, von Leeb was called back to active duty to command Army Group C during the German offensive in 1940. Amongst his peers von Leeb was regarded as a defensive "position" specialist and considered to be somewhat out of date in his military thinking. He saw no further service after 1942. Ritter von Leeb died at the age of 80, in Hohenschwangau. Taylor, *The March of Conquest,* p. 19; and Keilig. *Das Deutsche Heer,* p. 193.

25. Jacobsen, *Fall Gelb,* p. 15.

26. Walter von Reichenau was born in Karlsruhe on October 8, 1884. During World War I he served in the 1st Prussian Guards Field Artillery Regiment and later as a staff officer. In February 1934 he became the Chief of the Ministerial-Amt (administrative office), Reichswehr-Ministerium (Ministry of War), and in October 1935 headed Kreis-Gruppenkommado VII (District Army Group Command) (later Wehrkreis VII), Munich. Von Reichenau, also known as "Hans dampf in allen Gassen" (Hans who gets into every alley) was labeled a Nazi officer because he always maintained good contacts with the party. In 1934 he played a leading role during the Röhm crisis, taking the initiative and convincing Hitler of Röhm's goals and intentions with regards to the Army. Promoted Colonel-General on October 1, 1939, he assumed command of the 6th Army. On July 19, 1940 he received his promotion to Field Marshal. Interestingly enough, when Guderian recommended von Reichenau to replace von Brauchitsch in November 1939, Hitler simply replied, "This general is too political for my taste." Von Reichenau was a modern officer who understood the technical innovations of the day. Even though labeled a Nazi officer, von Reichenau did not fold when confronted by Hitler; on the contrary, he always spoke his mind in a very confident manner. Von Reichenau later developed doubts and finally broke with Hitler altogether. Lewis, *Forgotten Legions,* p. 32; Taylor, *The March of Conquest,* pp. 399, 400; and Below, *Als Hitlers Adjutant,* pp. 72-73 and 443.

27. Günther von Kluge, born on October 30, 1882 in Posen, began his military career in the 46th Prussian Field Artillery Regiment in 1901. He remained in the Reichsheer and commanded an artillery regiment. 1933 he became Inspector of Signal Troops and in 1934 assumed command of the 6th Infantry Division. Von Kluge commanded the 4th Army during the Battle of France in 1940 and was promoted to Field Marshal on July 19, 1940. He led from the front. His personality was somewhat complex and rendered him un-approachable to many. Thus, von Kluge was a difficult person as a superior and for many subordinates. Linked to the resistance movement, he committed suicide after the failed

attempt on Hitler's life in 1944. Keilig, *Das Deutsche Heer,* p. 168; Lewis, *Forgotten Legions,* p. 105.

28. Von Brauchitsch requested von Bock's opinion on the planned offensive because he did not want anyone to have the impression that he was using von Reichenau's opinion to back his own. The military community was well aware of von Reichenau's opposition to the offensive in the West. Von Bock, in his diary, does not clearly state what his reply to von Brauchitsch was. One can only assume it to have been negative since the reply went by personal courier and aircraft to Berlin. General Feldmarschall Fedor von Bock, Tagebuchnotizen Western 4.10.39–9.5.40. National Archives and Records Service (NARS), T84/271, pp. 1-3; Deutsch, *The Conspiracy against Hitler in the Twilight War,* pp. 72-75.

29. Domarus, *Hitlers Reden,* vol. 2, p. 1394; a total of 17 directives for the conduct of war were issued between August 31, 1939 and August 1, 1940. Taylor, *The March of Conquest,* pp. 433-34; at the same time Germany experienced a monthly steel deficit of 600,000 tons. Demands on the three services exceeded their productive capacity, placing the services in a state of constant rivalry for higher quotas. Halder, obviously concerned with these developments, indicated in his journal that the "ObdH must make clear cut demands in the economic field. Not only military and political demands, also economic demands." Halder, *The Halder Diaries,* vol. 2, p. 17; and Burkhart Müller-Hillebrand, *Das Heer 1933-1945,* vol. 2 (Frankfurt am Main: Verlag von E. S. Mittler & Sohn, 1956), pp. 41-42, 105-7, and 141.

30. Jacobsen, *Fall Gelb,* p. 19; Müller-Hillebrand, *Das Heer,* vol. 2, pp. 41-42, 105-6, and 141.

31. Halder, *The Halder Diaries,* vol. 2, p. 25; Jacobsen, *Fall Gelb,* p. 19; and Müller-Hillebrand, *Das Heer,* vol. 2, pp. 41-42, 105-7, and 141.

32. Müller-Hillebrand, *Das Heer,* vol. 2, pp. 40-42.

33. Ibid., p. 42.

34. Halder, *The Halder Diaries,* vol. 2, p. 30; also, Generals Keitel and Jodl visited Zossen on October 22 to discuss the recently published operations plan. During their discourse Keitel mentioned Hitler's displeasure with the plan, and that OKW decided that it was no longer necessary to occupy Holland. (The Chief of Staff of the Luftwaffe became irate when he realized the operation plan of October 29, 1939 did not incorporate Holland. The Luftwaffe feared that the British would use Dutch airfields for their fighters. Thus, by November 20, 1939 Holland was again added to the offensive and scheduled for occupation.) Jodl also explained Hitler's ideas of using Special Operation Forces to capture bridges and the fort at Eben-Emael in Belgium. Lastly, they informed Halder that Hitler set a firm date for the offensive based on OKH's decision that all armored forces would be combat-ready by November 11, 1939. The new date was November 12. Jacobsen, *Fall Gelb,* pp. 38-39; and Halder, *The Halder Diaries,* vol. 2, p. 111.

35. Gerd von Rundstedt was born in Aschersleben on December 12, 1875. In 1892 he joined the 83rd Light Infantry Regiment. After World War I, he remained in the Reichsheer to command both a cavalry and infantry division. In 1938 he retired as Colonel-General and became the honorary Colonel of the 18th Infantry Regiment. Called back to active duty in 1939 he served initially as Commander, Army Group South, and subsequently as Commander in Chief, East during the Polish Campaign. Relocating his headquarters to the West after the end of the Polish Campaign he was redesignated Commander, Army Group A on October 25, 1939. In this capacity, he directed the German forces at the Schwerpunkt of the Western offensive. He enjoyed deep respect not only as the most

senior German general, but because of his very resourcefulness, ability, and flexibility. As commander he relied on the professional officers of his staff, providing them a great deal of flexibility. Field Marshal von Rundstedt, a true believer in Auftragstaktik, displayed immense ability. Keilig, *Das Deutsche Heer,* p. 281; Taylor, *The March of Conquest,* p. 19; and Lewis, *Forgotten Legions,* p. 106.

36. Foreign Armies West. A division on the Army General Staff's intelligence section whose sole purpose was to collect intelligence and information on foreign armies west of Germany. Foreign Armies West was subdivided into smaller sections with duties for specific countries.

37. Wilhelm Keitel was born in Helmscherode on September 22, 1882. He entered the 46th Field Artillery Regiment in 1902. After World War I Keitel held several Reichsheer positions until he became Military Commandant of Bremen and was promoted to Major-General in 1934. In 1935 Keitel became chief of the Wehrmachtamt (Armed Forces Offices, principal department handling interservice planning amongst the three services) in the Ministry of War. By 1938 Keitel achieved the rank of Colonel-General. When Hitler, during the Blomberg-Fritsch crisis in 1938, asked von Blomberg for recommendations on a replacement, Keitel's name came into play. Hitler previously observed Keitel in the War Minister's office and actually questioned von Blomberg about him. Von Blomberg replied that Keitel was simply in charge of running the routine daily operations of the Wehrmachtamt. Hitler immediately indicated that that was exactly the type of officer he required. Hitler appointed him Chief of OKW, the successor agency to the Ministry of War. Although an impressive title, Keitel, unlike von Blomberg, was not a commander in chief of the Wehrmacht, hence he had no power over the three services. Behind his back, fellow officers would refer to him as "Lakeitel" (lackey). Keitel remained in his position until the end of the war. Condemned to hang as a war criminal by the Nürnberg War Tribunal, his execution was carried out in 1946. Keilig, *Das Deutsche Heer,* p. 160; Taylor, *the March of Conquest,* pp. 12-13; Lewis, *Forgotten Legions,* p. 43; Below, *Als Hitlers Adjutant,* pp. 66-67; and Horne, *To Lose A Battle,* p. 143; and Warlimont, *Inside Hitler's Headquarters,* pp. 12-13.

38. Alfred Jodl was born in Würzburg, Bavaria on May 5, 1890. He started his career as a cadet and subsequently joined the 4th Bavarian Field Artillery Regiment in July 1910, and was promoted Lieutenant in October 1912. After World War I, he served in the Reichsheer. He would become one of the most dominant figures in the OKW. In September 1939 Jodl took over as Chief, Plans and Operations Division of OKW, and became Hitler's principal military advisor throughout the war. More forceful than his superior, Keitel, Jodl often stated his views to Hitler. Jodl, overwhelmed by Hitler's early successes, became infatuated by his style of leadership. Consequently, Jodl treated his staff much the same way Hitler treated the leadership of OKH, simply providing them with detailed instructions for execution, rather than drawing on them for consultation. Jodl, tried for war crimes before the Nürnberg War Tribunal, was condemned to death and executed in 1946. Keilig, *Das Deutsche Heer,* p. 152; Taylor, *The March of Conquest,* p. 13; Lewis, *Forgotten Legions,* p. 63; and Warlimont, *Inside Hitler's Headquarters,* pp. 12-13.

39. Jacobsen, *Fall Gelb,* pp. 28-37; Horne, *To Lose a Battle,* pp. 124-25, 189-90; Ulrich Liss, *Westfront 1939/40: Erinnerungen des Feindbearbeiters im O.K.H.* (Neckargemünd: Scharnhorst Buchkameradschaft, 1959), pp. 102-3; and Donald S. Detweiler, *World War II Germany Military Studies,* vol. 7 (New York and London: Garland Publishing, Inc., 1979), pp. 29-30 (a collection of 213 special reports for the

United States on World War II prepared by former officers of the Wehrmacht); also, since the armored formations were scheduled to be fully combat-ready on November 11, 1939, Hitler opted for November 12 as the offensive date.

40. Halder, *The Halder Diaries,* vol. 2, p. 38.

41. Ibid., p. 39.

42. Ibid., p. 39; also the three Belgian forts were Eben-Emael, Liege, and Namur.

43. It is not clearly understood how many Panzer and motorized units Hitler intended for these Panzer groups. He worried about placing all Panzer and motorized forces at one main effort, south of Liege. Hitler felt that a simultaneous advance in two directions, north and south of Liege, would lead to a better chance for success. One must keep in mnd that Hitler, not a trained general staff officer, acted strictly on intuition. Halder, in the course of developing the final plan, eliminated this diluted main effort. The actual size of the Panzer group employed in May 1940 consisted of three corps (two Panzer and one motorized); later Panzer groups were renamed Panzer armies.

44. Jacobsen, *Fall Gelb,* p. 41.

45. Erich von Lewinski, known as Manstein, was born to a family of nine children in Berlin on November 24, 1887. His father was an artillery general and a member of an old aristocratic military family that produced several generals during the nineteenth and twentieth centuries. The von Mansteins were childless and adopted Erich at an early age. Hedwig von Manstein, Erich's new mother, was his birth mother's sister. In 1906, he entered the 3rd Prussian Foot Guard Regiment and during World War I served on General von Gallwitz's staff throughout most of the worst fighting at Verdun. Von Manstein became convinced that attrition warfare was obsolete. After the war he remained in the Reichsheer, and in 1935 became Army chief of operations under General Ludwig Beck. In 1938, after the Blomberg-Fritsch crisis, von Manstein took command of the 18th Infantry Division. General von Rundstedt managed to get von Manstein in 1939 as his chief of staff at Army Group A. Von Manstein played a key role in the development of the final operation plan for the Battle of France. He commanded from corps to army group, and was perhaps the most able field general the German Army produced in the twentieth century. His interests were purely professional. When the resistance movement approached him in 1942 to join in a coup, von Manstein replied that he would only participate after first being allowed to capture Sevastopol. Hitler relieved Field Marshal von Manstein in March 1944 because of the sharp differences separating them. He saw no further service during the war. After World War II, von Manstein was tried for war crimes and was sentenced to 12 years imprisonment. After his sentence was markedly reduced, he retired to Essen. Von Manstein assisted the new German Bundeswehr in "Amt Blank" and died on June 10, 1973. Keilig, *Das Deutsche Heer,* p. 196; Erich von Manstein, *Verlorene Siege,* 9th ed. (München: Bernhard & Gräfe Verlag, 1981), pp. 658-59; Horne, *To Lose a Battle,* pp. 150-51; and von Mellenthin, *German Generals,* p. 19.

46. Horne, *To Lose a Battle,* pp. 140-42; and Jacobsen, *Fall Gelb,* pp. 50-53.

47. Horne, *To Lose a Battle,* pp. 143-44; also Hitler realized that relieving the Commander in Chief of the Army at this stage of the war would have a destabilizing effect on the Army and public relations.

48. OKW (Oberkommando der Wehrmacht). Hitler created OKW to replace the Ministry of War in 1938. After Hitler relieved Field Marshal von Blomberg in 1938, War Minister and Commander in Chief of the Wehrmacht, he personally assumed the position of Commander in Chief. The position of War Minister remained vacant. Instead, Hitler appointed Wilhelm Keitel Chief of Staff, OKW. This assured Hitler that the three service chiefs would answer to him directly. Army staffs routinely referred to OKW as "Oben

Kein Wiederstand,'' no resistance at the top.

49. Heinz Guderian was born in Kulm on June 17, 1888. After attending the Karlsruhe Cadet School and the Cadet School at Gross-Lichterfelde, Berlin, he joined the 10th Hannoverian Jäger Battalion in 1908. After transferring with the battalion to Goslar in the Harz Mountains, Guderian fell in love with Margarete Görne. However, when they wanted to marry, Herr Görne disapproved because Margarete was only 18 years old. Guderian agreed to a two-year waiting period and asked for a reassignment during this time. His father, a Brigadier-General, suggested signal troops rather than machine guns. Guderian agreed, and transferred to the 3rd Telegraph Battalion in Koblenz. The time with the telegraph battalion shaped his future ideas on warfare. In 1913 Guderian earned one of 168 slots at the Potsdam War Academy. In the same year he married Margarete. Guderian, quick on his feet, earned the nickname "Schneller Heinz" in years to come. During World War I, Guderian served as intelligence officer at 5th Army headquarters, 4th Army headquarters, and the 4th Infantry Division. He served as the logistician for the Xth Corps, and commanded the 2nd Battalion, 14th Infantry Regiment. During the interwar period, Guderian commanded the 2nd Panzer Division, and XVIth Corps. On September 1, 1939, he assumed command of XIXth Corps (renamed XIXth Panzer Corps for the Battle of France). He held numerous command positions at echelons above corps and served as Army chief of staff from July 1944 until March 1945. After his release as prisoner of war in 1948, he settled in Schöngau. Colonel-General Guderian a.D. died on May 14, 1954. Keilig, *Das Deutsche Heer*, p. 111; Horst Scheibert, *Das war Guderian* (Friedberg: Podzun-Pallas-Verlag, 1975), pp. 15 and 165; and Kenneth Macksey, *Guderian: Creator of the Blitzkrieg* (New York: Stein and Day Publishers, 1976), pp. 33-37; also, Guderian's new motorized group was scheduled to be composed of one motorized division, one SS regiment (Leibstandarte-SS "Adolf Hitler"), Infanterie Regiment "Grossdeutschland," and the 4th Light Division. Army Goroup A operation order, dated November 17, 1939, the SS regiment is Leibstandarte-SS "Adolf Hitler." NARS T311/246, Beilage 1 zu Anlage 1 z. H. Gr. Befehl Nr. 3 den 17. November 1939.

50. Jacobsen, *Fall Gelb*, pp. 52-53.

51. Halder, *The Halder Diaries*, vol. 2, p. 48; Jacobsen, *Fall Gelb*, pp. 52-53; Feld Marschall Fedor von Bock, *Tagebuchnotizen Westen 4.10.39–9.5.40*, p. 18.

52. Jacobsen, *Fall Gelb*, p. 50-53; and Heinz Guderian, *Panzer Leader* trans. by Constantine Fitzgibbon (New York: Ballatine Books, 1957; 5th printing, 1972), pp. 67-68; also there were a total of 29 postponements of the offensive date throughout the winter and spring period of 1939-40:

No. of postponements:	Decision date:	D-Day:	No. of days shifted:
	5 Nov 39	12 Nov 39	(7 days to deploy)
1	7 Nov 39	15 Nov 39	3
2	9 Nov 39	19 Nov 39	4
3	13 Nov 39	22 Nov 39	3
4	16 Nov 39	26 Nov 39	4
5	20 Nov 39	3 Dec 39	7
6	27 Nov 39	9 Dec 39	6
			(5 days to deploy)
7	4 Dec 39	11 Dec 39	2
8	6 Dec 39	17 Dec 39	6
9	12 Dec 39	1 Jan 40	15

No. of postponements:	Decision date:	D-Day:	No. of days shifted:
10	27 Dec 39	(13 or 14 Jan 40)	12
11	9 Jan 40	14 Jan 40	-
12	10 Jan 40	17 Jan 40	3
13	13 Jan 40	20 Jan 40	3
14	16 Jan 40	sometime in the spring	(24 hours to deploy)
15	(6 Mar 40	18 Mar 40	-)
16	(13 Mar 40	nothing definite	-)
17	(14 Mar 40	not before 22 Mar 40)	
18	(26/27 Mar 40	probably on 14 Mar 40)	
19	(10 Apr 40	13 Apr 40	-)
20	(14 Apr 40	21/22 Apr 40	-)
21	(18 Apr 40	not before 24 Apr 40)	
22	(22 Apr 40	nothing definite	-)
23	(27 Apr 40	betw. 1-7 May)	
24	(3 May 40	5 May 40	-)
25	3 May 40	6 May 40	1
26	4 May 40	7 May 40	1
27	5 May 40	8 May 40	1
28	7 May 40	9 May 40	1
29	8 May 40	10 May 40	final

Note: Dashes do not indicate the recall of marching orders, rather Hitler's suspenses (i.e., Hitler thinks).
Source: Jacobsen, *Fall Gelb,* p. 141.

53. Ibid., p. 53.

54. Von Bock diary, pp. 10-20, covering the dates October 27 to November 15, 1939.

55. Jacobsen, *Fall Gelb,* pp. 148-52; von Manstein, *Verlorene Siege,* pp. 103-4; and Horne, *To Lose a Battle,* pp. 152 and 155.

56. Von Manstein, *Verlorene Siege,* pp. 101-3.

57. Jacobsen, *Fall Gelb,* p. 152.

58. Ibid., pp. 148-52; von Manstein, *Verlorene Siege,* pp. 101-3; Horne, *To Lose a Battle,* pp. 124-25; also Robert Allen Doughty's *The Seeds of Disaster: The Development of French Army Doctrine 1919-1939* (Hamden, CN: Archon Books, 1985) provides an excellent account of French doctrine for that time period.

59. Based on Keitel's visit on October 22, OKH removed the occupation of Holland from its October 29 operation plan. OKH published its plan without consulting OKL. This resulted in an immediate complaint by the Luftwaffe, because its chief of staff felt that once Belgian neutrality was violated, Britain would use Dutch fighter bases. Consequently, OKW issued Directive No. 6 for the conduct of war on November 20 with the following changes to the basic October 29 plan:

a. The Army must occupy Holland.

b. The main effort remains with Army Group B, however, OKH must be prepared to shift to Army Group A, should the opportunity arise.

On November 23, Hitler assembled about 120 leading generals and admirals of the three services at the Chancellory to explain his offensive philosophy. His monolog began at noon and lasted several hours. Among other things, Hitler attacked the Army leadership for not conforming to his offensive ideas. He labeled OKH as "Zossen Geister" (Defeatists from Zossen), and declared personal war on "Miesmacher" (troublemakers) who dared to oppose his aims. He praised the Luftwaffe and Navy for their achievements. The entire theme of Hitler's speech was a rebuttal of von Brauchitsch's accusations of November 5. Hitler called General von Brauchitsch to the Chancellory for another meeting at 1800 hours to again denounce the Army commander in chief. Von Brauchitsch offered his resignation, but Hitler refused on the grounds that he (von Brauchitsch) like any other soldier must perform his duty. Later that evening, Guderian spoke to Hitler and recommended that von Brauchitsch be relieved as a result of the Führer's lack of confidence in his Army commander in chief. Guderian recommended von Reichenau as a replacement. Hitler, however, declined. Domarus, *Hitler's Reden,* vol. 2, *Untergang,* pp. 1420-27; and, directives referred to in the January 17, 1940 offensive date, were those issued on October 10, November 11, 15, 20, and 28, 1939.

60. Major Hellmuth Reinberger, a Luftwaffe paratroop officer, against strict orders, carried the top secret operation plan while on a flight from Münster to Köln. His pilot, Captain Erich Hönmann, because of poor visibility, strayed into Belgian territory. While attempting to return to the German border their ME 108 (Typhoon) developed engine trouble. Unable to restart the engine, Hönmann made an emergency landing near the village of Mechelen, Belgium. Reinberger, borrowing matches from a Belgian farmer, attempted to burn the plans behind a hedge not far from the wreckage. Hönmann in the meantime tried to act as the sole German when Belgian officers and troops arrived. The Belgian officers, spotting Reinberger's smoke, apprehended him also. Reinberger later had another opportunity to burn additional papers when Belgian officers left him and Hönmann unattended. The Belgians stopped him again and, finally realizing that Reinberger carried something important, confiscated the papers. Consequently, portions of the operation plan fell into Allied hands. The German military attaché interviewed both officers shortly afterwards and reported that the Belgians only obtained nonessential information. Hitler remained unconvinced by the reports and postponed the offensive indefinitely. This proved fortunate for OKH because now, for the first time, an opportunity existed to fundamentally change the October 29 plan. Jacobsen, *Fall Gelb,* pp. 93-99; Horne, *To Lose a Battle,* pp. 156-57; and Halder, *The Halder Diaries,* vol. 2, p. 24.

61. Halder, *The Halder Diaries,* vol. 3, pp. 80-81; and Jacobsen, *Fall Gelb,* pp. 148-52.

62. Ibid., pp. 148-52; Guderian, *Panzer Leader,* pp. 69-71. During the war game at Mayen on February 14, 1940, Halder agreed to employing XIXth and XIVth Panzer Corps side by side through Belgium. It also became apparent to the Army chief of staff that this armored thrust required a separate army headquarters. Halder chose General Ewald von Kleist to command the armored force over Guderian. Guderian, *Panzer Leader,* pp. 69-70.

63. Jacobsen, *Fall Gelb,* p. 153; and Horne, *To Lose a Battle,* pp. 166-68.

64. Lewis, *Forgotten Legions,* pp. 94-98.

CHAPTER 2

1. Müller-Hillebrand, *Das Heer,* vol. 2, pp. 31-32.

2. Yearly draft group or wave is a translation of the German word "Welle." OKH

categorized the divisions into waves for mobilization purposes. The Army further segregated divisions into active, reserve, and Landwehr divisions. The first wave, active duty divisions, numbered from 1 through 36 and 44 through 46, a total of 39 divisions. The second wave, reserve divisions, totaled 16. The third wave, reserve/Landwehr divisions, totaled 21. The fourth wave, primarily composed of reservists, totaled 14.

	1st Draft	2nd Draft	3rd Draft	4th Draft
Active Duty	78%	6%	0%	9%
Reserve	18%	91%	58%	67%
Landwehr	4%	3%	42%	24%

Once fully mobilized the personnel strength of the 1st through 4th wave infantry divisions was composed of 35,781 officers, 191,238 noncommissioned officers, and 1,146,934 enlisted. Upon mobilization the 1st wave divisions provided active duty officers and NCOs to 2nd wave divisions as cadre, so they could immediately deploy into combat. Third wave divisions, consisting of age groups 1900 to 1913, had only received short-term training. Fourth wave divisions, although short-term enlistees, had active cadre. Interestingly, the 5th and 6th wave, hastily organized once Hitler decided to attack France, received only Czechoslovakian weapons. Werner Haupt, *Das Buch der Infantrie* (Friedberg: Podzun-Pallas Verlag, 1962), pp. 50-55; Franz Halder, *The Halder Diaries,* p. XXVII; and Müller-Hillebrand, *Das Heer,* vol. 2, pp. 32-36 and 47.

   3. Müller-Hillebrand, *Das Heer,* vol. 2, pp. 32-33.
   4. Lewis, *Forgotten Legions,* p. 89.
   5. The MG 34 was a gas pressure, recoil-operated gun. The MG 34 replaced the MG 08/15, a World War I vintage light machine gun, in 1934. The MG 34, however, was not officially accepted into the Army until shortly before the Polish Campaign. The MG 34 was considered to be a light machine gun when operated with its bipod. When employed with a tripod, it was classified as a heavy machine gun. Subsequent to the reorganization of the rifle squad, after the Polish Campaign, each squad was equipped with the MG 34, providing a platoon of four squads with immense firepower. The MG 34 gun section consisted of a gunner, assistant gunner, and an ammunition bearer. Technical data are as follows:

Caliber	7.92 mm
Weight	12.1 kg (24.4 lbs)
Length	1.22 meters
Barrel length	59.2 cm
Sight adjustment	200 to 2,000 meters
Maximum range	3,000 meters
Initial muzzle velocity	755 meters/second
Rate of fire	800 to 900 rounds/minute
Maximum effective range	1,500 meters

These light machine guns provided the rifle companies with their main firepower. The light weight and low profile of the MG 34 facilitated its forward employment in all types of combat. The MG 34 could easily be operated by a single gunner, when necessary. Alex Buchner, *Das Handbuch der Deutschen Infanterie 1939-1945: Gliederung Uniformen-Bewaffnung-Ausrüstung-Einsätze* (Friedberg: Podzun-Pallas-Verlag, 1987), p. 25.

6. Halder, *The Halder Diaries,* pp. 80-82; and Lewis, *Forgotten Legions,* pp. 65-67.

7. Halder, *The Halder Diaries,* pp. 80-82; and Lewis, *Forgotten Legions,* pp. 65-67.

8. S. J. Lewis, "Reflections on Military Reforms: One German Example" (accepted for publication by *Military Review,* January 1988), p. 2.

9. Williamson Murray, "The German Response to Victory in Poland," *Armed Forces and Society,* Winter 1981, vol. 7, no. 2, pp. 285-98.

10. General der Infanterie a. D. Günther Blumentritt, *The German Armies 1914 and 1939,* trans. M. Otto (Fort Leavenworth: Combat Studies Institute, U.S. Army Command and General Staff College, 1986), pp. 267-73.

11. Murray, "The German Response," pp. 285-98; and Lewis, *Forgotten Legions,* pp. 60-64.

12. Müller-Hillebrand, *Das Heer,* vol. 2, p. 40; Gordon A. Craig, *The Politics of the Prussian Army 1640-1945* (New York: Oxford University Press, 1972), p. 482. Police officers inducted into the Reichsheer maintained their equivalent Army rank. Army officers showed distaste for this procedure since advancement in the Reichsheer was much slower than in the police.

13. The Abitur is equivalent to an Associate Arts Degree. In the German school system children begin their Hochschule and Gymnasium (high school) education at the end of their fourth grade. Thus the German Hochschule and Gymnasium encompass subjects in the humanities and sciences that are only taught in colleges and universities in the United States.

14. Lewis, *Forgotten Legions,* pp. 60-64; Murray, "The German Response," p. 287; Müller-Hillebrand, *Das Heer,* vol. 2, p. 37; Claus Meyer, "Geschichte der Feldjägertruppe," in Helmut Damerau, ed., *Deutsches Soldatenjahrbuch 1988: 36. Deutscher Soldatenkalender* (München: Schild Verlag, 1988), pp. 340-41; and Edgar Röhricht, *Pflicht und Gewissen: Erinnerungen eines deutschen Generals 1932 bis 1944* (Stuttgart: W. Kohlhammer Verlag, 1965), p. 158.

15. Der ObdH, Gen St d H/Ausb. (Ia), Nr. 400/39g. 13.10.39, Betr.: "Ausbildung des Feldheeres"; see Appendix H, German Military Documents for an explanation of the format of preceding citation; and Halder, *The Halder Diaries,* vol. 3, pp. 5 and 22.

16. Murray, "The German Response," p. 291.

17. ObdH, Gen St d H/Ausb. (Ia), Nr. 400/39g. 13.10.39, Betr.: "Ausbildung des Feldheeres"; and Hermann Balck, *Ordnung im Chaos* (Osnabrück: Biblio Verlag, 1981), pp. 265-66.

18. Lewis, *Forgotten Legions,* p. 94; and Buchner, *Das Handbuch der Deutschen Infanterie,* pp. 15-17.

19. Murray, "The German Response," p. 293.

20. Murray, "The German Response," pp. 285-98; and ObdH, 24.10.39., Zustandsberichte, NARS T315/1025/357.

21. Murray, "The German Response," pp. 285-98.

22. Halder, *The Halder Diaries,* vol. 3, p. 117; and Lewis, "Reflections on Military Reforms."

23. Lewis, *Forgotten Legions,* p. 97.

24. ObdH, Gen St d H/Ausb. (Ia), Nr. 900/39g. 12.12.39, Betr.: "Ausbildung des Feldheeres."

25. Ibid.; Müller-Hillebrand, *Das Heer,* vol. 2, p. 42; and Halder, *The Halder Diaries,* vol. 3, pp. 88-89.

26. ObdH, Gen St d H/Ausb. (Ia), Nr. 900/39g. 12.12.39, Betr.: "Ausbildung des Feldheeres."

27. OKH, Gen St d H/Gen d. Inf. 1964/40g. III, 28.2.40, Betr.: Truppenpioniere bei den M. G. Bataillonen; OKH did not expect to have any armor vehicle launch bridges until the end of March 1940. These hydraulically emplaced bridges were mounted on a Panzer Mark IV chassis. The bridge span was nine meters for a water depth of two meters. Four divisions were scheduled to receive three units each. There was also a shortage of infantry foot bridges, of which two were to be ready sometime in February 1940. Halder, *The Halder Diaries,* vol. 3, p. 27.

28. Halder, *The Halder Diaries,* vol. 3, pp. 88-89.

29. A.O.K. 12, O. Qu I, 5.3.40, Betr.: Persöhnlicher Brief des Oberbefehlshabers A.O.K. 12 an den Oberbefehlshaber Heeresgruppe A.

30. Heeresgruppe A, O. Qu I Nr. 145/40geh, 26.1.40, Betr.: Verkehrskontrolle der Heeresgruppe A; Heeresgruppe A, ObdH, A. H. Qu, den 14.12.39, Betr. Heeresgruppen-Befehl zur Besserung der Verkehrsverhältnisse im Bereich der Heeresgruppe A; Nachschubkompanie 32, Wasser-Kol. Mot Zug 162/561, 18.4.40. General Guderian sent a letter to his division commanders on February 14, 1940 in an effort to make safe driving everyone's concern. Between October 1, 1939 and January 31, 1940, XIXth Panzer Corps suffered 22 fatalities, 101 serious injuries, and 300 light injuries from traffic related accidents. A thorough investigation revealed that all accidents resulted from poor driver discipline. Guderian also emphasized the corps' equipment losses, especially in vehicles, for which no replacements existed. Generalkommando XIX. Armeekorps, den 14.2.40.

31. Of the 25,360 authorized vehicles in 12th Army, 24,457 were on hand; of the 569 vehicles not on hand, 1 ton or larger capacity trucks precipitated a transport hauling short-fall of 1,707 tons. The 12th Army also had many motorcycles, ¼ to ½ ton trucks, and 1 ton or higher capacity trucks in maintenance shops. Its total hauling shortfall in 1 ton or higher capacity trucks amounted to 16.9 percent or 4,773 tons. A.O.K. 12, O.Qu I, 1/Kf. 7.1.40, Betr.: Kfz-Bestand der Armee; and A.O.K. 12, 38/40g. Kdo, 15.1.40, Betr.: Kfz-Bestand der Armee, Persöhnlicher Brief des Oberbefehlshaber der 12. Armee an den Herrn Oberbefehlshaber der Heeresgruppe A.

32. Wilhelm List was born in Oberkirch on May 14, 1880. He entered the Army as an officer cadet on July 15, 1898, and joined the 1st Bavarian Engineer Battalion in 1900. After World War I, List remained in the Reichsheer and commanded the Infantry School in 1930, the 4th Division in 1933, the 4th Corps in 1935, and 2nd and 5th Army Groups in 1938. During World War II, he commanded 14th Army in Poland, assumed command of 12th Army on October 25, 1939, and was Commander Southeast from July to October 1941. From July to September 1942, List commanded Army Group A. List was promoted to Field Marshal on July 19, 1940 for his services in the Battle of France. List settled in Garmisch after World War II. Keilig, *Das Deutsche Heer,* p. 201.

33. A.O.K. 12, 38/40g. Kdo, 15.1.40, Betr.: Kfz-Bestand der Armee, Persöhnlicher Brief des Oberbefehlshaber der 12. Armee an den Herrn Oberbefehlshaber der Heeresgruppe A.

34. Generalkommando XIX. A. K., O. Qu I, Nr. 065/40g., 12.1.40; Fedor von Bock, *Tagebuchnotizen Westen,* diary entry of November 6, 1939; also, in early March 1940 OKH received a report that 2nd Panzer Division had hoarded seven railroad boxcars of vehicle repair parts. This caused the initiation of an investigation which in fact located the boxcars in 2nd Panzer Division's deployment area. The division commander, rather embarrassed, returned the parts within ten days. Armee-Oberkommando 12 O. Qu/Qu 1/Kf. A. H. Qu, den 10.3.40, Bezug: OKH Gen St d H, Gen Qu/Qu3 Abt IIb Nr. 5031/40 vom 6.3.40, Betr.: Kfz-Ersatzteile der 2. Pz. Division.

35. Müller-Hillebrand, *Das Heer,* vol. 2, p. 42.

36. Halder, *The Halder Diaries,* vol. 3, pp. 15-16; and Lewis, "Reflections on Military Reforms," p. 9.

37. OKH, Gen St d H/Ausb. Abt (Ia), Nr. 135/40g. 19.01.40, Betr.: "Ausbildung des Feldheeres," Bez. ObdH/Gen St d H/Ausb. Abt (Ia), Nr. 400/39g. von 13.10.39 und Nr. 900/39g. von 12.12.39.

38. Aggressor forces provide a certain realism to training because they dressed as enemy soldiers and employed the enemy's doctrine and tactics.

39. OKH, Gen St d H/Ausb. Abt (Ia), Nr. 135/40g. 19.01.40, Betr.: "Ausbildung des Feldheeres," Bez. ObdH/Gen St d H/Ausb. Abt (Ia), Nr. 400/39g. von 13.10.39 und Nr. 900/39g. von 12.12.39.

40. Ewald von Kleist was born on August 8, 1881 in Braunfels. He entered the 3rd Light Field Artillery Regiment in 1901. In 1912, von Kleist transferred to a Hussar regiment. During the interwar period, he commanded an infantry regiment, the 2nd Cavalry Division, and VIIIth Corps. Von Kleist retired as General of Cavalry in 1938. Called back to active duty when war broke out in 1939, von Kleist commanded the XXII Corps during the Polish Campaign. After the Polish Campaign, XXII Corps headquarters transferred to Rheinberg on the Western Front. In March 1940, XXII Corps headquarters, renamed Panzer Gruppe von Kleist, transferred for operational control to Army Group A. Panzer Group von Kleist became the higher headquarters for XIXth and XLIst Panzer Corps and XIVth Motorized Corps. Von Kleist led the first echelon and main effort in the advance through the Ardennes to the Channel coast. He was promoted to the rank of Field Marshal in 1943. Initially a prisoner of war of the British, von Kleist was handed over to the Yugoslavians in 1946 and subsequently to the Soviet Union in 1948. Field Marshal Ewald von Kleist died in 1954, his ninth year of imprisonment in the Soviet Union, Keilig, *Das Deutsche Heer,* p. 166; and Robert Wistrich, *Who's Who in Nazi Germany* (New York: Macmillan Publishing Co., 1982), pp. 172-73.

41. General Headquarters Troops are those units assigned to army level or higher headquarters.

42. Generalkommando XXII. A. K. Nr. 882/40 geh., K. H. Qu, den 6.3.40. Assumption of command orders.

43. Ulrich Liss, *Westfront 1939/40: Erinnerungen des Feindbearbeiters im O.K.H.* (Neckargemünd: Scharnhorst Buchkameradschaft, 1959), p. 104.

44. Ibid., p. 143.

45. Ibid., p. 144.

46. Ibid.

47. The 1st Chasseurs Ardennais was a Belgian light infantry division specially trained for delaying action. E. T. Melchers, *Kriegsschauplatz Luxemburg, August 1914-May 1940* (Luxemburg: Sankt-Paulus Druckerei, A. G., 1979), p. 383.

48. Liss, *Westfront,* p. 144.

49. *ObdH, Gen St d H Op Abt (Ia) Nr. 130/40 g. Kdos H Qu OKH, 24.2.40, Betr.: Geheime Kommandosache: Die zur Zeit* gültige Aufmarschanweisung "Gelb" (Der ObdH Gen St d H Op Abt (Ia) Nr. 074/40 g. Kdos Chefs vom 30.1.40) ist durch anliegende Neufassung im Sinne meiner Ausführungen von den Oberbefehlshabern am 24.2.40 zu ersetzen. gez. Brauchitsch; Anlage 1 zu ObdH Gen St d H Op Abt (Ia) Nr. 130/40 g. Kdos vom 24.2.40, Betr.: Neufassung der Aufmarschanweisung "Gelb"; and XXII A. K. (Gruppe von Kleist Kriegstagebuch (KTB)) Nr. 3, (March 6, 1940 to May 9, 1940), entry for March 6, 1940.

50. Ernst Busch was born in Essen-Steele on July 6, 1885. He joined the 13th Infantry

Regiment in 1904. After World War I, he remained in the Reichsheer and commanded the 9th Infantry Regiment in 1932, the 23rd Division in 1935, and the 8th Corps in 1938. During World War II, Busch continued to command the 8th Corps in the Polish Campaign. In February 1940, he assumed command of 16th Army for the Battle of France. From October 1943 to June 1944, Busch commanded Army Group Center on the Eastern Front and in March 1945, Army Group Northwest. Busch was promoted to Field Marshal on February 1, 1943. He died as a prisoner of war in England in 1945. Keilig, *Das Deutsche Heer,* p. 51.

51. Anlage B. Generalkommando XXII. A.K. (Gruppe von Kleist) Chef des Generalstabes, 10.8.40, Betr.: Vorläufige Erfahrungen mit grossen motorisierten Verbänden.

52. Georg-Hans Reinhardt was born in Bautzen on March 1, 1887. He entered the 107th Infantry Regiment in 1907. In the interwar period Reinhardt commanded the 1st Infantry Brigade (mot) and the 4th Panzer Division, maintaining command of the division through the Polish Campaign. In February 1940 Reinhardt assumed command of XLIst Panzer Corps. Reinhardt, promoted to Colonel-General in 1942, maintained this rank until 1945. General Reinhardt died in November 1963. Keilig, *Das Deutsche Heer,* p. 266.

53. Gustav von Wietersheim was born in Breslau on February 11, 1884. He entered the 4th Guard Grenadier Infantry Regiment in 1902. During the interwar period von Wietersheim commanded the 29th Infantry Division. In 1938 he assumed command of XIVth Corps, renamed XIVth Motorized Corps shortly before the Battle of France. Von Wietersheim, promoted to General of Infantry, received no further promotions. He retired in the latter part of 1942 and saw no further service. Keilig, *Das Deutsche Heer,* p. 364.

54. Anlage B, Generalkommando XXII. A.K. (Gruppe von Kleist) Chef des Generalstabes, 10.8.40, Betr.: Vorläufige Erfahrungen mit grossen motorisierten Verbänden; also, General von Kleist's concept envisioned two corps abreast, instead of three corps in depth. Von Rundstedt wanted to lead with one corps, three divisions abreast. Von Kleist felt that in combat a corps commander could only successfully command and control two divisions abreast. Von Rundstedt's concept totally committed XIXth Panzer Corps. With two corps leading, the Group's first echelon would consist of four divisions instead of three. Von Kleist's concept pitted more combat power up front, rather than echeloning in such great depth. KTB Nr. 3 (Gruppe von Kleist) 6.3.40; and Anlage B, Generalkommando XXII. A.K. (Gruppe von Kleist) Chef des Generalstabes, 10.8.40, Betr.: Vorläufige Erfahrungen mit grossen motorisierten Verbänden.

55. *The Encyclopedia Americana,* international ed. (Danbury, Conn.: Grolin Incorporated, 1984), 30 vols., p. 248.

56. Hans von Dach, "Panzer durchbrechen eine Armeestellung," *Schweizer Soldat* (47) 1972, no. 2, p. 58.

57. Anlage I zu Gr von Kleist Ia/Op Nr. 217/40 g. Kdos Chefs von 21.3.40 (Neuauffassung vom 3.5.40) Betr.: Besondere Anordnungen für die Strassenzuteilung, Marsch und Verkehrsregelung (zum "Befehl für den Durchbruch bis zur Maas"); and Verkehrsregelung, NARS T315/558/01329.

58. 1) Tactical March Routes (TMR) assigned to Panzer Group von Kleist.

TMR A Geichlingen: Start: Mosbach, Daun, Wallenborn, Weidenbach, Steinborn, Kyllburg, Malberg, Malbergweich, Seffern Süd, Bickendorf, Rittersdorf, Oberweis, Neuhaus, Sinspelt, Nieder-Geckler, *Geichlingen,* Roth, Vianden, Merscheid, Gralingen, Hoscheid, Niederschlinder, follow the road north of the Sauer to intersection 1 km east of Esch, Buderscheid, to intersection 800 m northeast of Schumann, Mecher, Böwen, to intersection 3 km southeast of Böwen, Harlange.

TMR B Wallendorf: Start: Horperath, Ulmen, Steiningen, Mehren, to intersection 1 km southwest of Oberwinkel, Gillenfeld, Eckfeld, Manderscheid, Eisenschmitt, Oberkail, Gindorf, Badem, Erdorf, Bitburg, Messerich, Bettingen, Peffingen, Mettendorf, Freilingerhöhe, *Wallendorf,* Bettendorf, Diekirch, Ettelbrück, Niederfeulen, Grossbus, Grewels, Martelingen.

TMR C Bollendorf: Start: Kaisersesch, Driesch, Ober Scheidweiler, Hasborn, Wittlich/ north, Hupperath, Landscheid, Niederkeil, Binsfeld, Hersforst, Speicher, Röhl, Scharfbillig, to intersection 1 km east of Esslingen, continue on road intersection 2 km east of Meckel, Niederweis, Echternacherbrück, *Bollendorf,* (cross river), Befort, Müllerthal, to intersection 1 km west of Breitweiler, Christnach, Fels (east), Medernach, Schrondweiler, Cruchten (8 km southwest of Diekirch), continue to railway station 1 km east of Berg, Bissen, Redingen, Attert.

TMR D Echternach: Start: Cochem, Moseltalstrasse to Alf, Kinderbeuren, Wittlich (south), Salmrohr, Hetzerath, Föhren, Ehrang, Kordel, Welschbillig, Eisenach, Menningen, Mindin, Rosport, Steinheim, *Echternach,* Michelshof, Alttrier, Heffingen, Fels (south), Angelsberg, Reckingen, Säul, Nördingen, Beckerich, Oberpallen, Tontelingen.

2) Main Supply Route assigned to Panzer Group von Kleist. Begin railway station Bitburg follow road to Trier to 1 km east of Masholder, Nieder Stedem, Wolsfeld, Echternach, Michelshof, Onsdorf, Müllerthal, follow TMR C to Medernach, Bissen to Redingen.

3) Feeder roads controlled by Panzer Group von Kleist.

Road Wallendorf: Hachenburg, Herschbach, Wölferlingen, Herschbach, Marienhausen, Rüscheid, Neuwied, Plaidt, Mayen, Monreal, Bermel, Oberelz, Horperath. *Road Bollendorf:* Reichsautobahn from Limburg to Koblenz, cross Rhine at Koblenz-Kesselheim, continue on autobahn to Kaisersesch. *Road Echternach:* Limburg, Hirschberg, Dörnberg, Badem, cross Rhine at Niederlahnstein, follow Moselstrasse to Cochem. *Feeder road Herborn–Wölferlingen:* Herborn, Höhn, Ailertchen, Langenhahn, Wölferlingen. *Feeder road Heuchelheim–Limburg:* Reichstrasse 49 from Heuchelheim to Limburg. *Feeder roads for 8th Panzer Div.:* All roads within the left and right boundaries are available for movement of the division. Left boundary: Wittlich, Platten, Wehlem, Bernkastel, Longkamp, Mosbach, Allenbach, Kirschweiler, Idar-Oberstein. Right boundary: Alf, Bullay, Moritzheim, Hesweiler, Panzweiler, Kappel, Dickenschied, Rhauen, Bundenbach, Kellenfels, Kirn. The division received orders to utilize every available crossing over the Moselle to feed into TMR B. XIX. A.K. Studie für Korpsbefehl Nr. 1. Für den "Fall Gelb," March 28, 1940.

59. Anlage I zu Gr von Kleist Ia/Op Nr. 217/40 g. Kdos Chefs von 21.3.40 (Neuauffassung vom 3.5.40), Betr.: Besondere Anordnungen für die Strassenzuteilung, Marsch und Verkehrsregelung (zum "Befehl für den Durchbruch bis zur Maas"); und Verkehrsregelung, NARS T315/558/01329; and Dach, "Panzer durchbrechen eine Armeestellung," p. 60.

60. XXII.A.K. (Gr von Kleist) KTB, 8.3.40.

61. Kurt Zeitzler was born in Gossmar/Luckau on June 9, 1895. He entered the 72nd Infantry Regiment in 1914. After World War I, Zeitzler remained in the Reichsheer. In the spring of 1939 he took command of the 60th Infantry Regiment. During World War II, Zeitzler served as chief of staff of the XXIInd Corps (later Panzer Group von Kleist) throughout the Polish and French Campaigns, and as chief of staff of Army Group D in 1942. On September 24, 1942, he replaced Halder as the Army chief of staff and served in that capacity until July 1, 1944. Zeitzler was discharged from the Army on January 31, 1945. In September 1942, Zeitzler was promoted to General of the Infantry, bypassing the rank of Major-General. The highest rank he achieved was Colonel-General on January 30,

1944. Zeitzler retired to Hamburg after the war, and died in September 1963 at the age of 68. Keilig, *Das Deutsche Heer,* p. 374.

62. Dach, "Panzer durchbrechen eine Armeestellung," p. 60; and XXII. A.K. (Gr von Kleist) KTB, 8.3.40.

63. Anlage I zu Gr von Kleist Ia/Op Nr. 217/40 g. Kdos Chefs von 21.3.40 (Neuauffassung vom 3.5.40), Betr.: Besondere Anordnungen für die Strassenzuteilung, Marsch und Verkehrsregelung (zum "Befehl für den Durchbruch bis zur Maas"); Gr von Kleist O. Qu/Qu I, 175/40 geh. Kdos, 1.4.40; and Heeresgruppe A O. Qu I, Nr. 457/40 geh., 20.3.40, Betr.: Verkehrsregelung an den Rheinbrücken im Bereich der Heeresgruppe A.

64. Beilage B zur Anlage I Gr von Kleist Ia/Op 217/40 geh. Kdos vom 21.3.40, Betr.: Besondere Anordnungen für die Verkehrsregelung; Anlage I zu Gr von Kleist Ia/Op Nr. 217/40 g. Kdos Chefs von 21.3.40. (Neuauffassung vom 3.5.40), Betr. Besondere Anordnungen für die Strassenzuteilung, Marsch und Verkehrsregelung (zum "Befehl für den Durchbruch bis zur Maas"); and Der Kommandierende General der Gr von Kleist, Einsatzort, den 11.5.40, NARS T315/558.

65. Anlage I zu Gr von Kleist Ia/Op Nr. 217/40 g. Kdos Chefs von 21.3.40 (Neuauffassung vom 3.5.40), Betr.: Besondere Anordnungen für die Strassenzuteilung, Marsch und Verkehrsregelung (zum "Befehl für den Durchbruch bis zur Maas").

66. Halder, *The Halder Diaries,* vol. 3, p. 91; Melchers, *Kriegsschauplatz Luxemburg,* pp. 191-210; and Jacobsen, *Fall Gelb,* p. 163.

67. Regular infantry divisions were equipped with two type B bridges only. Type K bridges were found in Panzer and motorized infantry divisions.

68. Anlage 5 zu Gr von Kleist Ia/Op 217/40 g. Kdos Chefs, vom 21.3.40, Betr.: Besondere Anordnungen für das überwinden der Befestigungen, Sperrungen u. Flüsse im Vormarschstreifen.

69. Buchner, *Das Handbuch der Deutschen Infanterie 1939-1945,* pp. 60-66.

70. The type B bridges developed in 1934 consisted of heavy pontoon and trestle bridge equipment: 16 half pontoons (eight full pontoons), 8 piles, 2 ramps, 8 stills, 8 crossing rails (16 ton capacity), 6 storm boats, 1 motor boat, 20 small pneumatic boats, and 24 large pneumatic boats. The personnel in the type B and K bridge columns were only equipment caretakers and transporters. Bridges or ferries were constructed and operated with personnel from the three engineer companies within the battalion. Thus, during bridge construction, engineers were in short supply for other missions. This is the primary reason why the German Army trained infantrymen in routine engineers' tasks. Having infantrymen trained in engineer skills left more engineers available for both routine and technical missions. Type B bridge characteristics and capabilities are: Pontoon bridges: four ton capacity = 130 meters, eight ton capacity = 80 meters, 16 ton capacity = 50 meters. Trestle bridge capacity:

3.9 meter span		6.4 meter span		19 meter span		32 meter span	
8 ton	*16 ton*	*8 ton*	*16 ton*	*8 ton*	*16 ton*	*8 ton*	*16 ton*
21*	9	13	7	2	2	1	1

Number of ferries: 4 ton capacity = 8; 8 ton capacity = 4; and 16 ton capacity = 2.

*Number of separate spans a type B bridge column could support for the given span distance/tonnage.

Buchner, *Das Handbuch der Deutschen Infanterie,* pp. 60-66; and OKH, *Handbuch für den Generalstabsdienst im Kriege,* vol. 2, pp. 218-19.

71. Type K bridge capabilities:

Gaps				Bridges			
9 meter span		*18 meter span*		*37 meter span*		*72 meter span*	
8 ton	*16 ton*	*8 ton*	*16 ton*	*8 ton*	*16 ton*	*8 ton*	*16 ton*
8*	4	4	2	2	1	1	–

Ferries: 8 ton capacity = 4; 16 ton capacity = 2.
*Number of separate spans a type K bridge column could support for the span distance/tonnage.
OKH, *Handbuch für den Generalstabsdienst im Kriege,* vol. 2, pp. 222-23.

72. Walther Nehring was born in Stretzin on August 15, 1892. He entered the 152nd Infantry Regiment in 1911. Remaining in the Reichsheer after World War I Nehring, promoted Colonel in 1937, commanded the 5th Panzer Regiment. In July 1939 he became Chief of Staff, XIXth Panzer Corps and remained with the corps through the Battle of France. Nehring took command of the 18th Panzer Division in October 1940 and subsequently served with the Afrika Corps from March to August 1942 and as Commander in Chief Tunisia, November-December the same year. Nehring achieved the rank of General of Panzer Troops in July 1942. General Nehring served in many other high command positions throughout the war. Keilig, *Das Deutsche Heer,* p. 232-33.

73. The Fieseler Storch (Fi 156) was a single engined aircraft capable of holding the pilot and two passengers. Originally designed as an observation aircraft, the Storch had a wing span of 14 m, length of 10 m, and a 240 hp engine capable of flying 170 km/h. Flying range was 800 km or 5½ hours. Maximum carrying capacity, including the pilot, was 470 kg (1034 lbs). Required minimum take-off distance was 120 m and required minimum landing distance 80 m, at maximum weight. Since several other similar operations were planned for May 10, 1940, only 100 aircraft became available for Garski's battalion. Dach, ''Panzer durchbrechen eine Armeestellung,'' p. 67.

74. Anlage 1 zu: Generalkommando XIX. A.K., Abt la Nr. 35/40 g. Kdos, 1.2.40.

75. Halder, *The Halder Diaries,* vol. 3, p. 95; Generalkommando XIX. A.K., Abt Ia Nr. 273/40g. Kdos den 10.4.40. and Generalkommando XIX. A.K., Abt Ia Nr. 280/40 g. Kdos den 11.4.40; Anlage 1 zu: Generalkommando XIX. A.K. Abt Ia Nr. 35/40 g. Kdos 1.2.40. Crailsheim served as training area for special operations units.

76. Codename NIWI was derived from the first letters of the towns of *Ni*ves and *Wi*try; Generalkommando XIX. A.K. Abt Ia 16.4.40, Betr.: Befehl für den Einsatz der Abteilung Förster-Garski; and Abt Ia Nr. 536/40g Kdos, den 13.4.40.

77. Hugo Sperrle was born in Ludwigsburg on February 7, 1885. He joined the 126th Royal Würtemberg Infantry Regiment at an early age and was promoted to Lieutenant in 1913. During World War I, Sperrle served in the air force. After the war he remained in the Reichsheer, worked at the Reichswehr Ministry in 1925, and held several commands between 1929 and 1933. In 1935 he transferred to the newly formed Luftwaffe as a Brigadier-General and, recognized for his leadership and organizational abilities, quickly rose in rank. During the Spanish Civil War, Sperrle commanded the German Condor Legion in Spain. In November 1937 he was promoted to General of Fliers and in 1938 he assumed command of Luftflotte III (Air Corps). Luftflotte III supported von Kleist's advance and breakthrough operation in May 1940. In July 1940 Sperrle was promoted, along with many other generals, to the rank of Field Marshal. Sperrle held many other high ranking positions during the war. Acquitted of all war crimes by the Allied Tribunal, Sperrle lived out his life in Munich. He died on April 7, 1953. Wistrich, *Who's Who in*

Nazi Germany, pp. 294-95; and Helmut Damerau, ed., *Deutsches Soldatenjahrbuch 1963* (Tettnang: Lorenz Senn Verlag, 1963), p. 169.

78. Melchers, *Kriegsschauplatz Luxemburg,* p. 380; Generalkommando XIX. A.K., Abt Ia 16.4.40, Betr.: Befehl für den Einsatz der Abteilung Förster-Garski; Generalkommando XIX. A.K., den 1.5.40., Betr.: Studie zum Korpsbefehl Nr. 1. Besondere Anordnungen über die Unterstützung des XIX. A.K. am A-Tag durch den Nahkampfführer II.

79. Generalkommando XIX. A.K. Abt Ia Nr. 273/40g. Kdos, den 10.4.40 and Abt Ia Nr. 280/40 g. Kdos, den 11.4.40.

80. Ibid.; Dach, "Panzer durchbrechen eine Armeestellung," p. 61.

81. Rigging or to rig is a U.S. Army term used to describe the preparation of an aircraft, i.e.: the proper loading, storing, and tying down of equipment on an aircraft.

82. H-Hour is the time at which combat operations commence.

83. Generalkommando XIX. A.K. Abt Ia Nr. 221/40 g. Kdos, den 18.4.40; Dach, "Panzer durchbrechen eine Armeestellung," p. 62; and Gr von Kleist Abt Ia Nr. 636/40 g. Kdos, K. H. Qu, den 23.4.40.

84. Generalkommando XIX. A.K. Abt Ia Nr. 597/40 g. Kdos, den 22.4.40; see also for the problem of soldiers firing on the Fieseler Storch aircraft. After the Mechelen Affair, Hitler demanded extreme security measures throughout the Armed Forces. Army commanders in Army Group A's sector probably had knowledge of the operation, but the infantryman ready to advance across Luxembourg certainly had no idea of the impending air assault. Thus Garski's had a valid concern. Within XIXth Panzer Corps only several officers of the 1st Panzer Division received prior briefings.

85. Guderian, *Panzer Leader,* pp. 69-70.

86. Hermann Balck, in *Ordnung im Chaos,* vividly describes the situation at Guderian's command post on the morning of May 13, 1940. The Meuse River crossings turned into a hastily organized operation because General von Kleist did not want to wait for the infantry divisions, which would have allowed the defender to improve his defenses. Von Kleist, on the morning of May 14, ordered Guderian to conduct assault crossings with his motorized infantry (dismounted) that afternoon. With no time to write elaborate orders, Colonel Nehring simply ordered: "Mission: Duplicate War Game Koblenz, H-hour is 1600 hours today."

87. The first German Flak (antiaircraft) units of corps size were activated at the conclusion of the Polish Campaign. Each Panzer division had organic antiaircraft battalions, however, for the Battle of France these were insufficient. The German Army was also ill-prepared for antitank warfare since their 37 mm antitank guns were obsolete. The Flak's 88 mm antiaircraft gun proved itself in Poland as a definite antitank asset. The 88 mm guns with their armor-piercing ammunition seemed a viable solution. The Flak could engage aircraft, tanks, and bunkers. The Luftwaffe, in organizing these new Flak corps, initiated some fundamental changes in the ammunition allocation. Flak units would carry 50 percent time fuze, used in antiaircraft missions, 30 percent percussion fuzes, for ground targets, and 20 percent armor-piercing ammunition. First Flak Corps was organized from the III Airforce Administrative Headquarters (Luftgaukommando III) in October 1939. For more information see Appendix E. Generaloberst Hubert Weise, *Organization of Air Defense in the Field Experiences of I Flak Corps,* manuscript data sheet originally prepared for Headquarters European Command, Office of the Chief Historian (Washington, D.C.: Department of the Army Office of the Chief of Military

History, 1952), pp. 1-3; and Georg Tessin, *Verbände und Truppen der Deutschen Wehrmacht und Waffen-SS im Zweiten Weltkrieg 1939-1945*, vol. 2, *Die Landstreitkräfte 1-5* (Osnabrück: Biblio Verlag, 1973), pp. 15-16.

88. Adalbert Koch, *Die Geschichte der Deutschen Flakartillerie 1935-1945* (Friedberg: Podzun-Pallas Verlag, 1954), pp. 30-32.

89. Kenneth Macksey, *Guderian: Creator of the Blitzkrieg* (New York: Stein and Day Publishers, 1976), pp. 124-25.

90. Ibid., p. 127; and Horst Scheibert, *Das war Guderian: Ein Lebensbericht in Bildern* (Friedberg: Podzun-Pallas Verlag, 1975), pp. 42-44.

91. KTB Nr. 3, Gr von Kleist, entry for March 13, 1940.

92. Liss, *Westfront,* p. 126.

93. Fritz Bayerlein was born in Würzburg on January 14, 1899. He joined the Army in 1917. During the interwar period Bayerlein served in the 21st Infantry Regiment in 1922, in the logistics section (Ib) of the 15th Corps in 1938, and then joined the 10th Panzer Division as operation officer (Ia) in the spring of 1939. During World War II, Bayerlein remained the operation officer of the 10th Panzer Division in Poland. In February 1940, Bayerlein transferred to XIXth Panzer Corps as the operation officer. Subsequent assignments were: Chief of Staff, German Africa Corps in 1941; Chief of Staff, German-Italian Panzer Army in 1942; Chief of Staff, 1st Italian Army in 1943; commander of the 3rd Panzer Division in 1943; Panzer-Lehr Division in 1944; and the 53rd Corps in 1945. Bayerlein achieved the rank of Major-General on April 1, 1944. He retired to Würzburg after the war and died on January 30, 1970. Keilig, *Das Deutsche Heer,* p. 17.

94. Generalkommando XIX. A.K. Abt Ia Nr.306/40 g. Kdos, den 17.4.40, Betr.: Zielübermittlung und Zielanweisung.

95. Generalkommando XIX. A.K. Ia/Naka Nr. 367/40 g Kdos, den 6.5.40.

96. Class I is food or rations, Class III fuel, and Class V ammunition.

97. Dach, "Panzer durchbrechen eine Armeestellung," p. 60; Halder, *The Halder Diaries,* vol. 3, pp. 270, 298-300, 328, 395, and 401; and Eduard Wagner, *Der General-Quartiermeister: Briefe und Tagebuchaufzeichnungen des Generalquartiermeisters des Heeres, General der Artillerie Eduard Wagner,* ed. Elisabeth Wagner (München: Günter Olzog Verlag, 1963), pp. 153 and 155.

98. General Eduard Wagner was born on April 1, 1894, in Kirchenlamitz/Hof. He joined the Army as a cadet in 1912, and the 12th Bavarian Field Artillery Regiment in 1914. In 1936, Wagner became section chief in the Army General Staff, and in the spring of 1939 assumed command of the 10th Artillery Regiment. During World War II, Wagner was the Quartermaster-General (Generalquartiermeister) of the Army General Staff from August 1940 until July 1944, when he committed suicide because of his connection to the failed attempt on Hitler's life. Wagner achieved the rank of General of Artillery on August 1, 1943. Keilig, *Das Deutsche Heer,* p. 353; and Wagner, *Der General-Quartiermeister.*

99. Generalkommando XIX. A.K. Abt Qu Nr. 500/40 geh. 7.3.40; and Halder, *The Halder Diaries,* p. 278.

100. Heeresgruppe A O. Qu I Nr. 172/40 g. Kdos H. Qu, den 14.3.40, Betr.: Versorgung auf dem Luftwege.

101. Telegraphic message ordering the resupply exercise dated April 2, 1940. The originator of the message based his authority on a previous General Staff document. That document was Gen St d H/Gen Qu/Qu 3 (Ia) Nr. 502/40 g. Kdos vom 3.3.40, Betr.: Versorgung auf dem Luftwege.

102. Balck, *Ordnung im Chaos*, p. 266; Halder, *The Halder Diaries*, p. 168; Macksey, *Guderian: Creator of the Blitzkrieg*, p. 124; also, the Army grew in personnel from 2.76 million in September 1939 to 3.3 million by May 1940. Production did not keep pace with the rapid growth of the Army, thus no weapons reserves existed in 1940. For the time being the German Army relied heavily on captured Polish and Czechoslovakian equipment. Müller-Hillebrand, *Das Heer,* vol. 2, pp. 40-41.

CHAPTER 3

1. Von Below, *Als Hitlers Adjutant 1937-45,* p. 229.

2. XIX. A.K. KTB Verlauf des 9.5.40, Der Durchbruch zum Ärmelkanal. Herstellung der Marschbereitschaft des XIX. A.K. The tactical command post of XIXth Panzer Corps consisted of General Guderian, his chief of staff, the operation officer, the close air support officer, two messenger officers, a signal officer, the corps engineer, and several clerks.

3. Ibid.

4. XIX. A.K. KTB, 10.5.40, Verlauf des 10.5.40, Vormarsch durch Luxembourg, Durchbruch durch die südbelgischen Befestigungen u. Ardennen.

5. The Lehr und Bau Bataillon z. b. V. 800 (800th Instruction and Construction Battalion for special disposition) is more commonly known as the "Brandenburgers." This unit originated in upper Silesia as an Industrial Complex Protection Unit (Industrieschutz Oberschlesien) after World War I, when local Silesians feared an invasion by Poland. The members were primarily of Polish origin who were, however, sympathetic to Germany. If Poland invaded, the unit would seize important industrial complexes and hold them until relieved by German troops. The cadre of Lehr and Bau Batallion z. b. V. 800 came from the Industrial Complex Protection Unit. In October 1939 Admiral Canaris instructed its leader Captain von Hippel to occupy an empty barracks in Brandenburg, and organize the Lehr and Bau Kompanie z. b. V. Hence the unit was nicknamed the "Brandenburgers." This company later grew to division size, and participated in every German theater of the war. Melchers, *Kriegsschauplatz Luxemburg,* pp. 300-1; Generalkommando XIX. A.K. Abt Ic Nr. W 606/40 g. Kdos, den 25.4.40, Betr.: Studie "Sonderkommandos"; Generalkommando XIX. A.K. Ic Nr. W 614/40 g. Kdos; Armee-Oberkommando 16 Abt Ia/Ic Nr. 157/40 g. Kdos, A.H.K., den 24.4.40, Betr.: Reichsdeutsche in Luxembourg; and Generalkommando 12 Ia/Ic/Ao. Nr. 1860/40g. A.H.Qu, den 11.4.40, Betr.: Zuweisung eines Sonderkommandos für Aufgaben Abw. II. For a more thorough history of the Brandenburgers, see Sepp de Giampietro's *Das Falsche Opfer Ein Südtiroler in der Division Brandenburg zwischen seinem Gewissen und der Achse Berlin-Rom* (Stuttgart: Leopold Stocker Verlag, 1984).

6. Melchers, *Kriegsschauplatz Luxemburg,* pp. 302-48.

7. Heeresgruppe A Abt O. Qu I., den 3.5.40. Intelligence update on enemy activity in Luxembourg and Belgium from April 20-28, 1940.

8. Melchers, *Kriegsschauplatz Luxemburg,* pp. 322-25.

9. Ibid., pp. 330-31.

10. Ibid., pp. 308-12.

11. At the end of the first day, the Luftwaffe destroyed 40 percent or 320 airplanes of the French Northeast-Zone air force assets. The British lost 474 planes; Dach, "Panzer durchbrechen eine Armeestellung," pp. 63-64.

12. Melchers, *Kriegsschauplatz Luxemburg,* p. 383; Dach, "Panzer durchbrechen eine Armeestellung," p. 66; and XIX. A.K. KTB, 10.5.40.

13. Krüger's group landed at two locations about 10 km from the designated landing zone. Garski's group also landed at two locations, but only three km from their intended landing zone. Dach, "Panzer durchbrechen eine Armeestellung," pp. 66-67; XIX. A.K. KTB, 10.5.40; and Tagesmeldung by XIXth Panzer Corps to Panzer Group von Kleist, signed by Colonel Nehring.

14. Horne, *To Lose a Battle,* pp. 214-15; Dach, "Panzer durchbrechen eine Armeestellung," p. 66; and Melchers, *Kriegsschauplatz Luxemburg,* pp. 385-86.

15. Dach, "Panzer durchbrechen eine Armeestellung," p. 66; XIX. A.K. KTB, 10.5.40; and Abendmeldung 1700 Uhr. Gen. Kdo XIX. A.K. and Gr von Kleist (Major Beyerlein and Rittmeister Klewitz).

16. Melchers, *Kriegsschauplatz Luxemburg,* p. 385.

17. Rudolf Veil was born in Stuttgart on December 10, 1883. He joined the Army as cadet in 1904 and became a Lieutenant in the 19th Uhlan Regiment in 1905. After World War I, Veil remained in the Reichsheer. In 1938 he assumed command of the 2nd Panzer Division. During World War II, Veil commanded the 2nd Panzer Division throughout the French Campaign. Other commands included: 48th Panzer Corps from February 1942 to May 1942; Commander Reorganization and Refit Staff Center from September 1942 to June 1943; acting Commander 5th Corps from September 1943 to July 1944. Because of his connection to the resistance, Veil was relieved of his duties in July 1944. Highest rank achieved during World War II was General of Armored Troops on April 1, 1942. After the war, General Veil retired to Stuttgart where he died in 1956. Keilig, *Das Deutsche Heer,* p. 348.

18. Franz Josef Strauss, *Geschichte der 2. (Wiener) Panzerdivision* 3d ed. (Forschheim: Buchdruckerei Sperl, 1987), pp. 46-47.

19. Friedrich Kirchner was born in Zöbigker/Leipzig on March 26, 1885. He entered the 107th Infantry Regiment in 1906 and received his Lieutenant's commission in 1907. In 1911 he transferred to the 17th Uhlan Regiment. After World War I, Kirchner remained in the Reichsheer. Between 1933 and 1938 he commanded a cavalry regiment, an infantry regiment (mot), and an infantry brigade (mot). In 1938, Kirchner became a general officer and in November 1939 he assumed command of the 1st Panzer Division. From 1941-45 he commanded the 57th Panzer Corps. Highest rank achieved: General of Panzer Troops in 1942. Keilig, *Das Deutsche Heer,* p. 163.

20. Walter Krüger was born in Zeitz on March 23, 1892. He entered the 181st Infantry Regiment in 1910. Krüger received his commission in 1911 in the 19th Hussar Regiment. After World War I he remained in the Reichsheer. Krüger commanded the 10th Cavalry Regiment in 1937, and in November 1939 he took command of the 1st Infantry Brigade (mot), 1st Panzer Division. He assumed command of the 1st Panzer Division in 1941, 58th Panzer Corps in 1944, and became acting commander of 4th Corps in April 1945. Highest rank achieved: General of Panzer Troops in 1944. Keilig, *Das Deutsche Heer,* p. 183.

21. Anlage 5 zu Gruppe von Kleist Ia/Op 217/40 g. Kdos Chefs, 9.5.40, Betr.: Besondere Anordnungen für das überwinden der Befestigungen, Sperrungen u. Flüsse im Vormarschstreifen; Korpskommando XV. A.K., Abt Ia Nr. 76/40 g. Kdos, 16.3.40, Korpsbefehl für den Angriff. OKW allocated the use of Special Operations type forces for Fall Gelb, in particular to prevent the demolition of seven road and railroad bridges in the

Ettelbrück-Diekirch area. Twenty-three members of the Brandenburg Regiment, dressed in civilian clothes, infiltrated ahead of 1st Panzer Division's sector with the mission of preventing the destruction of those bridges. Pro-German Luxembourg men were also recruited and some even trained in Germany, but their sloppy work alerted the Luxembourg authorities in their attempt to capture police and border guards. By 0200 hours on May 10, 1940, the Luxembourg government ordered the closing and locking of obstacles. Generalkommando XIX. A.K. Abt Ic Nr. W 606/40 g. Kdos, den 25.4.40, Betr.: Studie "Sonderkommandos"; Generalkommando XIX. A.K. Ic Nr. W 614/40 g. Kdos; Armee-Oberkommando 16 Abt Ia/Ic Nr. 157/40 g. Kdos, A.H.K., den 24.4.40. Betr.: Reichsdeutsche in Luxembourg; and Generalkommando 12 Ia/Ic/Ao. Nr. 1860/40g., A.H.Qu, den 11.4.40, Betr.: Zuweisung eines Sonderkommandos für Aufgaben Abw. II.

22. Hermann Balck was born in Danzig-Langfuhr on December 7, 1892. He entered the 10th Jäger Battalion in 1913 and received his commission in 1914. After World War I, Balck remained in the Reichsheer. From 1938-39 he worked at OKH and, in October 1939, he assumed command of the 1st Infantry Regiment (mot). Other commands in World War II included: 3rd Panzer Regiment, December 1940; 2nd Panzer Brigade, May 1941; 11th Panzer Division, May 1942; Infantry Division "Grossdeutschland," April 1943; 40th Panzer Corps, November 1944; 4th Panzer Army and later Army Group G at the end of the war. Highest rank achieved: General of Panzer Troops in 1943. Keilig, *Das Deutsche Heer,* p. 13; and Balck, *Ordnung im Chaos.*

23. XIX. A.K. KTB, 10.5.40; and Balck, *Ordnung im Chaos,* p. 268.

24. Horne, *To Lose a Battle,* pp. 199-200.

25. Balck, *Ordnung im Chaos,* p. 268; and Melchers, *Kriegsschauplatz Luxemburg,* pp. 378-79.

26. Gerhard Schmidt, *Regimentsgeschichte des Panzer-Artillerie-Regiments 73* (Bremen: Walther Böttscher Verlag, 1959), p. 32; and Dach, "Panzer durchbrechen eine Armeestellung," p. 65.

27. Ibid.; and Gen. Kdo XXII. A.K. KTB (Gr von Kleist), Betr.: Durchbruch zum Ärmelkanal und die Schlacht in Flandern und im Artoir vom 10.5-31.5.40.

28. Ferdinand Schaal was born in Freiburg im Breisgau on February 7, 1889. He entered the 22nd Dragoon Regiment in 1908 and received his commission in 1909. After World War I he remained in the Reichsheer. Between 1934 and 1939 Schaal commanded the 16th Cavalry Regiment and the 1st Panzer Brigade. In August 1939 he assumed command of the 10th Panzer Division. Other commands during World War II were: 34th Corps, September 1, 1941; XLI Panzer Corps, September 13, 1941. From September 1943 until July 1944 Schaal was the Commander of Wehrkreis Bohemia and Moravia and plenipotentiary with the Reichsprotector in Bohemia and Moravia. Keilig, *Das Deutsche Heer,* p. 286.

29. XIX. A.K. KTB, 10.5.40; also, IR "GD" had the specific mission of protecting the corps' left flank from advancing Allied forces.

30. For May 11, XIXth Panzer Corps received operational control of: 49th Artillery Regiment, 2nd Battalion/69th Artillery Regiment (10 cm), the 511th Engineer Regiment, and the 41st Engineer Battalion with two type B bridges. XXII. A.K. (Gr von Kleist) Abt Ia/Op K. Gef. Std., den 10.5.40, Betr.: Gruppenbefehl Nr. 1 für den 11.5.40.

31. XIX. A.K. KTB, 10.5.40; and Dach, "Panzer durchbrechen eine Armeestellung," p. 64.

32. Gruppenbefehl, Der Kommandierende General der Gruppe von Kleist, Einsatzort, den 11.5.40.

33. Dach, "Panzer durchbrechen eine Armeestellung," p. 65; Anlage B, General-kommando XXII. A.K. (Gr von Kleist) 10.8.40, Vorläufige Erfahrungen mit grossen mot. Verbänden.

34. XIX. A.K. KTB, 10.5.40; Tagesmeldung des XIX. A.K., 10.5.40 signed by Colonel Nehring; and Gruppenbefehl Nr. 1 für den 11.5.40.

35. XIX. A.K. KTB, 10.5.40.

36. XIX. A.K. KTB, 11.5.40.

37. Liss, *Westfront*, p. 150.

38. Message from Panzer Group von Kleist at 0745 hours, May 11, 1940 to Army Group A, signed by the operation officer.

39. XIX. A.K. KTB, 11.5.40.

40. Strauss, *Geschichte der 2. (Wiener) Panzerdivision*, p. 46; and XIX. A.K. KTB, 11.5.40.

41. Dach, "Panzer durchbrechen eine Armeestellung," p. 68; XIX. A.K. KTB, 11.5.40; and Schmidt, *Regimentsgeschichte*, p. 32.

42. Karl Keltsch was born in Tröstau on May 7, 1892. He entered the Army in 1912 and joined the 7th Bavarian Infantry Regiment in 1914. After World War I Keltsch remained in the Reichsheer. In January 1938 he assumed command of the 2nd Panzer Regiment. During World War II he continued to command the 2nd Panzer Regiment in Poland, and in February 1940 assumed command of the 1st Panzer Brigade. In November of the same year Keltsch commanded the 18th Panzer Brigade. Other commands included: Commander, 6th Transportation Depot, 6th Army from November 1941 to July 1942; Commander, 12th Transportation Depot in April 1943; Commander, Central Transportation West from January to November 1944; and Commander, Transportation Depot, 3rd Military Administrative Area Headquarters. Keilig, *Das Deutsche Heer*, p. 160.

43. Stoves, *Die 1. Panzer Division*, pp. 84-85; Dach, "Panzer durchbrechen eine Armeestellung," p. 68; Schmidt, *Regimentsgeschichte*, p. 32; and XIX. A.K. KTB, 11.5.40.

44. Stoves, *Die 1. Panzer Division*, p. 85; Dach, "Panzer durchbrechen eine Armeestellung," p. 68; XIX. A.K. KTB, 11.5.40; Schmidt, *Regimentsgeschichte*, p. 32; and Liss, *Westfront*, pp. 148-49.

45. Stoves, *Die 1. Panzer Division*, p. 85; and Schmidt, *Regimentsgeschichte*, p. 32.

46. Dach, "Panzer durchbrechen eine Armeestellung," p. 68; Stoves, *Die 1. Panzer Division*, p. 85; and XIX. A.K. KTB, 11.5.40.

47. XIX. A.K. KTB, 11.5.40.

48. Ibid.

49. Ibid.

50. Ibid., entry at 2100 hours.

51. XIX. A.K. KTB, 11.5.40; XXII. A.K. (Gr von Kleist) KTB (Abschrift) 10.5 bis 11.7.40, entry for May 5, 1940.

52. XIX. A.K. KTB, 11.5.40, Luftlage.

53. Liss, *Westfront*, p. 153.

54. XIX. A.K. KTB, 11.5.40, Abschlusslage am Abend.

55. XIX. A.K. KTB, 11.5.40, Zusammenfassung.

56. The distance between the two headquarters probably caused the delay. XIXth Panzer Corps' tactical command post was located at Neufchâteau, whereas Panzer Group von Kleist located its command post at Erpeldingen. XIX. A.K. KTB, 11.5.40; Generalkommando XIX. A.K. Abt la K. Gef. Std. Neufchâteau, den 11.5.40, Betr.:

Korpsbefehl Nr. 2 für den 12.5.40; and Gr von Kleist Abt Ia/Op K. Gef. Std., den 11.5.40, Erpeldingen 2100 Uhr, Betr.: Gruppenbefehl Nr. 2 für den 12.5.40.

57. XIX. A.K. KTB, 12.5.40.

58. XIX. A.K. KTB, 12.5.40, entry at 0900 hours and Abschlusslage am Abend (Feind); Dach, "Panzer durchbrechen eine Armeestellung," p. 69; and Strauss, *Die 1. Panzerdivision,* p. 46.

59. XIX. A.K. KTB, 12.5.40; Dach, "Panzer durchbrechen eine Armeestellung," p. 69; and Stoves, *Die 1. Panzer Division,* p. 86.

60. Dach, "Panzer durchbrechen eine Armeestellung," p. 69; and Stoves, *Die 1. Panzer Division,* p. 86.

61. Dach, "Panzer durchbrechen eine Armeestellung," p. 69; Stoves, *Die 1. Panzer Division,* p. 86; and XIX. A.K. KTB, 12.5.40.

62. Dach, "Panzer durchbrechen eine Armeestellung," p. 69; and XIX. A.K. KTB, 12.5.40.

63. Schmidt, *Regimentsgeschichte,* pp. 32-33.

64. XIX. A.K. KTB, 12.5.40.

65. Guderian, *Panzer Leader,* pp. 78-79; XIX. A.K. KTB, 12.5.40; and General-kommando XIX. A.K. Abt Ia K. Gef. Std., den 12.5.40, 1750 Uhr, Betr.: Vorbefehl für Angriff über die Maas.

66. General von Kleist's refusal of Guderian's concept of the Luftwaffe's employment to only fly bombing missions on May 12 does not support the actual events of May 13, 1940. From XIXth Panzer Corps' war diary it can be clearly determined that Guderian and von Stutterheim coordinated the Luftwaffe's employment for the Meuse River crossing in early May. In the Panzer Group's war diary one notes that von Kleist and Sperrle conducted their own coordination on the morning of May 12. During the actual events on May 13, the Luftwaffe employed Guderian's technique. Guderian, without knowing this, complained all day on the 13th that the air offensive was a failure until he met with von Stutterheim in the evening. Von Stutterheim informed him that there was not enough time to make the necessary changes von Kleist and Sperrle had wanted and thus decided on his own to execute the plan he and Guderian coordinated. We can safely assume that von Stutterheim's decision for this course of action resulted as a consequence of pilots and crews being trained for their mission well in advance. Many historians fault Guderian for wanting to postpone the crossings for one day. From both the XIXth Panzer Corps and the Panzer Group von Kleist war diaries it is fairly evident that Guderian only asked for a postponement because he considered the use of the Luftwaffe and its systematic attack on the French artillery positions as essential. Von Kleist's concept concerned him because he thought that there would not be enough artillery available to support the crossings, thus a postponement would have provided the necessary time to deploy all the artillery assets forward. Guderian, *Panzer Leader,* p. 79; XIX. A.K. KTB, 12.5.40. and 13.5.40; and XXII. A.K. (Gr von Kleist) KTB, 12.5.40. and 13.5.40.

67. The Panzer Group in its Operation Order Nr. 2, issued on May 11, 1940, paragraph 3, "Missions to Corps," specially directed XIXth Panzer Corps to "use May 12 to make preparations for the planned Meuse River crossing on May 13. The main effort must be west of the Ardennes Canal." Gr von Kleist Abt Ia/Op K. Gef. Std., den 11.5.40, Erpeldingen. 2100 Uhr, Betr.: Gruppenbefehl Nr. 2 für den 12.5.40.

68. Guderian, *Panzer Leader,* p. 79.

69. XXII. A.K. (Gr von Kleist) KTB, 12.5.40; Heeresgruppe A, Arbeitsgebiet Qu I (Abendmeldung) Zeitabschnitt 12.5.40.

70. The French Army was convinced that the German Army would not attack without first bringing forward all artillery assets, ammunition, and bridging equipment. They anticipated a two to three day time period which could be used for their preparation along the Meuse River. The French High Command, however, did take some precautionary measures by transporting the 1st Armored Division towards Charleroi. The 14th Infantry Division moved to Novion-Porcier, and two additional artillery regiments were added to 10th Corps, defending west of Sedan. The 71st Infantry Division also hastily deployed into the defensive sector. The 55th Infantry Division, taken out of the front early on May 12, occupied the west bank of the Meuse, and took the brunt of the attack on the following day. They were disorganized throughout the night of May 12 to 13, and planned to use the 13th to get their defensive positions in order. During the night, however, it became apparent to some French commanders that the Germans would attack. All vehicle columns moving toward Sedan were using full headlights without regard to security. Dach, "Panzer durchbrechen eine Armeestellung," p. 48; also, for a detailed study of the French Army's actions during the battle of France, see Horne's *To Lose a Battle;* Liss, *Westfront,* pp. 156-59; XIX. A.K. KTB, 12.5.40; Generalkommando XIX. A.K. Abt Ia K. Gef. Std. Bellevaux 13.5.40, 815 Uhr; and Gr von Kleist Abt Ia/Op Gruppen-Gef. Std. Ebly, den 12.5.40, 2330 Uhr.

71. The war game referred to was "War Game Koblenz" conducted along the Moselle River. Although the basic plan remained the same, changes, based on the meeting conducted at the Panzer Group's Command Post on the afternoon of May 12, had to be incorporated. That explains why the order was not issued until 0815 hours on May 13, 1940. XIX. A.K. KTB, 12.5.40; Generalkommando XIX. A.K. Abt Ia K. Gef. Std. Bellevaux 13.5.40, 815 Uhr; and Gr von Kleist Abt Ia/Op Gruppen-Gef. Std. Ebly, den 12.5.40, 2330 Uhr.

CHAPTER 4

1. Guderian, *Panzer Leader,* p. 80.

2. Gr von Kleist, Abt Ia/Op Gruppen-Gef. Std. Ebly, den 12.5.40, 2330 Uhr, Betr.: Gruppenbefehl Nr. 3 für den Angriff über die Maas am 13.5.40.

3. Von Stutterheim executed the plan he coordinated with Guderian since the available time was too short to incorporate the Group's changes. He filled the skies above Sedan with up to 20 aircraft, continuously, throughout the day. Only at 1500 hours did von Stutterheim attack en masse with 900 to 1,000 aircraft, shifting to targets in depth after 1600 hours. Guderian complained the entire day about the faulty air bombardment. However, he was rather satisfied when he found out through Nehring later in the evening that the air bombardment had been executedas previously coordinated. XIX. AK KTB, 13.5.40.

4. Ibid.

5. Wend von Wietersheim was born in Neuland/Löwenberg on April 8, 1900. He joined the Army in 1918 and entered the 4th Hussar Regiment in 1919. After the imposition of the Versailles Treaty and the reduction to a 100,000-man army, von Wietersheim was allowed to remain in the Reichsheer. In 1938, he served as aide-de-camp to the 3rd Panzer Division commander, remaining in that position until he assumed command of the 1st Motorcycle Battalion. From 1941 to 1943 he commanded the 113th Panzer Grenadier Regiment, and in August of 1943 took command of the 11th Panzer Division. Von Wietersheim achieved the rank of Major-General in July 1944. He was a highly decorated officer, earning the German Cross in Gold and the Knights Cross with oak leaves and swords. After the war von Wietersheim settled in Bad Godesberg. Keilig, *Das Deutsche Heer,* p. 364.

6. Walther Wenck was born in Wittenberg on September 18, 1900. He began his military career by entering Freikorps von Oven in 1919. In the Reichsheer Wenck served in the 9th Infantry Regiment. In April 1939 he became the operations officer of the 1st Panzer Division. From February to September of 1942 he taught at the Kriegsakademie (War Academy). Other duties during World War II included: Chief of Staff, LVII Panzer Corps in September 1942; Chief of Staff, 3rd Romanian Army in November 1942; Chief of Staff, Army Hollidt (later 6th Army) in December 1942; Chief of Staff, 1st Panzer Army in March 1943; Chief of Staff, Army Group Southern Ukraine in March 1944; Chief, Operations Section in the Army General Staff (OKH) and acting Chief of Staff of OKH at the Führer headquarters from July 1944 to February 1945. From April 1945 to the end of the war he commanded the 12th Army. Wenck achieved the rank of General of Panzer Troops in April 1945. He settled at Bochum after the war, and died at the age of 81 on May 1, 1982. Keilig, *Das Deutsche Heer,* p. 361.

7. Stoves, *Die 1. Panzer Division,* p. 89; also, the change in attack time for the Luftwaffe was made late in the evening at Panzer Group von Kleist's headquarters. XXII. A.K. (Gr von Kleist) KTB, 13.5.40.

8. XIX. A.K. KTB, 13.5.40.

9. Ibid., Stoves, *Die 1. Panzer Division,* pp. 89-90; Schmidt, *Regimentsgeschichte,* p. 33; and Balck, *Ordnung im Chaos,* pp. 269-70.

10. Dach, "Panzer durchbrechen eine Armeestellung," p. 48; and XIX. A.K. KTB, 13.5.40; also Horne, *To Lose a Battle,* pp. 304-9.

11. ARKO referred to Artilleriekommandeur (artillery commander). In the case of ARKO 101 he was the corps artillery commander with a staff to coordinate the corps' fire support.

12. XIX. A.K. KTB, 13.5.40; Dach, "Panzer durchbrechen eine Armeestellung," p. 76; and Stoves, *Die 1. Panzer Division,* p. 90.

13. Dach, "Panzer durchbrechen eine Armeestellung," p. 77; Stoves, *Die 1. Panzer Division,* p. 93; and XIX. A.K. KTB, 13.5.40.

14. Ibid; Balck, *Ordnung im Chaos,* pp. 269-70; and Dach, "Panzer durchbrechen eine Armeestellung," p. 77.

15. XIX. A.K. KTB, 13.5.40; and Balck, *Ordnung im Chaos,* pp. 270-71; and Stoves, *Die 1. Panzer Division,* pp. 88 and 94.

16. Ibid.; Stoves, *Die 1. Panzer Division,* p. 88.

17. XIX. A.K. KTB, 13.5.40.

18. Ibid.

19. Only selected elements of the 2nd Panzer Division reached the Meuse River in time to conduct the river crossing. It was not until late in the night that the entire division closed in the vicinity of Donchery. XIX. A.K. KTB, 13.5.40.

20. Dach, "Panzer durchbrechen eine Armeestellung," pp. 78-79.

21. Ibid., pp. 79-80.

22. The XIXth Panzer Corps only identified elements of a fortress brigade, the 2nd, 3rd, and 5th Cavalry Divisions, and the 55th Infantry Division in its sector. Liss, *Westfront,* pp. 162-63; and XIX. A.K. KTB, 13.5.40.

23. Generalkommando XIX. A.K., Abt Ia, K. Gef. Std., Wald bei La Chapelle, den 13.5.40., Betr.: Korpsbefehl Nr. 4.

24. Generalkommando XIX. A.K. Abt Ia, K. Gef. Std., Wald bei La Chapelle, den 13.5.40; and XIX. A.K. KTB, 13.5.40.

25. Dach, "Panzer durchbrechen eine Armeestellung," pp. 49 and 54; and Horne, *To Lose a Battle*, pp. 288-92.

26. The Germans reported 53 French and 47 British aircraft shot down and another 65 severely damaged. Of the 100 aircraft shot down over the Sedan area, 56 succumbed to the Flak gunners and 44 to Me 109's. These losses represented 22 percent of the remaining Allied air forces. Another 15 percent were severely damaged and 8 percent lightly damaged. German forces had 90 Me 109's at their disposal for fighter protection. Dach, "Panzer durchbrechen eine Armeestellung," pp. 56, 84; and Horne claims the losses were probably closer to 90; Horne, *To Lose a Battle*, p. 334.

27. XIX. A.K. KTB, 14.5.40.

28. Ibid.

29. Ibid.; Dach, "Panzer durchbrechen eine Armeestellung," p. 84; Stoves, *Die 1. Panzer Division*, pp. 97-98; F. W. von Mellenthin, Panzer Battles: A Study of the Employment of Armor in the Second World War, trans. H. Betzler (Norman: University of Oklahoma Press, 1956), p. 15; also see Chapter 14, Horne, *To Lose a Battle*, pp. 319-46.

30. Dach, "Panzer durchbrechen eine Armeestellung," p. 84; Balck, *Ordnung im Chaos*, pp. 272-73; Stoves, *Die 1. Panzer Division*, pp. 97-99; also, in Balck's book, *Ordnung im Chaos*, Chehery and Chemery are interchanged. It remains especially difficult to reconstruct the exact curse of these engagements. Colonel Keltsch was wounded seriously. Colonel Johannes Nedtwig, commander of the 1st Panzer Regiment, replaced Keltsch. Different authors provide various figures on the number of destroyed French tanks. Dach and Balck claim at least 70, while von Mellenthin only reports 50 destroyed. Suffice it to say, the French suffered significant losses of tanks on the 14th.

31. Mark III Panzers carried 99 rounds of 3.7 cm main gun, and 2,000 rounds of machine gun ammunition. Mark IV's carried 87 rounds of 7.5 cm main gun, and 3,150 rounds of machine gun ammunition. Armin Halle, and Carlo Demand, *Panzer: Illustrierte Geschichte der Kampfwagen* (Herrsching: Verlag Manfred Pawlak, 1971), pp. 83 and 84; XIX. A.K. KTB, 14.5.40; Dach, "Panzer durchbrechen eine Armeestellung," pp. 84-85; and Schmidt, *Regimentsgeschichte*, pp. 33-34.

32. Thirty artillery pieces were of 155 mm caliber and 10 were 105 mm. Dach, "Panzer durchbrechen eine Armeestellung," p. 86.

33. XIX. A.K. KTB, 14.5.40; Dach, "Panzer durchbrechen eine Armeestellung," p. 86; and Stoves, *Die 1. Panzer Division*, p. 100.

34. XIX. A.K. KTB, 14.5.40; and Stoves, *Die 1. Panzer Division*, p. 100. One troop of the Armored Reconnaissance Battalion attempted to penetrate the northern edge of the Bois du Mont Dieu at about 1800 hours, but was repulsed by the French defenders in the woodline.

35. XIX. A.K. KTB, 14.5.40; Stoves, *Die 1. Panzer Division*, p. 100; and Strauss, *Geschichte der 2 (Wiener) Panzerdivision*, p. 46.

36. Strike with a determined fist instead of feeling around with your fingers (Klotzen, nicht Kleckern), was the phrase Guderian used when explaining armored tactics and doctrine. His aim was to impress the idea of one main thrust and not to piecemeal forces at several places, accomplishing nothing. Stoves, *Die 1. Panzer Division*, p. 102.

37. XIX. A.K. KTB, 14.5.40; Guderian, *Panzer Leader*, p. 83.

38. Stoves, *Die 1. Panzer Division*, p. 101.

39. XIX. A.K. KTB, 14.5.40; Dach, "Panzer durchbrechen eine Armeestellung," p.

86; Balck, *Ordnung im Chaos,* p. 274; and Stoves, *Die 1. Panzer Division,* p. 100.

40. XIX. A.K. KTB, 14.5.40, and XXII. A.K. (Gr von Kleist) KTB 14.5.40.

41. The noncommitted divisions Guderian referred to were the 8th Panzer Division and the 2nd Infantry Division (mot). XIX. A.K. KTB, 14.5.40; and XXII. A.K. KTB, 14.5.40.

42. Gr von Kleist Abt Ia/Op, Gruppen-Gef. Std. Bellevaux, den 14.5.40, 2315 Uhr, Betr.: Gruppenbefehl Nr. 5 für den 15.5.40, XIX. A.K. KTB, 14.5.40.

43. Actually only one and one-half divisions of the corps were repelling the counterattacks at any one time. Neither 2nd nor 10th Panzer Divisions were involved in the main tank battles of May 14. Heeresgruppe A, Arbeitsgebiet Qu I 14.5.40.

44. Von Mellenthin, *Panzer Battles,* p. 16.

45. XIX. A.K. KTB, 14.5.40; for a thorough study on French doctrine read Robert Allan Doughty's *The Seeds of Disaster: The Development of French Army Doctrine 1919-1939* (Hamden: Archon Books, 1985).

46. Liss, *Westfront,* p. 165.

47. The Spahi Brigade was an Algerian native cavalry unit serving in the French Army.

48. XXII. A.K. (Gr von Kleist) KTB, 15.5.40; XIX A.K. KTB, 15.5.40; Balck, *Ordnung im Chaos,* p. 276; and Stoves, *Die 1. Panzer Division,* p. 104.

49. Balck, *Ordnung im Chaos,* p. 277.

50. When Guderian visited 1st Infantry Regiment on the morning of May 16, Balck told him of the episode during the night. Balck explained that his men were so exhausted and fatigued from combat that orders became meaningless. He realized that the only way to get them to move was for him to go at it alone. Balck went on to explain that he felt confident no German soldier would allow an officer to walk into certain death alone. Balck, *Ordnung im Chaos,* p. 106; XXII. A.K. (Gr von Kleist) KTB, 15.5.40; XIX. A.K. KTB, 15.5.40; Guderian, *Panzer Leader,* pp. 85-86; and Stoves, *Die 1. Panzer Division,* p. 106; and Strauss, *Geschichte der 2 (Wiener) Panzerdivision,* p. 47.

51. XXII. A.K. (Gr von Kleist) KTB, 15.5.40; XIX. A.K. KTB, 15.5.40; and von Mellenthin, *Panzer Battles,* p. 16.

52. Wagner, *Der General Quartiermeister,* p. 171; and Gr von Kleist Abt Ia/Op, Gruppen-Gef. Std. Bellevaux, den 14.5.40, 2315 Uhr, Betr.: Gruppenbefehl Nr. 5 für den 15.5.40.

53. XXII. A.K. (Gruppe von Kleist) KTB 15.5.40; XIX. A.K. KTB 15.5.40; and Heeresgruppe A, Arbeitsgebiet Qu I, 15.5.40.

54. Guderian, *Panzer Leader,* pp. 70-71. At the Berlin meeting on February 14, 1940, General Busch, commander of the 16th Army, expressed a lack of confidence in Guderian's plan to cross the Meuse River, to which Guderian hotly replied that it was not Busch's mission and not to worry about it in any case. During the night of May 13-14, Guderian sent a teletype message to inform Busch of the successful river crossing. Guderian, *Panzer Leader,* p. 82.

CHAPTER 5

1. Although there were 4,000 active officers in the Reichswehr in 1934, 500 transferred to the Luftwaffe in 1935, and another 450 were doctors and veterinarians. The Army really only had a core of 3,050 active officers to expand on.

2. David N. Spires, *Image and Reality: The Making of German Officers, 1921-1933* (Westport, Conn.: Greenwood Press, 1984), p. 126.

3. Ibid., pp. 121-22.

4. The Officer Evaluation Report (OER) system was also a legal way around the restrictions of the Versailles Treaty, because for every officer the Reichswehr dismissed a new one could be enrolled. In this manner the Reichswehr built an unofficial officer reserve pool. Under von Seeckt, officers received OER's biannually. However, Wilhelm Heye, von Seeckt's replacement in 1926, introduced an annual system which would double the number of dismissals.

5. Spires, *Images and Reality*, p. 129.

6. Ibid., pp. 127-28 and 129; also Lewis, "Reflections on Military Reform," p. 8.

7. Lewis, "Reflections on Military Reform," p. 10.

8. Ibid., pp. 9-12.

9. Lewis, *Forgotten Legions*, pp. 97-98.

10. Lewis, "Reflections on Military Reform," pp. 9-12.

11. In 1938 the German General Staff removed co-responsibility from its Officer's Handbook. The commander held sole responsibility for all decisions under his command. However, commanders realized that in some situations during a battle, their chiefs of staff were in a much better position to make a decision concerning the overall operation. It is also important to note that when chiefs of staff took this unauthorized prerogative, it was carried out within the limitations of the commander's intent. Oberkommando des Heeres, *Handbuch für den Generalstabsdienst im Kriege*, pp. 14-15.

12. Der Völkischer Beobachter was the official National Socialist party newspaper.

13. Wilhelm Weiss, *Triumph der Kriegskunst* (München: Zentralverlag der NSDAP, Franz Eher Nachf., 1941), pp. 14, 16, and 84.

14. Weiss, *Triumph der Kriegskunst*, p. 100.

15. Ibid., p. 101; and Wagner, *Der General-Quartiermeister*, p. 169.

16. Generalkommando XXII. A.K. (Gr von Kleist) Chef des Generalstabes, den 10.8.40, Betr.: Vorläufige Erfahrungen mit grossen mot. Verbänden.

17. Weiss, *Triumph der Kriegskunst*, p. 102.

APPENDIX A

1. Jacobsen, *Fall Gelb*, p. 4; and Oberkommando des Heeres (OKH), *Der Feldzug in Frankreich vom 10. Mai bis 25. Juni 1940*. Lage West am 9.9.39 (7714 Engr Base Repro, October/November 1949, Reproduced at the Command and General Staff College, Fort Leavenworth, 1983), p. 83-3183/2.

2. Jacobsen, *Fall Gelb*, p. 28; and OKH, *Der Feldzug in Frankreich*, p. 83-3183/3.

3. Jacobsen, *Fall Gelb*, p. 30.

4. Ibid., p. 42; Taylor, *The March of Conquest*, p. 166; and OKH, *Der Feldzug in Frankreich*, p. 83-3183/4.

5. Jacobsen, *Fall Gelb*, p. 96; and OKH, *Der Feldzug in Frankreich*, p. 83-3183/7.

6. Jacobsen, *Fall Gelb*, p. 142; and Taylor, *The March of Conquest*, p. 167.

7. Von Manstein, *Verlorene Siege*, p. 102.

APPENDIX B

1. Anlage 1 zu Gr von Kleist, Ia/Op Nr 217/40 g. Kdos Chefs vom 21.3.40 (Neuauffassung) vom 3.5.40, Betr.: "Besondere Anordnungen für die Strassenzuteilung, Marsch und Verkehrsregelung" (zum "Befehl für den Durchbruch bis zur Maas").

2. Nebelwerfer is a rocket projector.

3. Anlage 1 zu Gr von Kleist, Ia/Op Nr 217/40 g. Kdos Chefs vom 21.3.40.

4. Ibid. "Bewegungsübersicht für Gelb."

APPENDIX C

1. The Army commander in chief planned to personally lead the Army in time of war. In order to do this, he streamlined OKH and reduced some of his daily burdens. Von Brauchitsch split the organization of OKH, taking only the Army chief of staff and necessary operational sections to Zossen. He appointed a commander of the Replacement Army to deal with all other duties. This was, however, dependent on a short war scenario. As indicated on the chart, von Brauchitsch did maintain a nominal crew in Berlin. Müller-Hillebrand, *Das Heer,* vol. I, pp. 116-19 and 177-78; also for a detailed explanation of each section or office within the General Staff at Zossen, in Berlin, and the Replacement Army, see Müller-Hillebrand's *Das Heer,* vol. I. OB Ost refers to Berbefehlshaber Ost (Commander in Chief, East).

2. Armies and corps are placed from left to right and top to bottom, generally corresponding to their actual locations from west to east on May 10, 1940. Seventh Army is strictly north to south. The geographic areas above the armies are target areas, whereas the geographic areas above the corps are deployment areas. Taylor, *The March of Conquest,* pp. 429-31.

APPENDIX E

1. Müller-Hillebrand, *Das Heer,* vol. I, pp. 141-44; Stoves, *Die 1. Panzer Division,* p. 830; and OKH, *Handbuch für den Generalstabsdienst im Kriege,* vol. 2.

2. Müller-Hillebrand, *Das Heer,* vol. I, pp. 139-41; and OKH, *Handbuch für den Generalstabsdienst im Kriege,* vol. 2.

3. Dach, "Panzer durchbrechen eine Armeestellung," p. 62; and OKH, *Handbuch für den Generalstabsdienst im Kriege,* vol. 2, p. 62.

4. Müller-Hillebrand, *Das Heer,* vol. I, p. 140; and OKH, *Handbuch für den Generalstabsdienst im Kriege,* vol. 2.

5. OKH, *Handbuch für den Generalstabsdienst im Kriege,* vol. 2, p. 34.

6. Tessin, *Verbände und Truppen der deutschen Wehrmacht und Waffen-SS im Zweiten Weltkrieg,* vol. 2, pp. 15-16; and Dach, "Panzer durchbrechen eine Armeestellung, p. 82.

APPENDIX F

1. Pneumatic boats (Flosssäcke) were similar to the U.S. rubber raft. They had a wooden bottom and came in two sizes. The small pneumatic boat was 3 m long, 1.15 m wide, and had a tube diameter of 35 cm. Uninflated weight was 110 pounds. The small raft could carry three to four men, and up to 660 pounds. Using a bellows the boat could be inflated in five minutes. The large pneumatic boat was 5.5 m long, 1.85 m wide, and had a tube diameter of 60 cm. Uninflated, it weighed 330 pounds. Total carrying capacity was 1.5 metric tons. Six oarsmen (infantry) and one helmsman (engineer) were required to operate the boat. It could carry 12 men and one light machine gun (normally one squad), or one 3.7 mm antitank gun with crew. Each engineer battalion's TOE allowed for

38 small and 36 large boats. Provided a stream's current was not too swift, five small boats, covered with two parallel rows of boards, could be used to construct ferries that carried larger vehicles. The ferries were propelled by assault boats. These pneumatic boats were handy when confronted with a surprise river crossing and no engineer bridging companies were available. Assault boats (Sturmboote) were very shallow and constructed of wood. This boat floated empty in 10 centimeters of water. It was propelled by a four-cylinder outboard motor and reached a top speed of 30 km/hour. The crew consisted of one operator (helmsman, engineer in rear of boat) and one assistant (engineer) in the front. The assault boat had a capacity to transport six men. Buchner, *Das Buch der deutschen Infanterie*, pp. 63-65.

2. Dach, "Panzer durchbrechen eine Armeestellung," p. 70; and Generalkommando XIX. A.K. Abt Ia, K. Gef. Std. Bellevaux 13.5.40, 815 Uhr, Betr.: Korpsbefehl für den Angriff über die Maas am 13.5.40.

3. Wilhelm Berlin was born in Köln on April 28, 1889. He entered the Army in 1909 and joined the 14th Artillery Regiment in 1910. After World War I, Berlin remained in the Reichsheer. In 1938, he commanded the 33rd Artillery Regiment, and when the war broke out Berlin became the Commander of Artillery Command 101 (ARKO 101). In his capacity as ARKO 101, Berlin planned the artillery support plan for XIXth Panzer Corps. From October 1940 until April 1943, Berlin commanded the Artillery School at Jüterborg. Subsequent duties included: Commander, 58th Infantry Division in May 1943; Commander, 227th Infantry Division in June 1943; Commander, 26th Corps in June 1944; Chief Artillery Officer at OKH from November 1944 to February 1945; and Commander, 101st Corps from February 1945 until the end of the war. Berlin's highest rank was General of Artillery. He retired in Köln after the war. Keilig, *Das Deutsche Heer*, p. 24.

4. Anlage 5 zum Korpsbefehl für den 13.5.40. Besondere Anordnungen für den Maasübergang am 13.5 40 für die Artillerie.

5. Anlage 3 für den Korpsbefehl für den 13.5.40. Besondere Anordnungen für den Maasübergang (Pionierwesen) am 13.5.40.

6. The following weapons were employed: 48 medium mortars, 48 light machine guns; 18 light infantry guns (7.5 cm); 9 heavy infantry guns (15 cm). The heavy weapons of the infantry battalions supported the crossing. Rifle companies were left with only two light machine guns and three 50 mm mortars. Dach, "Panzer durchbrechen eine Armeestellung," p. 74.

7. The following weapons were employed: 60×3.7 cm antitank guns, 6×5 cm antitank guns, 6 assault guns (7.5 cm), 4 Flak guns (88 mm). Dach, "Panzer durchbrechen eine Armeestellung," p. 74.

8. The following weapons were employed: 36 howitzers (105 mm/150 mm) of 1st Panzer Division's artillery; the fires of the reinforced corps assets: 40 howitzers (105 mm), 24 howitzers (150 mm), 8 field guns (100 mm), 8 210 mm mortars, and 18 rocket launchers (210 mm/108 tubes). Anlage 5 zum Korpsbefehl für den 13.5.40. Besondere Anordnungen für den Maasübergang am 13.5.40 für die Artillerie.

9. Dach, "Panzer durchbrechen eine Armeestellung," p. 74.

10. Anlage 1 zum Korpsbefehl Nr. 3. Zeittafel für den Angriff über die Maas am 13.5.40.

11. Dach, "Panzer durchbrechen eine Armeestellung," p. 75.

12. Ibid., p. 72.

13. Ibid., p. 73.

14. Ibid.

APPENDIX G

1. General Headquarters Troops are those units assigned, attached, or under operational control of a headquarters authorized a general staff (corps or higher).

2. The normal artillery regiment of a Panzer division consisted of two battalions of three batteries. The 1st, 2nd, and 10th Panzer Divisions artillery regiments were reinforced by General Headquarters Troops heavy artillery battalions. In 2nd and 10th Panzer Divisions the heavy battalion consisted of three batteries (two batteries of heavy field howitzer 150 mm, and one battery of 100 mm field guns. The 1st Panzer Division's heavy artillery battalion consisted of three batteries of 150 mm howitzers. A battery normally consisted of four artillery pieces. Müller-Hillebrandt, *Das Heer,* vol. 2, p. 143.

3. The heavy artillery battalion was a pure 150 mm battalion (also General Headquarters Troops). Müller-Hillebrandt, *Das Heer,* vol. 2, p. 125.

4. Ibid.

5. The artillery regiment of a motorized infantry division consisted of two light battalions of 105 mm howitzers and one heavy battalion of 150 mm howitzers. Müller-Hillebrandt, *Das Heer,* vol. 2, p. 139.

6. Gliederung der Truppen der Gruppe von Kleist, stand vom 15.3.40; XIX. A.K. Abt Ia, den 28.3.40., Studie für den Korpsbefehl Nr. 1 für den Fall "Gelb."

7. George Tessin, *Verbände und Truppen der Deutschen Wehrmacht und Waffen-SS im Zweiten Weltkrieg,* pp. 15-16.

Bibliography

PRIMARY SOURCES

Archival Microfilm Sources

National Archives of the United States, Washington, D.C. (NARS):
T84/271, War diary of Field Marshal Fedor von Bock
T311/246, War records of Army Group A
T311/247, War records of Army Group A
T311/248, War records of Army Group A
T311/249, War records of Army Group A
T311/250, War records of Army Group A
T311/251, War records of Army Group A
T311/252, War records of Army Group A
T314/613, War records of XIXth Panzer Corps
T314/614, War records of XIXth Panzer Corps
T314/615, War records of XIXth Panzer Corps
T314/666, War records of XXIInd Army Corps (Panzer Group von Kleist)
T314/667, War records of XXIInd Army Corps (Panzer Group von Kleist)
T314/668, War records of XXIInd Army Corps (Panzer Group von Kleist)
T314/669, War records of XXIInd Army Corps (Panzer Group von Kleist)
T315/13, War records of 1st Panzer Division
T315/14, War records of 1st Panzer Division
T315/89, War records of 2nd Panzer Division
T315/92, War records of 2nd Panzer Division
T315/558, War records of 10th Panzer Division
T315/559, War records of 10th Panzer Division

Published Documents

Detweiler, Donald S. *World War II German Military Studies.* 27 vols. New York and London: Garland Publishing, Inc., 1979.

Domarus, Max. *Hitlers, Reden und Proklamationen 1932-1945:* Kommentiert von einem deutschen Zeitgenossen. 4 vols. Wiesbaden: R. Löwit, 1973.

Jacobsen, Hans-Adolf. *Dokumente zur Vorgeschichte des Westfeldzuges 1939-1940.* Göttingen: Musterschmidt Verlag, 1956.

Snyder, Louis C. *Encyclopedia of the Third Reich.* New York: McGraw Hill, 1976.

Oberkommando des Heeres. *Handbuch für den Generalstabsdienst im Kriege.* 2 vols. Berlin: Reichsdruckerei, 1939.

Diaries and Memoirs

Balck, Hermann. *Ordnung im Chaos.* 2d ed. Osnabrück: Biblio Verlag, 1981.

Below, Nicolaus von. *Als Hitlers Adjutant, 1937-1945.* Mainz: v. Hase & Köhler Verlag, 1980.

Erfurth, Waldemar. *Surprise,* trans. Dr. Stefan T. Possony and Daniel Vilfroy. Harrisburg: Military Service Publishing Company, 1943.

Guderian, Heinz. *Panzer Leader,* trans. Constantine Fitzgibbon. New York: Ballantine Books, Inc. 1957, 5th printing 1972.

Halder, Franz. *The Halder Diaries: The Private War Journal of Colonel General Franz Halder.* Boulder, Colo.: Westview Press, 1976.

Leeb, Generalfeldmarschall Wilhelm Ritter von. *Tagebuchaufzeichnungen und Lagebeurteilungen aus zwei Weltkriegen,* edited and biographical notes by Georg Meyer. Stuttgart: Deutsche Verlags-Anstalt, 1976.

Liss, Ulrich. *Westfront 1939/40: Erinnerungen des Feindbearbeiters im O.K.H.* Neckargemünd: Scharnhorst Buchkameradschaft, 1959.

Manstein, Erich von. *Verlorene Siege.* 9th ed. München: Bernhard & Gräfe Verlag, 1981.

Röhricht, Edgar. *Pflicht und Gewissen: Erinnerungen eines deutschen Generals 1932 bis 1944.* Stuttgart: W. Kohlhammer Verlag, 1965.

Wagner, Eduard. *Der General-Quartiermeister: Briefe und Tagebuchaufzeichnungen des Generalquartiermeisters des Heeres, General der Artillerie Eduard Wagner,* ed. Elisabeth Wagner. München und Wien: Günter Olzog Verlag, 1963.

Warlimont, Walter. *Inside Hitler's Headquarters 1939-45,* trans. R. H. Barry. New York: Praeger Publishers, 1964.

SECONDARY SOURCES

Books

Berlin, Paul, Dr. *Deutschland Stirbt Nicht! Eine politische Analyse mit nationalem Zitatenlexikon.* München: DSZ-Verlag, 1988.

Buchner, Alex. *Das Handbuch der Deutschen Infanterie 1939-1945; Gliederung-Uniformen-Bewaffnung-Ausrüstung-Einsätze.* Friedberg: Podzun-Pallas Verlag, 1987.

Craig, Gordon A. *The Politics of the Prussian Army 1640-1945. London: Oxford University Press, 1955.*

Damerau, Helmut, ed. *Deutsches Soldatenjahrbuch 1963: Elfter Deutscher Soldatenkalender.* Tettnang: Lorenz Senn Verlag, 1963.

_____. *Deutsches Soldatenjahrbuch 1988: 36. Deutscher Soldatenkalender.* München: Schild Verlag, 1988.

Davis, W.J.K. *The German Army Handbook 1939-1945.* New York: ARCO Publishing, Inc., 1974.

Deutsch, Harold C. *The Conspiracy Against Hitler in the Twilight War.* Minneapolis: The University of Minnesota Press, 1968.

Dieckhoff, G., and M. Holzmann, *Infanterie Gestern und Heute: Bildbericht der ehemaligen 3, Infanterie-Division und des Jäger-Bataillons 41.* Friedberg: Podzun-Pallas Verlag, 1978.

Doughty, Robert Allan. *The Seeds of Disaster: The Development of French Army Doctrine 1919, 1939.* Hamden, Conn.: Archon Books, 1985.

Engelmann, Joachim, and Horst Scheibert, *Deutsche Artillerie 1934-1945: Eine Dokumentation in Text, Skizzen und Bildern.* Limburg/Lahn: C. A. Starke Verlag, 1974.

Frischauer, Willi. *The Rise and Fall of Hermann Göring.* Boston: Houghton Mifflin, 1951.

Giampietro, Sepp de. *Das Falsche Opfer: Ein Südtiroler in der Division Brandenburg zwischen seinem Gewissen und der Achse Berlin-Rom.* Stuttgart: Leopold Stocker Verlag, 1984.

Görlitz, Walter. *History of the German General Staff 1657-1945,* trans. Briar Battershaw. New York: Praeger Publishers, 1967.

Halle, Armin, and Carlo Demand. *Panzer: Illustrierte Geschichte der Kampfwagen.* Herrschimg: Verlag Manfred Pawlak, 1971.

Hart, Liddell B. H. *The German Generals Talk.* New York: William Morrow & Co., 1948.

Haupt, Werner. *Das Buch der Infanterie: Marschiert-gesiegt-gelitten-geopfert.* Friedberg: Podzun-Pallas Verlag, 1962.

Horne, Alistair. *To Lose a Battle: France 1940.* Boston: Little, Brown and Company, 1969.

Irving, David. *Hitler's War.* 2 vols. New York: The Viking Press, 1977.

Jacobsen, Hans-Adolf. *Fall Felb: Der Kampf um den Deutschen Operationsplan zur Westoffensive 1940.* Wiesbaden: Franz Steiner Verlag, GmbH, 1957.

Keilig, Wolf. *Das Deutsche Heer 1939-1945.* 3 vols. Bad Nauheim: Podzun-Pallas Verlag, 1957.

Kielmansegg, Adolf Graf von. *Der Fritsch Prozess 1938.* Hamburg: Hoffman and Campe Verlag, 1949.

Koch, Adalbert. *Die Geschichte der Deutschen Flakartillerie 1935-1945.* Friedberg: Podzun-Pallas Verlag, 1954.

Lewis, S. J. *Forgotten Legions: German Army Infantry Policy 1918-1941.* New York: Praeger Publishers, 1985.

Macksey, Kenneth. *Guderian: Creator of the Blitzkrieg.* New York: Stein and Day Publishers, 1976.

Meissner, Hans Otto. *Die Machtergreifung 30. Januar 1933.* Esslingen: Bechtle Verlag, 1983.

Melchers, E. T. *Kriegsschauplatz Luxemburg: August 1914-Mai 1940.* Luxemburg: Sankt-Paulus Druckerei, A. G., 1979.

Mellenthin, F. W. von. *German Generals of World War II As I Saw Them.* Norman: University of Oklahoma Press, 1977.

_____. *Panzer Battles: A Study of the Employment of Armor in the Second World War,* trans. H. Betzler. Norman: University of Oklahoma Press, 1956.

Müller-Hillebrand, Burkhart. *Das Heer 1933-1945: Entwicklung des Organisatorischen Aufbaues.* 3 vols. Frankfurt am Main: Verlag von E. S. Mittler & Sohn, 1956.

Nofi, Albert A. *The War Against Hitler: Military Strategy in the West.* New York: Hippocrene Books, Inc., 1982.

Raeder, Erich. *My Life,* trans. Henry W. Drexel. Annapolis: United States Naval Institute, 1960.

Scheibert, Horst. *Das war Guderian: Ein Lebensbericht in Bildern.* Friedberg: Podzun-Pallas Verlag, 1975.

_____. *Die 6. Panzer Division 1937-1945: Bewaffnung-Einsätze-Männer.* Friedberg: Podzun-Pallas Verlag, 1975.

_____. *Panzer Grenadier Division Grossdeutschland und Ihre Schwesterverbände.* Dorheim: Podzun-Pallas Verlag, 1975.

Schmidt, Gerhard. *Regimentsgeschichte des Panzer-Artillerie-Regiments 73.* Bremen: Walther Böttscher Verlag, 1959.

Spires, David N. *Image and Reality: The Making of German Officers 1921-1933.* Westport, Conn.: Greenwood Press, 1984.

Steinzer, Franz. *Die 2. Panzer Division 1935-1945 Bewaffnung-Einsätze-Männer.* Friedberg: Podzun-Pallas-Verlag, 1975.

Stoves, Rolf O. G. *Diel. Panzer Division 1935-1945: Chronik einer der drei Stamm Divisionen der deutschen Panzerwaffe.* Bad Neuheim: Verlag Hans-Henning Podzun, 1961.

_____. *Die 1. Panzer Division 1935-1945.* Dorheim: Podzun-Pallas Verlag, 1961.

Strauss, D.F.J. *Friedens und Kriegserlebnisse einer Generation: Ein Kapitel aus der Sicht der Panzerjäger-Abteilung 38 (SF) in der ehemaligen 2. (Wiener) Panzerdivision.* Schweinfurt: Schweinfurter Tagblatt, 1960.

_____. *Geschichte der 2. (Wiener) Panzerdivision.* 3d ed. Forschheim: Buchdruckerei Sperl, 1987.

Sydnor, Charles W. Jr. *Soldiers of Destruction: The SS Death's Head Division 1933-1945.* Princeton, N.J.: Princeton University Press, 1977.

Taylor, Telford. *The March of Conquest: The German Victories in Western Europe, 1940.* New York: Simon & Schuster, 1958.

Tessin, Georg. *Verbände und Truppen der deutschen Wehrmacht und Waffen-SS im Zweiten Weltkrieg 1939-1945.* vol 2: Die Landstreitkräfte. Osnabrück: Biblio Verlag, 1973.

Weiss, Wilhelm. *Triumph der Kriegskunst.* München: Zentralverlag der NSDAP, Franz Eher Verlag Nachf., 1941.

Wistrich, Robert. *Who's Who in Nazi Germany.* New York: Macmillan Publishing Co., Inc., 1982.

Young, Peter. *Der Grosse Atlas zum II. Weltkrieg.* Stuttgart: Fackelverlag, 1973.

Articles

Dach, Hans von. "Panzer durchbrechen eine Armeestellung." *Schweizer Soldat* (47) 1972, no. 2.

German Military Training. "A Study of German Military Training." Produced at GMDS by a combined British, Canadian, and U.S. staff, May 1946.

Lewis, S. J. "Reflections on Military Reform: One German Example." Accepted for publication by *Military Review*, January 1988.

Murray, Williamson. "The German Response to Victory in Poland." *Armed Forces and Society*, Winter 1981, vol. 7, no. 2, pp. 285-98.

Military Studies

Weise, Generaloberst Hubert. *Organization of Air Defense in the Field: Experiences of I Flak Corps.* Manuscript data sheet originally prepared for Headquarters European Command, Office of the Chief Historian, Washington, D.C.: Department of the Army, Officer of the Chief of Military History, 1952.

Index

About the Author

FLORIAN K. ROTHBRUST, a major in the U.S. Army, was born in Heidelberg, West Germany, on February 27, 1954. In 1967, he immigrated with his parents to the United States and settled in San Jose, California. He received his B.A. from Santa Clara University and a Master of Military Art and Science (History) from the U.S. Army Command and General Staff College. A career military officer, Major Rothbrust entered the Army in 1976 and recently graduated from the U.S. Army Command and General Staff College. He has served all his troop assignments with parachute units at Fort Bragg, North Carolina, and in Vicenza, Italy. He is currently stationed at Fort Bragg, assigned as the Executive Officer, 2d Battalion (Airborne), 325th Airborne Infantry Regiment.